ABOUT ISLAND PRESS

Island Press is the only nonprofit organization in the United States whose principal purpose is the publication of books on environmental issues and natural resource management. We provide solutions-oriented information to professionals, public officials, business and community leaders, and concerned citizens who are shaping responses to environmental problems.

In 1998, Island Press celebrates its fourteenth anniversary as the leading provider of timely and practical books that take a multidisciplinary approach to critical environmental concerns. Our growing list of titles reflects our commitment to bringing the best of an expanding body of literature to the environmental community throughout North America and the world.

Support for Island Press is provided by The Jenifer Altman Foundation, The Bullitt Foundation, The Mary Flagler Cary Charitable Trust, The Nathan Cummings Foundation, The Geraldine R. Dodge Foundation, The Ford Foundation, The Vira I. Heinz Endowment, The W. Alton Jones Foundation, The John D. and Catherine T. MacArthur Foundation, The Andrew W. Mellon Foundation, The Curtis and Edith Munson Foundation, The National Fish and Wildlife Foundation, The National Science Foundation, The New-Land Foundation, The David and Lucile Packard Foundation, The Surdna Foundation, The Winslow Foundation, The Pew Charitable Trusts, and individual donors.

The Global Commons

To my daughter, Bethany

The Global Commons
An Introduction

SUSAN J. BUCK
University of North Carolina-Greensboro

ISLAND PRESS

Washington, D.C. • Covelo, California

Copyright © 1998 by Island Press

All rights reserved under International and Pan-American Copyright Conventions. No part of this book may be reproduced in any form or by any means without permission in writing from the publisher: Island Press, 1718 Connecticut Avenue, N.W., Suite 300, Washington, DC 20009.

ISLAND PRESS is a trademark of The Center for Resource Economics.

Library of Congress Cataloging-in-Publication Data

Buck, Susan J.
    The global commons: an introduction / Susan J. Buck
        p. cm.
    Includes bibliographical references and index.
    ISBN 1-55963-550-9 (cloth). — ISBN 1-55963-551-7
    1. Environmental policy. 2. Commons. 3. Natural resources,
Communal. 4. Environmental management. I. Title.
GE170.B83 1998
363.7—dc21   97-49587
                                                            CIP

Printed on recycled, acid-free paper

Manufactured in the United States of America
10 9 8 7 6 5 4 3 2 1

Contents

Acknowledgments

Many excellent scholarly works rooted in international relations and comparative politics have discussed the global commons. This book is written to bring another perspective to the discussion: the extensive and rich analytic frameworks in public administration, political science, and economics that have been developed to study common pool resources.

As most works do, this book took on a life of its own, and I could not have completed it without help.

Dr. Albert Utton at the University of New Mexico School of Law generously gave me an office during the fall and spring of 1991–1992. Support for a related project on the management of transboundary resources in Central Asia came from the National Science Foundation (grant number SES#-914766). My university, the University of North Carolina at Greensboro, provided a course release during the fall of 1992 to prepare an honors seminar on the global commons, an activity that was very useful to me in organizing my thoughts.

Two dear friends, Betty Morgan and Pam Mason, read drafts of various chapters; their constructive comments helped me to clarify my ideas and my writing. Joe Morgan, cartographer extraordinaire, made the map of the Antarctic region that appears in chapter 3. Dr. Milton Moss reviewed the critical chapters setting out the definitions and analytic framework. Lynda Kellam was my cyberspace research lifeline during the copyedit stage while I was in Scotland under the auspices of a Fulbright award examining Scottish wildlife management.

I have been singularly fortunate in my research assistants. Tiffany Bolick saw me through the first draft of this book with many trips to the library and requests for interlibrary loans. Karen Titus Markovics researched and wrote the descriptive material that eventually became the boxed text, and she also helped throughout the early stages of manuscript preparation. Mitchel Jofuku, now a member of the New Mexico State Bar but then a third-year student at the University of New Mexico School of Law, performed miracles, unearthing books and articles and steering me through the arcane corridors of his law library. Andrew Esposito organized and reconciled all the notes and the bibliography over a long holiday weekend.

The second draft of this book was written between 1996 and 1997. Mary Hennessey, my indispensable graduate research assistant, carried out all the library work, from locating the latest research to picking up books on inter-library loan. She spent one lovely spring week proofreading the manuscript, verifying notes, and generally catching my sins of omission and commission. Her thoroughness was remarkable.

Pat Harris was the copyeditor for this book. She used the Internet to ver-ify treaties and dates, which spared me a great deal of time-consuming work, and her editing was meticulous and even creative.

I am especially grateful to Todd Baldwin, senior editor at Island Press, for his guidance during the writing of this book. His comments on the text clar-ified my thinking and strengthened my writing. He bolstered my confidence when it flagged. He restored my sense of humor as the deadline loomed and the project lagged. It is a true blessing to have an editor who knows content as well as style.

To Elinor Ostrom I owe an incalculable intellectual debt because it was her work on economics and institutions in the governance of common pool resources that broke me out of my narrative rut.

I gladly share with these friends and colleagues any plaudits won by this book; any criticisms should be laid at my door alone.

Susan J. Buck
Greensboro, North Carolina
May 1997

Foreword

Susan Buck recognizes that technology has caught up with desire. For most of human history, the four global commons addressed in this book—Antarctica, the high seas and deep seabed, the atmosphere, and space—remained unclaimed due to a lack of technology for extracting their value and for establishing and sustaining property rights. To our peril, the technology for extracting value from these four domains has developed more rapidly than have the appropriate legal mechanisms for establishing an effective property regime. The treasured resources for all mankind are threatened by the very technological abilities that we have mastered during recent eras. This is indeed a Grotian moment.

Not only does Susan Buck introduce the reader to the key analytical concepts necessary to study both local and global commons, but she has written excellent in-depth case studies of each of the four domains. Often, scholars have approached only segments of global commons. Some have studied the renewable fisheries of the oceans, but have neglected to consider the nonrenewable minerals lying below. We all know that people overuse the atmosphere by pumping too much waste into it and they overuse the oceans by extracting too many fish; but it is important to recognize the negative externalities that are involved as the activities of one participant spill external costs onto others who share in the use and consequence of the global commons. Buck combines a deep knowledge of the law with the necessary tools for analyzing this series of important problems, as well as myriad other problems in modern society.

Students, faculty, and citizens interested in the problems of survival on Earth must begin to understand the macro consequences of their individual actions. A choice as simple as to when and how you travel to work affects others. Choosing to drive yourself in your own car during rush hour has more impact on local traffic patterns and the atmosphere than does creating a carpool or using available public transportation. But what are the ways you can take those external costs into account in making any individual decision?

The externalities are too far removed to facilitate easy solutions. When there are joint owners of local commons, the interdependencies may be far more obvious. Suppose I own a grazing commons with a small number of other families and we overstock it. This will lead to a depleted resource for all of us. If we continue to overstock with sheep and sheer for wool every year, we receive immediate feedback in the poor quality of our wool as a cumulative effect of our actions. Through the centuries, humans have developed various mechanisms for coping with their interdependence on the local commons, but it is only recently that we have had the technological capacity to affect global commons significantly. Not only do we now have the technical competence without the full evolution of legal institutions, but the set of interactions leads through such a long chain of reactions that awareness of the full consequences of our actions is rare. A mundane task such as shopping in the supermarket may seem far removed from the well-being of the atmosphere, but the choice of products we put in our market basket drives a very complex set of production activities that impact on the atmosphere in diverse ways.

Since our future is dependent on our joint use of the global commons, we either must face up to the issues discussed in this volume or find ourselves destroyed by our own indifference to the major set of problems facing us as we near the twenty-first century.

Elinor Ostrom

Chapter 1

Organizing the Commons: Definitions and Assumptions

> There is nothing which so generally strikes the imagination, and engages the affections of mankind, as the right of property; or that sole and despotic dominion which one man claims and exercises over the external things of the world, in total exclusion of the right of any other individual in the universe.
>
> —William Blackstone, *Commentaries on the Laws of England* (1776)

"That sole and despotic dominion which one man claims and exercises over the external things of the world": this is how in 1776 English jurist Sir William Blackstone described the right of property. Much of human history can be described as an effort to establish such sole and despotic dominion. Historically, human response to vast areas of valuable resources unfettered by legal rights recognized by the dominant culture usually has been appropriation by governments and individuals, followed by exploitation as soon and as rapidly as physical force and technology would permit.

Global commons—Antarctica, the high seas and deep seabed minerals, the atmosphere, and space—have remained exceptions only because access to them has been difficult and the value of the resources they contain has not been enough to justify the effort of acquiring them.[1] Today, however, technology has caught up with desire. Fortunately, the vulnerability of the global commons can be addressed in an era of remarkable peace among the superpowers. We have the luxury of engaging in public policy debates over the design of management regimes, and decisions are made at the negotiation table rather than on the battlefield.

Some scholars have suggested that recent developments in international

1

law foreshadow remarkable societal change. B. V. A. Röling recognizes the current era as a *Grotian moment* (named for Dutch scholar and humanist Hugo Grotius): "a time in which a fundamental change of circumstances [creates] the need for a different world structure and a different international law."[2] Others concur that the late twentieth century is a time of fundamental change.[3] If we are indeed facing a Grotian moment, the story of the recent changes in international law should provide key indicators of impeding change. This question is revisited in chapter 7.

The purpose of this book is to examine how legal and political contexts have affected the evolution of management regimes for the global commons. The approach is both narrative and analytic. The historical development of each commons management regime is described, with particular attention given to the role of law. Historical events are then examined through the lens of the analytic framework proposed in chapter 2.

This chapter begins by setting out the terms, definitions, and concepts used throughout the book. The second section discusses the influence of national politics, scientific uncertainty, and interest groups on the formation of international regimes.

The third section of this chapter presents the assumptions that undergird the discussions of international and global commons that follow. The first assumption is that a knowledge of historical and institutional history is important in regime design and sustainability. The second assumption is that sustainability is the appropriate goal for public policy outcomes in international and global commons.

The chapter concludes with a narrative outline of the remaining chapters.

Definitions and Concepts

Language matters in the law, perhaps more so than in other professions and academic pursuits. Words are used with precision, and because of this, complex ideas can be expressed succinctly. Once a second or third discipline is represented in an academic discussion, discourse becomes more complicated and much time is spent in clarification. This is not to say that the scholars in each discipline are at war with one another; they may simply be unaware that terms familiar to them have different meanings in other disciplines. For example, in the law, *alienation* is a term from real property law meaning "the transfer of the property and possession of lands, tenements or other things, from one person to another."[4] However, in the literature of common pool resources, alienation is "the right to sell or lease collective choice rights to manage resources or to exclude others from them."[5] Thus, in the common pool resource literature, alienation applies to a much broader category of behavior, and the legal scholar, who knows quite well what *alienation* means, loses the full meaning of the discourse. In this volume, I have mingled the ideas and the vocabulary of several disciplines: law, economics, ecology, political science, public administration, and cultural anthropology. It is therefore critical that the meaning of the core terms is clear from the outset.

To understand commons and common pool resources, we must first understand the differences and connections between resources, resource domains, property, and property regimes.

A resource is anything that is used to meet the needs of an organism. Some resources are *natural resources*, that is, material that has economic or social value when extracted from its natural state.[6] Others are *spatial-extension resources*, which have value because of their location. For example, geostationary orbits are not natural resources because they are not extracted or converted from their natural state; they are, however, spatial-extension resources in that they may be used to meet telecommunications needs.

Resources are located in fixed spatial dimensions known as *resource domains*. For example, fish are a natural resource found in the ocean resource domain. Geostationary orbits are resources found in the space resource domain. In some situations, the domain and the resource are coterminous. For example, when sailors use the oceans as roads to transport people and goods, the oceans themselves are a resource. When the sailors are fishing, the oceans are also a resource domain and the fish stocks are the resource.

Property is not used here in the "vulgar and untechnical sense of the physical thing with respect to which the citizen exercises rights recognized by law."[7] It is instead "an aggregate of rights which are guaranteed and protected by the government."[8] Property rights may be held by individuals or by groups of individuals such as communities, corporations, or nation-states. The property right to a resource is not a single right but rather a bundle of rights, such as rights of access, exclusion, extraction, or sale of the captured resource; the right to transfer one's rights to a second person; and the right of inheritance. The specific composition of each bundle of rights varies. For example, all nations that are members of the Antarctic Treaty System have the right to establish Antarctic research stations in their bundle of rights, but they cannot transfer their access rights to nonmember states. In contrast, nations that have been assigned geostationary orbit slots may lease those slots to other countries. Both groups have rights to the resource, but one may transfer access rights and the other may not.

Thus far, a resource domain has been defined as the fixed spatial dimension in which resources are found; resources, as things used to meet needs; and property in resources, as a bundle of rights protected by the government. The bundles of rights may be categorized in a number of ways. One of the earliest ways to organize property regimes is derived from the Roman law of property.

In Roman law, property was thought to exist in one of four property regimes: *res publica, res communes, res nullius,* and *res privatae.*[9] Objects for which the property rights are held by the government for the use and benefit of the public, such as navigable rivers, highways, and territorial seas, are *res publica.* Those things, such as light and air, that are accessible to any user but can never be exclusively acquired as a whole by any individual or government are *res communes.* Some objects have no property rights attached to them at all, either because they have been abandoned (stray cats) or because no person has acquired them (whales). These objects are *res nullius,* but once they are taken into possession by one or more individuals, they become *res privatae.*

I present these categories because they are so well known that they are often used by modern scholars to describe contemporary property regimes. However, despite the deceptive neatness of these categories, they are of limited usefulness in labeling common pool resources because they lack dimensions that incorporate the flow of resources from the resource domain, the nature of the resource itself, and the resource domain in which it is found.

A more helpful approach is to consider two attributes of resources: the difficulty or feasibility of excluding others from using the resources (*exclusion*) and the degree to which one appropriator's use of the resource diminishes the amount of the resource left for others (*subtractability*).[10] For example, it is fairly easy to exclude people from driving my car (a private good) but it is virtually impossible to exclude people from enjoying the benefits of a strong national defense policy (public good). Similarly, since only one person can drive my car at any given time, the good is highly subtractable, but the total amount of national defense available is not dependent on how many people are under its umbrella. Table 1.1 illustrates these categories.

This table is a useful heuristic device because it helps us categorize various resources, but we should not fall into the trap of confusing heuristic categories with immutable taxonomy. These four cells do not have absolute, impermeable boundaries. For instance, the classic example of a public good is the lighthouse, which casts its lifesaving beam across the water regardless of who will make use of it. It is impossible to exclude anyone from using the lighthouse beacon. However, in practical terms, all ships must eventually come into port, and most do so with predictable regularity. Thus, when the

Table 1.1 Categories of Goods

	SUBTRACTABILITY	
EXCLUSION	High	Low
Easy	Private goods	Toll goods
Difficult	Common pool goods	Public goods

need for more efficient lighthouses became apparent in Scotland in 1787, Parliament created the Northern Lighthouse Board, which imposed a duty on all ships and decked vessels navigating the North Sea area. In effect, these Scottish lighthouses were not public goods but rather a form of toll good.[11] Thus, most government-financed lighthouses would fit comfortably in the lower-right-hand cell of table 1.1 as public goods, but some would move toward the upper-right-hand cell as toll goods.[12]

Common pool goods have high subtractability and are difficult to exclude others from using. For example, in the Swiss alpine village of Töbel, villagers own the forests in common. Every villager is entitled to cut a limited amount of timber (low exclusion), and once cut, the timber is no longer available for other villages (high subtractability).[13] The timber is a common pool resource. Similarly, space is a resource domain from which it is difficult to exclude nations or businesses (low exclusion), but locations within space (spatial-dimension resources) such as geostationary orbits may be occupied by only one satellite at a time (high subtractability). Thus, geostationary orbits are common pool resources.

Each type of good implies a different bundle of property rights. For example, most private goods may be sold, but public goods cannot, and because common pool goods are subtractable, the right of access is usually limited to a legally defined user pool. The sets of rules (laws, treaties, regulations, customs) that define property rights are *property regimes*.

This leads to the definition of common pool resources: *Common pool resources are subtractable resources managed under a property regime in which a legally defined user pool cannot be efficiently excluded from the resource domain.*[14]

International and Global Commons

Commons are resource domains in which common pool resources are found. They may be very small (the parking lot for an apartment complex) or quite large (the high seas or the solar system). The very large resource domains that do not fall within the jurisdiction of any one country are termed international commons or global commons.[15] *International commons* are resource domains shared by several nations, such as the Mediterranean Sea[16] and Antarctica (although recent United Nations environmental treaties have affected the Antarctic regime so that it has some of the characteristics of a global commons). *Global commons* are resource domains to which all nations have legal access, such as outer space. The distinction between the two is important, especially because international commons are exclusionary while global commons are not.

In this book, Antarctica is discussed as one of four global commons even though it is governed by a regime that admits only a small number of nations and therefore is technically an international commons. Other international commons are primarily regional; for example, only Mediterranean governments participate in the Mediterranean Action Plan.[17] The Antarctic regime has no such regional logic, and no group of nations has recognized territorial claims to the resource domain.[18]

International Regime Formation

The processes that governments follow in making national policy are complex, and adding an international dimension complicates the process further. Some factors have unique attributes that magnify their impact on the formation of international regimes. Three of these factors are particularly germane to this discussion of regime formation for the global commons: the effect of national (i.e., internal) concerns, the accumulation and use of scientific information, and the influence of government and nongovernmental organizations at both the national and international levels. Treaty ratification and compliance following ratification also affect regime formation.

Nations have many international concerns that affect regime formation. For example, one American impetus to participate in forming an Antarctic regime was to have a location for military training in extreme cold that was far away from the Soviet presence in the northern polar regions. Nations must also reconcile domestic interests as well as international ones. For example, the United States refused to sign the 1982 United Nations Convention on the Law of the Sea (Law of the Sea Treaty) in part to protect domestic business interests in deep seabed mining. One of the many reasons why President George Bush refused to sign the Convention on Biological Diversity was a constitutional arrangement peculiar to the United States whereby the states hold much of the power to regulate wildlife conservation and management. President Bush claimed to be unwilling to commit the federal government to a treaty that would rely on the various states for implementation.[19]

There is also a great deal of uncertainty about scientific information on many international and global common pool resources.[20] Resource domains such as outer space and the deep seabeds are often inaccessible, and their sheer magnitude complicates data collection. Sometimes the resources contained within them are so complex that scientists cannot reach conclusions. The disagreement among scientists regarding the impact of chlorofluorocarbons on depletion of stratospheric ozone illustrates this problem. The scientific community could not agree on how to interpret the data it had collected, and thus politicians were able to delay regime decisions to accommodate economic and political pressures.[21]

Risk assessment is a second problem with scientific data. Risk assessment assigns probabilities to predicted outcomes; for example, if Pacific salmon stocks are decreasing, what is the probability that they will drop below the level of recovery within three or five or ten years? Because risk assessment is based on probabilities (that is, assumptions, guesses, and values), policy actors are less able to defend decisions based on risk assessments. Even when all policy actors agree on the data and the level of risk, their willingness to accept that risk may vary.[22] For example, small island nations are likely to endorse the precautionary principle when climate change is discussed; they are risk averse because if global warming does occur, some small island nations could disappear entirely.

Even if the data are not contested and probabilities are high, resource users may not be able to agree on a policy based on the data. Fisheries provide a clear example. Members of many fishing communities value their traditional ways of life and pursue sustainable harvests partly to preserve their communities. An external entrepreneur from outside the community, however, might logically invest in fishing equipment, harvest as many fish as possible until the stock is exhausted, and then move his or her capital to another venture, having maximized the return on the capital investment in as short a time as possible. Both the entrepreneur and the traditional fishermen recognize the economic arguments for massive exploitation, but fishermen will accept a regulatory regime that imposes a limited catch and therefore a limited income in order to preserve their communities and traditional lifestyles.[23]

Nongovernmental organizations (NGOs), both at the national and the international levels, also have substantial influence in the design and implementation of international and global common pool resource regimes.[24]

Patricia Birnie and Alan Boyle have identified the most important role of NGOs:

> They provide a permanent forum in which state members can engage in a continuous negotiating process to arrive at the compromises necessary to propel the law forward in a world consisting of states at very different stages of economic and social development and representing many different legal, cultural, and religious systems and values.[25]

They also act as policy watchdogs, notifying government institutions when problems arise.

Often, environmental policy networks have large popular bases that cut across national boundaries. During the 1992 United Nations Conference on the Environment and Development (UNCED, also known as the Rio Conference or Earth Summit), a parallel conference for more than 2,500 nongovernmental organizations was held. The 1992 Global Forum generated thirty-three alternative treaties covering a wide array of topics, such as forestry, biodiversity, and climate change.[26] NGOs frequently play a significant role in the initiation of international environmental programs.[27] NGOs may have observer status at international meetings, and official government delegations sometimes contain NGO members, as when a Greenpeace representative served on the New Zealand delegation to the 1972 Convention on the Prevention of Marine Pollution by Dumping of Wastes and other Matter (London Convention).[28] NGOs provide scientific or technical assistance; for example, the Recognized Private Operating Agencies (RPOAs) provide technical information to the formal Study Groups of the Standardization Bureau of the International Telecommunication Union, and they pay for the privilege. The benefit they receive is access to the policy-making process in the telecommunications regime. The impact of NGOs is substantial. Recent policies adopted in large part because of NGO influence include the designation of Antarctica as a world park, establishment of the Southern Ocean Whale Sanctuary, and a moratorium on high seas drift net fishing.[29] They may also affect implementation; for example, the World Conservation Union (IUCN, formerly the International Union for the Conservation of Nature and Natural Resources) drafted guidelines for implementation of the Convention on Biological Diversity signed at the Rio Conference.

Epistemic communities are policy networks formed by scientists, technical experts, and international organizations specializing in a particular policy area. As interest groups, epistemic communities have played important roles in the formation and legitimation of global commons regimes.[30] Certainly, the Antarctic regime was a child of the scientists; their insistence on a research focus and the exclusion of military concerns has helped maintain the stability of the regime. The International Telecommunication Union (ITU) has staunchly protected its apolitical character, and the Committee on Space Research (COSPAR), with its Interdisciplinary Scientific Commission (ISC), has sustained the scientific focus of much space policy. It is, of course, important to recognize that the scientific community has its own agenda in maintaining an avowedly neutral, scientific presence in the global commons regimes. Protection of research funds, government jobs, and access to policy decisions depend on their refusal to take sides in political disputes. There is also a culture of political neutrality within the sciences, although individual scientists may also hold policy positions (see, for example, the discussion of the International Telecommunication Union in chapter 6).

Global governance is essentially a matter of administration, and treaties may be stumbling blocks rather than useful guidelines for several reasons. First, the need for consensus and compromise often leads to the acceptance of the lowest common denominator for policy objectives, and second, even after a treaty has been negotiated, nations may delay ratification or even fail to ratify the treaty at all.[31]

Problems with ratification may occur for a number of reasons: other national priorities may move ratification down on the formal agenda, internal bureaucracies may object, or special interest groups may interfere.[32] On occasion, treaty negotiators forge agreements that exceed their mandates. In other cases, the government that sent the negotiators may fall or the administration may change. This was clearly the case when the Reagan administration withdrew American support from the Law of the Sea Treaty and when Prime Minister John Major of Great Britain supported the Maastricht Treaty only to face implacable domestic opposition led by Margaret Thatcher. Finally, the governments involved in negotiations may not have been negotiating in good faith; their agreements may be deliberate deceptions or mere expressions of solidarity with allies.[33]

To encourage cooperation and participation in international regimes, several inventive strategies have been used. Treaties and conventions may contain incentives to promote a higher level of cooperation or attainment than is strictly required by the treaty, a sort of international extra credit assignment. Treaties may impose unequal demands on nations in recognition that the nations involved have unequal resources or levels of technology. Treaty standards may also be put in place before ratification is complete, either through provisional treaty application or by "soft law," which sets agreed-on rules without the formal treaty apparatus. Governments may also assign responsibility for regime governance to an intergovernmental organization such as the International Telecommunication Union (see chapter 6).

General Assumptions

This book proceeds from several assumptions. First is the assumption that history matters.[34] Historical context is critical in understanding public policy. This may seem to be a truism, but much policy analysis neglects the historical evolution of the policy under study. A dramatic example of this is given by Lawrence Taylor in his account of an Irish fishing settlement.[35] Taylor describes how a parish priest with a national reputation for organizing successful collectives met with unexpected resistance in a small salmon fishery because his proposals for cooperative ownership of fishing rights failed to take into account the local history of intense conflicts over fishing rights. One fisherman was blunt in his assessment of the probable outcome of the priest's plan: if the proposal were implemented, he explained, "the river would run red with blood." A policy proposal that seemed sensible in the light of modern trends simply was not tenable given the history of the community.

Human nature has not altered dramatically over the centuries, but models used to interpret human motivations and actions certainly have.[36] We need to recognize that our analyses are colored by our own cultural biases, and to the extent possible, we need to compensate. Analytic techniques appropriate in one context may be inappropriate in another, and longitudinal changes may be as significant as cross-sectional variables.[37] Anthropologist Marshall Sahlins, describing the state of research into the lives of prehistoric hunter-gatherers, puts the problem succinctly: "Having equipped the hunter with bourgeois impulses and paleolithic tools, we judge his situation to be helpless in advance."[38]

My second assumption is that ecological and institutional sustainability are appropriate goals for policy outcomes in the global commons. This means that sustainability is the standard against which regimes should be measured.

The 1987 report of the World Commission on Environment and Development (Brundtland Commission) defined sustainable development as "development that meets the needs of the present without compromising the ability of future generations to meet their own needs."[39] The 1992 Earth Summit held in Rio established sustainable development as a substantial item on the world environmental agenda.[40] This is a "seductively simple concept, basic to human survival," easy to articulate but difficult to implement.[41] It has not yet emerged as a binding rule in international law,[42] but it has become an article of faith among environmentalists and many activists in development assistance.[43]

The legitimacy of sustainability as a policy goal is, of course, derived in part from normative considerations such as intergenerational equity and stewardship. There are, however, other justifications and logical arguments that support it as a guiding principle. First is the *precautionary principle*, which is succinctly expressed in the proverb "Better safe than sorry."[44] It is the precautionary principle that provides the utilitarian justification for protecting biological diversity: who knows what wonder drug might be missed if a small fungus were to become extinct? A second rationale derives from the illogic of the opposing principle, the *frontier ethic*,[45] which presents nature as unlimited bounty, a cornucopia.[46] It also supposes that science and technology will always find a way to reverse or bypass any environmental problem and that the human species is somehow divorced from and independent of the world ecosystem. The logic of this position is difficult to defend. The frontier ethic cannot be used as a guiding principle for policy outcomes, and sustainability is left by default as the remaining alternative principle.[47]

The Plan for this Book

The global commons are not easily compared with one another. They contain different kinds of resources, and the regimes that define their use have developed over dramatically different periods of time.

Antarctica is a domain in which numerous kinds of resources, from oil (nonrenewable and stationary) to penguins (renewable and fugitive), are found. Its geography provides unique opportunities for scientific research; thus, part of its resource base is spatial, just as space is a spatial-extension resource for telecommunications. A second commons, the oceans, contains resources that may be fugitive or stationary and renewable or nonrenewable. Technology to exploit the nonrenewable mineral resources of the deep seabed now exists, but the depressed price of minerals makes mining unprofitable. The atmosphere and outer space are, for now, primarily spatial-extension resources, but this may change as exploration uncovers new sources of exploitable resources and technology improves to allow access.

The time frames for regime formation in the global commons also differ dramatically. For the most part, the Law of the Sea Treaty (entered into force in November 1994) follows principles developed over centuries by custom, interpretation, and treaties; outer space is governed by a series of United Nations treaties, and the Antarctic Treaty system has strenuously resisted United Nations encroachment and has just as strenuously avoided any centralized administrative structure. Of the four commons discussed in this book (Antarctica, the oceans, the atmosphere, and space), the ocean regime is the oldest, with its modern roots in the thirteenth century. The regime for outer space, which was not seriously entertained until the 1950s, is the newest.

This variation in the time span of regimes raises a peculiar analytic difficulty. For instance, in the ocean regime, the amount of historical information is virtually infinite, but the content is often suspect. We do not know what filter of politics and culture the information has passed through: often it is the victors who write the histories of wars. The opposite problem exists with the atmospheric and outer space regimes, for which the descriptive detail of the United Nations bargaining sessions is so rich and so recent that interpretation must wait for some historical distance to provide perspective.

Given the varied characteristics of the global commons, it is not feasible to choose uniform time frames. What serves as a rule of thumb in this book is to begin at the point at which each commons became recognized as a resource domain susceptible to a property rights regime and to end at the time at which the current regime reached a recognizable or stable form. Although the chapter on the Antarctic contains some information on early exploration, the utility of such discussions is largely in establishing territorial claims, and the bulk of the historical material in the chapter centers on the late nineteenth century to the present. For the issue of the oceans, I have begun with the Romans (although they appear only briefly and the real tale begins in the thirteenth century) and continued to the most recent major round of the Law of the Sea negotiations. The atmosphere is an issue that is confined to the twentieth century as aircraft and communications issues are focused in that time frame. The final case study chapter, on outer space and telecommunications, covers from the mid-twentieth century to the present. In each of these domains, history provides a useful perspective on present-day issues of resource management.

Chapter 2 provides the analytic framework used in the subsequent chapters. It begins with the development of the law of nations, outlining the forces that shifted the feudal regimes of the Middle Ages (based on personal loyalties and mercantile considerations) to the modern era in which international law has incorporated the notion of contract and become systematized. The second section of the chapter begins with a brief discussion of regime theory and shows how the traditional literature for analyzing small-scale common pool resource regimes may also be applied to the global commons.

The next four chapters deal with specific international or global commons: Antarctica, the oceans, the atmosphere (airspace, acid deposition, stratospheric ozone, and climate change), and space (outer space and telecommunications). Each chapter first outlines the historical evolution of the commons: the development of interest in exploiting the resource domain; conflicts among nations over the use of the commons; and efforts to institutionalize access to and use of the domain. Each concludes with a description of the management regime that eventually emerged from the informal and formal negotiations.

Chapter 7 is a brief conclusion that addresses two areas. The first section summarizes what can be learned by applying the analytic framework developed in chapter 2 to the commons discussed in the following four chapters, and the second section revisits the idea that we may be in the midst of a Grotian moment.

Suggested Reading

Dales, J. H. *Pollution, Property, and Prices.* Toronto: University of Toronto Press, 1968. A classic and very readable essay that sets out the concept of pollution rights. Dales's presentation is persuasive even for those who are not economists.

Esty, Daniel. *Greening the GATT: Trade, Environment, and the Future.* Washington, D.C.: Institute for International Economics, 1994. A comprehensive analysis of the environmental issues in the General Agreement on Tariffs and Trade (GATT). Although Esty's recommendations may not appeal to all readers, the book is worthwhile for its discussion of the history of GATT and its annotated list of key cases and multilateral agreements.

Johnson, Stanley, and Guy Corcelle. *Environmental Policy of the European Communities.* London: Graham and Trotman, 1989. Patricia Birnie and Alan Boyle describe this book as "an exhaustive survey of the policy and lawmaking role of the European Communities" (p. 66, n. 103).

Neustadt, Richard, and Ernest R. May. *Thinking in Time: The Uses of History for Decision Makers.* New York: Free Press, 1988. A clear, well-organized, and readable discussion and illustration of the uses of history in policy analysis. The book is based on graduate seminars developed at the Kennedy School of Government at Harvard University.

Nugent, Neill. *Government and Politics of the European Community*, 3rd ed. Durham, N.C.: Duke University Press, 1994. The most up-to-date book about the European Community, with clear discussions of the European Community's policy-making process and private interest groups. Although it is not environmentally focused, it does discuss some environmental issues.

Ostrom, Elinor. *Governing the Commons; The Evolution of Institutions for Collective Action*. Cambridge: Cambridge University Press, 1990. If I could have only one book on the commons, this would be it. The focus is on small-scale common pool resources. The analytic framework, based on empirical data, has wide application. Very readable.

Notes

1. Antarctica is an international commons rather than a global commons (see the discussion of international and global commons that follows in the main text) because membership in the governing regime is limited. However, Antarctica is usually included in discussions of the global commons because it shares many of their attributes. It is the only international commons discussed in this volume.

2. B. V. A. Röling, "Are Grotius' Ideas Obsolete in an Expanded World?," in *Hugo Grotius and International Relations*, eds. Hedley Bull, Benedict Kingsbury, and Adam Roberts (Oxford: Oxford University Press, 1990), 297–298. Röling credits Richard Falk for the term *Grotian moment*. Richard Falk, "On the Recent Further Decline of International Law," in *Legal Change: Essays in Honour of Julius Stone*, ed. A. R. Blackshield (Sidney, Australia: n.p., 1983), 272. See also Hugo Grotius, *Freedom of the Seas*, or *The Right Which Belongs to the Dutch to Take Part in the East Indian Trade (Mare liberum)* (1608). trans. Ralph Van Deman Magoffin (New York: Oxford University Press, 1916; New York: Arno Press, 1972). For a related discussion of the fundamental changes occurring in Western law, see Harold Berman, *Law and Revolution: The Formation of the Western Legal Tradition* (Cambridge, Mass.: Harvard University Press, 1983).

3. Harold Berman writes that Western law has reached a crisis point:

> The traditional symbols of community in the West, the traditional images and metaphors, have been above all religious and legal. In the twentieth century, however, for the first time, religion has become largely a private affair, while law has become largely a matter of practical expediency. The connection between the religious metaphor and the legal metaphor has been broken.

Berman, *Law and Revolution*, vi. An interesting exploration of the connection between religious symbolism and civic symbolism is found in a recent article by Charles Goodsell, "Administration as Ritual," *Public Administration Review* 49 (1989): 161–166.

4. Henry Campbell Black, *Black's Law Dictionary: Definitions of the Terms and Phrases of American English Jurisprudence, Ancient and Modern* (St. Paul, Minn.: West, 1990).

5. Edella Schlager and Elinor Ostrom, "Property Rights Regimes and Natural Resources: A Conceptual Analysis," *Land Economics* 68, 3 (August 1992): 251.

6. Black, *Black's Law Dictionary.*

7. *United States* v. *General Motors Corporation*, 323 U.S. 373 (1945) at 377.

8. Black, *Black's Law Dictionary.*

9. The definitions in this section are drawn from Black, *Black's Law Dictionary*, and from Patricia Birnie and Alan Boyle, *International Law and the Environment* (Oxford: Clarendon Press, 1993), especially 117–122.

10. This typology is well established in the literature of common pool resources. See, for example, Elinor Ostrom, Roy Gardner, and James Walker, *Rules, Games, and Common-Pool Resources* (Ann Arbor: University of Michigan Press, 1994), especially chapter 1; Elinor Ostrom, "The Rudiments of a Theory of the Origins, Survival, and Performance of Common-Property Institutions," in *Making the Commons Work: Theory, Practice, and Policy*, ed. Daniel Bromley (San Francisco: ICS Press, 1992), 295–296; and Elinor Ostrom, *Governing the Commons: The Evolution of Institutions for Collective Action* (Cambridge: Cambridge University Press, 1990), especially chapter 2.

11. I stumbled across this tale of lighthouse fees in 1994 on a visit to the Arbroath Museum in Arbroath, Scotland. The information here is from a letter from Margaret King, the museum's curator. See also David Van Zandt, "The Lessons of the Lighthouse: 'Government' or 'Private' Provision of Goods," *Journal of Legal Studies* 22 (January 1993): 47–72. The classic work on this topic is Ronald H. Coase, "The Lighthouse in Economics," *Journal of Law and Economics* 17 (1974): 357–376.

12. It is also interesting to consider the analytic confusion caused by wreckers who displayed lights to lure passing vessels onto the rocks, where their cargoes could be plundered. The vessel operators thought they were using a common pool resource when in fact the lights were a private good.

13. Robert Netting, *Balancing on an Alp* (Cambridge: Cambridge University Press, 1981). See also Susan J. Buck, "No Tragedy on the Commons," *Environmental Ethics* 7, 1 (spring 1985): 49–61.

14. There is a subtle but important distinction between common prop-

erty resources and common pool resources. In this volume, I do not use the term *common property resources*, although it is frequently found in the commons literature. Since property is a variable bundle of rights, to speak of a common property resource regime has little analytic significance. It does not identify a particular arrangement of property rights, though it pretends to. On the other hand, *common pool resources* has no such disadvantage as a technical term. It is simply descriptive; denoting subtractable resources that are available to an identifiable group of users under an unspecified property regime. Thus, as an analytic term, *common pool resources* is preferable to *common property resources* and is used throughout this volume.

15. Marvin Soroos, "Conflict in the Use and Management of International Commons," in *Perspectives on Environmental Conflict and International Relations*, ed. Jyrki Käkönen (London: Pinter, 1992), 31.

16. See Peter Haas, *Saving the Mediterranean: The Politics of International Environmental Cooperation* (New York: Columbia University Press, 1990).

17. Haas, *Saving the Mediterranean*, xviii.

18. Although some member nations claim territory in the Antarctic, these claims have been temporarily set aside in the Antarctic Treaty.

19. Melinda Chandler, "The Biodiversity Convention: Selected Issues of Interest to the International Lawyer," *Colorado Journal of International Environmental Law and Policy* 4 (1993): 155. This apparently was not a difficulty for the Clinton administration, since President Bill Clinton signed the convention, although as of this writing the Senate has refused to ratify it. Certainly, similar conflicts have been resolved in favor of the federal government, notably in challenges to the Migratory Bird Treaty Act (1918). See *Missouri* v. *Holland*, 252 U.S. 416 (1920).

20. Michael McGinnis and Elinor Ostrom, "Institutional Analysis and Global Climate Change: Design Principles for Robust International Regimes," in *Global Climate Change: Social and Economic Research Issues* (Chicago: Midwest Consortium for International Security Studies and Argonne National Laboratory, 1992), 63.

21. An interesting case study on this topic is Forest Reinhardt, "Du Pont Freon® Products Division," in *Managing Environmental Issues: A Casebook*, eds. Rogene Buchholz, Alfred Marcus, and James Post (Englewood Cliffs, N.J.: Prentice-Hall, 1992), 261–286.

22. See Mary Douglas and Aaron Wildavsky, *Risk and Culture* (Berkeley: University of California Press, 1982). See also McGinnis and Ostrom, "Institutional Analysis," 63.

23. Apparently the mere study of economics diminishes cooperative behavior. Reporting on a study by Robert Frank, Thomas Gilovich, and Dennis Regan ("Does Studying Economics Inhibit Cooperation?," *Journal of*

Economic Perspectives [spring 1993]), *The Economist* notes that economists and economics students are less concerned about fairness, give less to charity, and are more likely to cheat than are their colleagues in other disciplines. "How Do You Mean, 'Fair?'," *The Economist*, 29 May 1993, 71.

24. See, for example, Paul Wapner, *Environmental Activism and World Civic Politics* (Albany: State University of New York Press, 1996); Grant Hewison, "The Role of Environmental Non-Governmental Organizations," in *Ocean Governance: Strategies and Approaches for the 21st Century*, ed. Thomas Mensah, 115–137 (Honolulu: Law of the Sea Institute, 1996); and Birnie and Boyle, *International Law and the Environment*, especially chapter 2.

25. Birnie and Boyle, *International Law and Environment*, 79.

26. "Chronological Summary: Events of 1992," *Colorado Journal of International Environmental Law and Policy* 4 (1993): 232.

27. Lynton Caldwell, "Beyond Environmental Diplomacy: The Changing Institutional Structure of International Cooperation," in *International Environmental Diplomacy*, ed. John Carroll (Cambridge: Cambridge University Press, 1988), 20.

28. Hewison, "Environmental Non-Governmental Organizations," 129.

29. Ibid., 137.

30. McGinnis and Ostrom, "Institutional Analysis," 63–64.

31. This discussion is based on Peter Sand, *Lessons Learned in Global Environmental Governance* (Washington, D.C.: World Resources Institute, June 1990).

32. Caldwell, "Beyond Environmental Diplomacy," 21. For example, the United States Senate has so far declined to ratify the Biodiversity Convention because Senator Jesse Helms, who chairs the Senate Foreign Relations Committee, has refused to let it out of his committee. He opposes the convention because he sees it as an attack on states' rights and because he and his fellow conservatives are unwilling to extend the environmental powers and responsibilities of the federal government.

33. Ibid., 14.

34. See Richard Neustadt and Ernest R. May, *Thinking in Time: The Uses of History for Decision Makers* (New York: Free Press, 1988), for a discussion and illustration of the uses of history in policy analysis.

35. Lawrence Taylor, "'The River Would Run Red with Blood': Community and Common Property in an Irish Fishing Settlement," in *The Question of the Commons: The Culture and Ecology of Communal Resources*, eds. Bonnie McCay and James Acheson (Tucson: University of Arizona Press, 1987), 290–307.

36. Work by Aaron Wildavsky and colleagues, which stresses the rela-

tionships between social preferences and social organizations, clarifies how changes in cultural biases lead to changes in policy outcomes. For example, preferences for the protection of individual liberty, as espoused in the documents of the American Revolution, led inexorably to legal protections for economic individualism, that is, laissez-faire capitalism. See Michael Thompson, Richard Ellis, and Aaron Wildavsky, *Cultural Theory* (Boulder, Colo.: Westview Press, 1990).

37. Hans Blomkvist, "The Soft State: Making Policy in a Different Context," in *History and Context in Comparative Public Policy*, ed. Douglas E. Ashford (Pittsburgh: University of Pittsburgh Press, 1992), 118.

38. Marshall Sahlins, *Stone Age Economics* (Chicago: Aldine-Atherton, 1972), 4. I am indebted to Todd Baldwin for suggesting this quotation.

Sir Henry Sumner Maine agrees:

> What mankind did in the primitive state may not be a hopeless subject of inquiry, but of their motives for doing it it is impossible to know anything. These sketches of the plight of human beings in the first ages of the world are effected by first supposing mankind to be divested of a great part of the circumstances by which they are now surrounded, and by then assuming that, in the condition thus imagined, they would preserve the same sentiments and prejudices by which they are now actuated,—although, in fact, these sentiments may have been created and engendered by those very circumstances of which, by the hypothesis, they are to be stripped.

Sir Henry Sumner Maine, *Ancient Law* (1861) (n.p.: Dorset Press, 1986), 210–211.

Douglas Ashford makes a similar point: "As provocative as some of the new international political economy analysis may be, it is difficult to link these studies to the institutional, political and organizational differences highlighted in, for example, French and British studies of industrial and economic policy in the nineteenth century. *The danger is that scholars may thereby be unaware that their macrotheories are quite inappropriate to the historical period.*" (emphasis added). Douglas E. Ashford, "Historical Context and Policy Studies," in *History and Context in Comparative Public Policy*, ed. Douglas E. Ashford (Pittsburgh: University of Pittsburgh Press, 1992), 32 (notes omitted).

39. World Commission on Environment and Development, *Our Common Future* (New York: Oxford University Press, 1987), 8. This is an anthropocentric definition, however. I prefer the one proposed by Helen Kolff in *Beyond War*: "the ability to support, provide for, [and] nurture the total life

system in our bioregion and all other bioregions on the planet; [and] the ability to supply in perpetuity all life forms with the necessities of life." Cited in Daniel Chiras, *Environmental Science: Action for a Sustainable Future*, 4th ed. (New York: Benjamin-Cummings, 1994), 6. Unfortunately, to adopt such an analytic standard in the present discussion would force radical conclusions about the propriety of most environmental policies and would move this book out of the realm of legal and institutional analysis.

40. Louis Henkin, *International Law: Politics and Values* (Boston: Martinus Nijhoff, 1995), 290.

41. Birnie and Boyle, *International Law and the Environment*, 5.

42. Ibid., 122–124.

43. See, for example, Chiras, *Environmental Science*, especially chapter 1.

44. See Timothy O'Riordan and J. Cameron, eds., *Interpreting the Precautionary Principle* (London: Earthscan, 1994), and E. Hey, "The Precautionary Concept in Environmental Policy and Law: Institutionalizing Caution," *Georgetown International Environmental Law Review* 4 (1992): 303–318.

45. Chiras, *Environmental Science*, 7–10.

46. Thompson, Ellis, and Wildavsky, *Cultural Theory*, especially chapter 1; Michael Thompson, "The Cultural Construction of Nature and the Natural Destruction of Culture," working paper prepared for the International Institute for Applied Systems Analysis, Laxenberg, Austria, 1984; and C. S. Holling, "Myths of Ecological Stability: Resilience and the Problem of Failure," in *Studies in Crisis Management*, eds. C. F. Smart and W. T. Stanbury, 97–109 (Montreal: Butterworth and the Institute for Research on Public Policy, 1978).

47. Here, I am following the logic of Sherlock Holmes: "Eliminate the impossible, and whatever remains, however improbable, must be the truth."

Chapter 2

A Framework for Analysis

Human history becomes more and more a race between education and catastrophe.

—H. G. Wells, *The Outline of History* (1920)

The parameters of a discussion of the global commons range across four dimensions: the height, breadth, and depth of the physical world and through the centuries of recorded human history. Because the concept of property rights is central to an understanding of the commons, the first purpose of this chapter is to establish a clear picture of property rights and the ways in which various property regimes evolve and are legitimated. The chapter begins with an overview of the Western legal tradition, showing how feudalism and domination by the Roman Catholic Church gave way to mercantilism and individualism. Mercantilism and individualism in turn led to our modern notions of property and ownership.

The chapter continues with a discussion of three of these modern concepts that have had a significant effect on the global commons regimes: the property rights paradigm, national sovereignty, and the "common heritage of mankind" (CHM) principle. The final section of this chapter presents the analytic model used throughout the remainder of the book. It is an amalgam of regime theory, the Institutional Analysis and Development (IAD) framework for small-scale common pool resources developed by Elinor Ostrom and others, and recent scholarship on multiple-use common pool resource domains.

The discussion begins with the evolution of law among nations and how it has affected our perspectives on the global commons.

Law and History

History matters in law as well as in politics. The story of the evolution of Western law provides the context for the property rights paradigm, national sovereignty, and the common heritage of mankind.

Development of Western Law

The Roman law of contract is the root of European government.[1] Roman law recognized the legal differences between the public law of the state, which was concerned with relations between governments and subjects, and civil law, which arbitrated relations among individuals. In Roman law, the *consensual contract*, completed by simple agreement without any legally binding sanction or symbolic act, was the ultimate form of agreement between individuals.[2] If contract law could function without direct intervention by a sovereign government, it could also be a regulating force between nation-states.[3] The impact of the Roman idea of contracts between individuals cannot be underestimated. The *Pax Romana* (the peace imposed by ancient Rome) extended to much of the known world, and Roman commerce, facilitated by a common understanding of contract, was the foundation of international law.[4] Even after the collapse of the Roman Empire, its legal legacy continued in the canon law of the Catholic Church.

In the Middle Ages, the Roman Catholic Church was the predominant social force in Europe, controlling education, science, and, of course, theology.[5] After the Reformation challenged the centrality of Catholic dogma, the church, with its hierarchy and entrenched support of the class structure, was no longer the arbiter of human behavior. Specialized legal systems emerged: canon law, mercantile law (the law merchant)[6], feudal and manorial law,[7] urban law, and royal law. A new merchant class developed, and new laws were needed to meet its changing needs. In the feudal system, landowners had contributed to the military demands of the king through servitude of knights and men. The new merchant class had neither and instead contributed to war efforts by loans and direct payments.[8] This gave kings obligations outside the old feudal society and an independent source of income; they were no longer completely dependent on the loyalty of their vassals to raise and to support the military. This was clearly to the advantage of the kings, allowing them more control over the feudal lords as well as independence.[9]

States also sought to distance themselves from the overweening authority of the church, thus replicating at the international level the rise of individualism at the national level.[10] Claims of national sovereignty were used to confound the Holy Empire, and the excuse of *raison d'état* was used to "subordinate the individual citizen to the needs of the state."[11]

Moneylenders and merchants supported the evolution of centralized power, partly because the new urban laws allowed them to buy exemptions from feudal responsibilities and to have their own urban courts administer justice.[12] The merchants themselves largely determined international mercantile law through international fairs, markets, and their own courts. Local customs were recorded so that visiting merchants would be able to conduct business properly.[13] Eventually, some portions of mercantile law were standardized and applied internationally; the merchants themselves enforced it to protect trade. They even invented credit (to enable businessmen to avoid the hazards of transporting large sums of money) and corporations (to limit personal liability).

Jurisprudence is the science of law; its function is to clarify the principles on which the law is based.[14] In the sixteenth century, two schools of jurisprudence—analytic jurisprudence, or legal positivism, and natural law—led to competing views of international relations. To oversimplify, legal positivism describes the law and identifies actors and policies in a context that supports, if not encourages, capitalism, whereas natural law assumes the existence of a moral code that is independent of human needs and desires and against which human activity can be measured. One school of thought is individualistic, the other is egalitarian or hierarchical.[15]

Analytic jurisprudence was expressed first in the work of Francis Bacon (1561–1626) and later seen in the social contract theories of Thomas Hobbes (1588–1679) and others: just as people had been in a state of nature prior to the formation of civil society, nation-states were now in an anarchic condition, and there was no international society in sight.[16] Because these states and their princes were not bound by an enforceable legal system or a single coherent society, they were free to pursue their own individual and national preferences.[17]

The alternative view of law that eventually prevailed was a new variation of natural law, although it was not a complete departure from medieval natural law theories. Building on the thirteenth-century work of Saint Thomas Aquinas, the new jurisprudence separated law from theology.[18] Hugo Grotius (1583–1645) wrote in this tradition; his *De jure belli ac pacis* (*On the law of war and peace*, 1625) had an enormous impact. He proposed a view of international relations that lent a normative order to the previous lawless condition among nations posited under the Hobbesian approach.

For Grotius, natural law held the actions of states to the same standard as the actions of individuals; natural law was the "body of moral rules known to all rational beings, against which the mere will or practice of states [could] be measured."[19] This approach to natural law laid the basis for modern Western law.

The shift in international law and relation was a reflection of a radical transformation in all of Western society:

> The attack against hierarchy which was waged in a number of countries in Europe in the sixteenth century was directed against the spiritual order of Catholicism as well as against the worldly order of feudalism. In the economic field, its chief target was the feudal system of economics, with its concomitant institutions of serfdom and vocational guilds. In the political field, the new orientation found expression in the fight against the feudal nobility and its privileges. Its ultimate effect in the countries in which the rebellion was successful was a strengthening of secular, individualistic, and liberalistic forces in the political, economic, and intellectual life.[20]

In the seventeenth and eighteenth centuries, as the modern notion of property rights was developing, the Industrial Revolution made its impact on European society. Men of low birth joined the ranks of the middle class, and the power of the guilds waned. Entrepreneurs abounded; class structures, though not disappearing, were shifting so rapidly as to be virtually impossible to map. Individualism was on the rise, and social and economic hierarchies were becoming increasingly unstable.

As the Industrial Revolution, with its mechanistic view of society, took hold, natural law fell out of favor and legal positivism became orthodoxy. Early legal positivists such as John Austin defined *law* as the command of a sovereign backed by a sanction.[21] International law as a field was challenged by this definition; when legal positivists applied Austin's definition of law to international law, they argued that international law could not be true law because it lacked both sovereign and sanction.[22] There is no central sovereign at the international level. The United Nations is a deliberative body; its members are instructed by their national governments and must return to their national governments for approval of decisions. Enforcement is also left to the individual member states. Although a critique of the legal positivists is beyond the scope of this volume,[23] the problem lies not with international law but rather with their theory.[24]

It is perhaps more helpful to think of international law as a process through which authoritative decisions are made in the transnational arena. Numerous policy actors (including nation-states, nongovernmental organizations, international nongovernmental organizations, and international government organizations) signal their acceptance of a particular international regime through custom, by incorporation of the principles of international law in treaties and conventions, by judicial decisions in both national and international courts, by the articulation of general principles of law, and by unilateral declarations.[25]

From the early days of Rome through the Middle Ages down to the present, perceptions of hierarchy and individualism have been reflected in the relationships among states. Rome was as much a commercial empire as a political one, and contractual relations between individuals led to expectations of contractual relations among nation-states. The ascendancy of the Catholic Church, with its rigid hierarchy, complemented feudal society. Individual liberties were subordinated to institutional welfare; people's rights—indeed, their very lives—were held at the whim of their overlords, who were in turn subject to papal authority. The Reformation and the Industrial Revolution changed the religious and economic institutions of society. Salvation became a reward for individual activity, and changes in technology and economic systems eroded the old class structures. Commerce established links among nations that were independent of papal supervision. The nation-states became as individualistic as their citizens, and international law reflected this individualism.

The Property Rights Paradigm

An individualistic, capitalistic society such as that found in the West requires a private property regime that permits property to be accumulated for individual benefit. The founding myth or "story" of the development of property rights must therefore rest on individualism and competition rather than on cooperation, although cooperation clearly is necessary for the formation of any regime.[26] This is the same paradox faced by economist Ronald Coase in 1937 when he addressed the problem of the formation of cooperative institutions within the firm: why would supposedly self-interested, rational actors expend their individual resources to form cooperatives that would then generate benefits which must be shared?[27]

In medieval notions of property, the idea that the use of property was regulated by custom and culture was an implicit underlying assumption of the regime. However, in the late eighteenth century, this concept was replaced by economic and political individualism.[28] The idea that the desire to acquire property rights is instinctive is a post-eighteenth-century doctrine. Eighteenth-century political theorists focused on the individual, a new creature recently discovered, partly through the Reformation, which had destroyed the medieval notion of humanity's place in a divinely directed hierarchy.

To explain the startling social and economic changes of the eighteenth century, new stories and myths were required, and they were written by individualists.[29] Seeing cooperation as not only undesirable but also impossible, political theorists exorcised the cooperative underpinnings of society in general and of property in particular. For example, in *Federalist 10*, James Madison explained how economic self-interest would protect society from the "violence of faction" by distributing property throughout the new commercial republic.[30] Economic growth became the "solid but low foundation" of American society, "magnifying and multiplying in American life the selfish, the interested, the narrow, the vulgar, and the crassly economic."[31] When the new American governments were formed, acquisitiveness became a solid, yeoman virtue, and avarice, the deadly sin, became a shadow of its former self.[32] The theorists could not do otherwise because their cultural context blinded them to other possibilities. These theorists, brilliant in their own day, lacked the "working rules"[33] derived from the modern concepts of institutionalism, political culture, and anthropology to help them organize the new world in which they found themselves. These working rules are prescriptions that define policy actors and the behaviors in which they may, must, or may not engage.[34] They are discussed more fully in the section on the institutional analysis and development (IAD) framework at the end of this chapter.

Thus, the modern Western legal view of property rights was shaped at a time when privatized rights were seen as both inevitable and—to the extent anyone cared about ethics—morally desirable. This view of social contract and the law, which seemed to clear the cobwebs from the old classical philosophies of Plato, Aristotle, and Cicero, went unchallenged by mainstream theorists until the twentieth century, although substantial and uncoordinated criticism by hierarchs (notably the churches) and egalitarians (e.g., utopians, transcendentalists, and New Age Aquarians) has never subsided completely. Modern criticisms of the mythology of property rights arise from new sources: political scientists and others trained in empirical methods who demonstrate that the theories no longer explain the data;[35] anthropologists and other social scientists who study cultures with belief systems that are fundamentally cooperative;[36] and legal historians who find that the law does not develop as the myth projects even in the West, and that in non-Western cultures the story makes even less sense.[37]

The final chapter in this entertaining story may come in the field of international law, in which the last of the open-access regimes (Antarctica, the high seas, the atmosphere, and space) are being changed to common pool resource regimes. Soon, and for the first time in history, there will be no place on Earth that is not governed under a management regime. There will be no more final frontier.[38] Now resource domains are finite, and resources become more valuable as they become more scarce. In response, the international law of property has begun to change. For example, the Convention on Biodiversity mandates equitable sharing of technological and financial benefits between the country of origin and developers who exploit genetic resources.[39] In the past, Western legal thought dominated international law, largely because Western nations dominated the international political arena. However, as the case discussions in the following chapters show, the developing nations have shifted some international regimes away from Western-style individualism and toward more egalitarian behavior.

The following two sections address national sovereignty and the common heritage of mankind (CHM) principle, both of which also suggest an emergent Grotian change.

National Sovereignty

Just as an individual holds a complex bundle of property rights in his or her own society, so does a nation-state exercise a complex bundle of rights in the international arena. Among the rights held by states is *national sovereignty*:

> The supreme, absolute, and uncontrollable power by which any state is governed; . . . the international independence of a state. The power to do everything in a state without accountability . . . ,—to make laws, to execute and to apply them, to impose and collect taxes and levy contributions, to make war or peace, to form treaties of alliance or of commerce with foreign nations, and the like.[40]

Sovereignty may be thought of as a special case of property rights. Of course, by entering into international agreements on trade, access to resources, pollution, and so forth, nations accept constraints on their absolute freedom of action. They agree in the Outer Space Treaty (see chapter 6), for example, to forgo the traditional right of territorial acquisition by discovery and occupation in exchange for peaceful access to the domain. Some of these limitations are on activities that have traditionally been the rights of national governments, such as the right to use any weapons in wartime. Some are restrictions on the activities of people and corporations that are under their national jurisdiction, such as the ban on the manufacture and use of chlorofluorocarbons.

The entire issue of transboundary resources and pollution makes it clear that absolute sovereignty is an idea whose time has passed.[41] Although global pollution problems are actually problems of externalities, they serve to underscore the importance of international cooperation and its inevitable restriction on national sovereignty. The dramatic depletion of fishery stocks in the high seas is attributable, in part, to ocean pollution, and the use of ozone-destroying chemicals in industrialized nations has serious consequences for public health and economic prosperity worldwide. In order to mitigate these effects, nations have chosen to cooperate in the formation of new international regimes (see the discussion on international regime formation in chapter 1), and in the process, their sovereign control over the affected resources and economic processes has changed.

The Common Heritage of Mankind

The old debates between positivists and proponents of natural law have been revived in recent years. This is perhaps inevitable, given the importance of environmental issues now shaping the international agenda, because the philosophical basis for environmental concerns rests on natural law and its twin concerns for human preservation and individual justice.[42] The positivist theories have faced a strong challenge in the claims of developing nations for a common-heritage approach to global and international commons and in the general rhetoric of the North–South debates in the United Nations.[43] The common heritage of mankind (CHM) principle (*res communes humanitatus*) is "a wholly new concept of property rights, a modern alternative to the traditional ideas of exclusive ownership or of free and unlimited access."[44] It was first proposed in 1967 by Arvid Pardo, Maltese ambassador to the United Nations.[45] CHM defines some resources, such as deep seabed minerals, as the property of the global human population. CHM proponents then argue that since a community (albeit a large one) already holds most of the bundle the property rights to the resources, the resources cannot legally be appropriated by any one individual or state. The benefits from their exploitation should be shared by all states (and presumably distributed to the people) regardless of the state's participation in resource extraction.[46]

The common heritage of mankind principle originated from two realizations in the international community. First, some valuable natural resource stocks, such as certain fisheries, are close to exhaustion. The developing countries are eager to ensure that the resources remain available for their own use, and the common heritage principle gives moral force to their arguments. Second, the developing nations were concerned that the first-come-first-served rule would be to their disadvantage in regimes such as deep-seabed mining and outer space. CHM was an assertion of their right to participate in exploitation and a moral claim to the development assistance needed for participation.

However, the developing countries have not seen many measurable benefits from the CHM principle. The seabed mineral regime was modified in 1994 to satisfy the developed nations before the Law of the Sea Treaty entered into force (see chapter 4). The CHM principle written into the Moon Treaty does not provide any special advantages for developing countries, and the major space-faring nations have yet to ratify the Treaty.[47]

Analytic Framework

Convergent evolution is defined by ecologists as "the independent evolution of similar traits among unrelated organisms resulting from similar selective pressures."[48] For example, the Tanzanian serval (a small cat) and the Brazilian maned wolf have developed similar body forms and hunting behaviors even though they are completely different species.[49] Convergent evolution may also occur in the social sciences, as an examination of regime theory and common pool resource literature demonstrates. The study of the global commons exists at a unique intersection of disciplines. International organizations and treaty regimes of all types have been predominantly the concern of scholars of international relations. Common pool resources, of which global commons may be considered a subset, have been almost exclusively the concern of students of economics, ecology, anthropology, and policy analysis.

Although the analytic approach used in this book is based primarily on the institutional and analytic development (IAD) framework, this section begins with a discussion of regime theory. Readers who are familiar with only one approach will find it helpful to have the parallels between regime theory and the IAD framework drawn explicitly.

Regime Theory

According to Oran Young, regimes are

> social institutions governing the actions of those involved in specifiable activities or sets of activities;. . . [They] are practices consisting of recognized roles linked together by clusters of rules or conventions governing relations among the occupants of these roles.[50]

The basis of regime analysis is the assumption that institutions are limiting factors; that is, existing institutions constrain policy options of individual actors. They may also establish rights, such as the right to conduct research in the Antarctic, but these established rights are limited in eligibility and exercise.

Institutions may be dependent variables: if individuals, constrained by factors such as geography, technology, finances, and cultural preferences, want to achieve certain effects, then particular institutions are likely to emerge. Institutions may also be independent variables: given certain institutional structures and rules, policies are affected in particular ways.[51]

Young posits three key components for international regimes: a substantive component, a procedural component, and implementation.[52] The substantive component includes rights and rules. *Rights* encompass "anything to which an actor (individual or otherwise) is entitled by virtue of occupying a recognized role."[53] *Rules* are guides to action, defining resource use through administrative regulations and incentive systems and outlining liability and procedures for daily activities. For example, how spacecraft must be marked for identification and when they must be registered are part of the substantive component.

The procedural component is at the aggregate level, where individual actors must make some collective choices. These decisions govern the allocation of resources, the distributive functions of the group, and the resolution of disputes. For example, determining the qualifications for national research stations in the Antarctic is part of the procedural component. Decisions in the procedural component differ from those in the substantive component primarily through the level of the choices involved. The rules at the procedural component are aggregate rules; those at the substantive level are individual.

The third component is implementation; here, compliance is affected by monitoring and enforcement. How whale harvests are monitored and what sanctions are imposed on nations that violate International Whaling Commission (IWC) directives are part of the implementation component. A recurrent criticism of both international relations and international law is that effective enforcement is virtually impossible because there is no routinized sanctioning mechanism. However, equally striking is the observation that international agreements work more often than they do not. Why should nations cooperate if the costs of noncooperation are low? One answer is that national leaders recognize that future cooperative ventures, which may be to their advantage, may be jeopardized if they become known as unreliable international actors.[54] A second answer is that although cooperation entails costs (especially transaction and monitoring costs), it also reduces economic uncertainty because international regimes provide predictability. Routinization is especially helpful in the global market economy because of the high transaction costs of negotiating exchange terms individually with all possible exchange partners.[55]

Institutional Analysis

Regime theory parallels important aspects of the Institutional Analysis and Development (IAD) framework developed for analysis of small-scale common pool resources by Elinor Ostrom and others.[56] Ostrom's definition of institutions is markedly similar to Young's definition of regimes:

> the sets of working rules that are used to determine who is eligible to make decisions in some arena, what actions are allowed or constrained, what aggregation rules will be used, what procedures must be followed, what information must or must not be provided, and what payoffs will be assigned to individuals dependent on their actions.[57]

Levels of Institutional Choice

In Ostrom's model, institutions operate within three levels of analysis: operational choice (appropriation, provision, monitoring, and enforcement), collective choice (policy making, management, and adjudication), and constitutional choice (formulation, governance, adjudication, and modification). Operational choice levels parallel Young's substantive component, and collective choice is similar to the procedural component. To take Antarctica as an example, operational choice decisions determine such issues as how waste will be disposed of, how many dogs may be kept at a station, and who has jurisdiction over interstation criminal activity. Analysis at the level of collective choice examines such issues as whether to have a permanent secretariat and whether decisions made by members of the Antarctic Treaty System (ATS) will be made by consensus or by some other method. Analysis at the constitutional level analysis examines who may become a party to the ATS.[58]

Design Principles

Ostrom's IAD framework identifies eight design principles for sustainable small-scale common pool resource regimes:

1. There must be *clearly defined boundaries* for the user pool (appropriators) and the resource domain.
2. *Appropriation rules* must be congruent with local conditions and with *provision rules* (which regulate user inputs for resource maintenance). Appropriation rules and provision rules together are called operational rules.
3. *Collective choice arrangements* ensure that the resource users participate in setting appropriation and provision rules.
4. *Monitoring* is done by the appropriators or by their agents.
5. *Graduated sanctions* are applied to appropriators who violate operational rules.
6. *Conflict resolution mechanisms* are readily available, low cost, and legitimate.
7. *Rights to organize regimes* are recognized by external authorities.
8. For common pool regimes that are part of larger systems: *Nested enterprises* aggregate institutions within local, regional, and national jurisdictions.[59]

Although all eight of the design principles are applicable to the analysis of global commons, five are particularly useful: clearly defined boundaries, congruency between operational rules and local conditions, monitoring, graduated sanctions, and nested enterprises.[60]

First is the need for clearly defined boundaries for the appropriators and the resource domain. For instance, one of the central problems with fisheries management is the fugitive nature of the resource, which moves through international waters and many national jurisdictions. Neither the resource domain nor the pool of users who are eligible to fish have clearly established boundaries. In contrast, the Antarctic Treaty System has both clear geographical boundaries and clear access rights to the domain, which have contributed to a relatively stable regime.

The second principle, that operational rules must be congruent with local conditions, is also important in global commons regimes. For example, Michael McGinnis and Elinor Ostrom note that

> although it might seem obvious that a global problem like green-house warming necessarily requires a solution that is similarly global in scope, no global regime can remain robust if it neglects to take account of local circumstances or the conflicting interests of smaller scale collective action organizations.[61]

Thus, the *operational rules* (appropriation and provision rules) must be nested (design principle 8) within local, regional, national, and international levels, as must *monitoring, sanctioning,* and *conflict resolution mechanisms.* Most international and global regimes cannot succeed if the participating national governments cannot or will not obtain compliance within their own jurisdictions. For example, the 1987 Protocol on Substances that Deplete the Ozone Layer (Montreal Protocol) depends on compliance by national governments, multinational chemical companies, retailers, and individuals. There is a lucrative smuggling trade for refrigerants between the United States and Mexico; if the United States is unwilling or unable to halt this trade, the effectiveness of the Protocol is diminished.

Issues of monitoring and sanctioning (design principles 4 and 5) are enduring, thorny problems in international regimes and international law.[62] For instance, in the telecommunications regime, corporations are especially vigilant because violations of regime rules gives economic advantages to their competitors; corporations will therefore influence their own national governments to negotiate compliance and sanctions in the international arena. National pressures were also brought to bear in 1985 by the U.S. Cetacean Society when it sued the American Secretary of Commerce to enforce national laws supporting the International Whaling Commission's moratorium on whaling, which had been violated by Japan.[63] Although the Cetacean Society won in the lower court, the United States Supreme Court reversed the lower court's decision; however, Japan notified the United States soon afterward that it would halt whaling operations by March 1988. Thus, the lack of an external, Austinian sovereign to apply sanctions may be a barrier to successful monitoring and sanctioning in global commons regimes. Clearly, the analytic structure of small-scale common pool resource regimes is similar to the structure of global commons regimes. The IAD framework has been tested in the field and in the laboratory, so it provides a base from which to analyze more complex common pool resource regimes. The next section examines the emerging literature on multiple-use commons.[64]

Multiple-Use, Multiple-User Commons

Property rights to a given resource in a resource domain may be held by a variety of groups or individuals who intend to exercise those rights in rather different ways. For example, water resources may be used for recreation, transportation, irrigation, industrial processes, municipal needs, human and animal consumption, waste disposal, and ecosystem maintenance.[65] Some of these uses are consumptive (drinking and, to some extent, irrigation), and others (transportation) are not. Some are more excludable (irrigation) than others (ecosystem maintenance). Some are really the result of negative externalities of nonrelated activities (waste disposal). To address these conflicts, some water resource regimes assign prioritized water uses; for example, in preindustrial America, residential and agricultural uses were preferred by law over manufacturing uses.[66] Other water resource regimes take a different tack, assigning use rights based on water quality, so that industrial waterways or shipping lanes are closed to fishing or swimming activities. In a commons, access to the resource domain is established by the property regime, but appropriators who have access rights may still be seeking different resources or planning to put the resources to different uses. This is seen at the international level in the Antarctic domain, where scientific research, exploration, hunting, fishing, mining, and tourism all take place simultaneously.

Victoria Edwards and Nathalie Steins have developed an analytic framework that incorporates multiple uses by multiple appropriators, emphasizing the need for nested enterprises.[67] Several of their findings are particularly useful in approaching the global commons. First, a sustainable regime must be able to support combined uses of the resource domain. Second, a lack of congruence in boundary rules, appropriation rules, and provision rules will threaten regime sustainability. Third, at a minimum, all the appropriators must be represented in the regime and share knowledge of the operational rules. If all the resource uses are to be sustainable, then decisions made at the collective choice level to establish the operational rules should include all the regime participants. If this does not occur, then those appropriators who participate at the collective choice level may diminish or eliminate altogether the rights of appropriators who have competing uses.

Summary

This section presents a summary of the analytic framework used throughout the remainder of the book. (See box 2.1, Analytic Framework for Global

---

Box 2.1 Analytic Framework for the Global Commons

I. Levels of Institutional Choice

   1. *Operational choice*: appropriation, provision, monitoring, and enforcement

   2. *Collective choice*: policy making, management, and adjudication

   3. *Constitutional choice*: formulation, governance, adjudication, and modification

II. Design Principles for Sustainable Regimes (principles especially important for global commons are indicated in bold)

   1. **Clearly defined boundaries**

   2. **Operational rules congruent with local conditions**

   3. Collective choice arrangements

   4. **Monitoring**

   5. **Graduated sanctions**

   6. Conflict resolution mechanisms

   7. Rights to organize regimes

   8. **Nested enterprises**

In addition, for multiple-use commons

   1. **Resource domain must be able to support all uses**

   2. **All users must be represented**

   3. **Knowledge of operational rules must be shared**

Sources: Edwards and Steins, "Developing an Analytical Framework"; McGinnis and Ostrom, "Institutional Analysis"; Ostrom, *Governing the Commons*

Commons.) Readers should be aware that the IAD framework developed by Elinor Ostrom and others is more complex and sophisticated than is presented here. Full use of the framework demands a depth of descriptive information that can be developed only in a series of independent volumes, each of which addresses just one global commons. Here we are looking through the lens of the IAD framework at a photomontage of management regimes; we are not peering through an IAD microscope at a single, discrete regime.

Sustainable management of the global commons requires an analytic framework that recognizes the fundamental institutional characteristics that define all common-pool resource regimes. The modified IAD framework, supplemented by new research on complex multiple-use commons, is the key to analysis of the global commons presented in the following four chapters.

The next chapter examines the most coherent of the global commons regimes: Antarctica.

Suggested Reading

Berman, Harold. *Law and Revolution: The Formation of the Western Legal Tradition*. Cambridge, Mass.: Harvard University Press, 1983. A magisterial work that is written simply and dramatically. It is accessible to the lay reader and satisfying for the scholar.

Kelly, John M. *A Short History of Western Legal Theory*. Oxford: Clarendon Press, 1992. An immensely readable history of jurisprudence from the Greeks to the late twentieth century.

Ponting, Clive. *A Green History of the World: The Environment and the Collapse of Great Civilizations*. New York: Penguin Books, 1991. A tour de force of readable, almost journalistic history that provides an excellent overview.

Rose, Carol M. *Property and Persuasion: Essays on the History, Theory, and Rhetoric of Ownership*. Boulder, Colo.: Westview Press, 1994. This volume collects Rose's articles on property over the previous decade. They are original, enlightening, and entertaining. I wish I had written them.

Notes

1. Andreas Wacke, "Freedom of Contract and Restraint of Trade Clauses in Roman and Modern Law," *Law and History Review* 11, 1 (Spring 1993): 1–19; Adda Bozeman, *Politics and Culture in International History* (Princeton, N.J.: Princeton University Press, 1960), 199–201. Grotius was heavily influenced by the Roman jurists, especially Cicero. Bozeman, *Politics and Culture*, 204.

2. Bozeman, *Politics and Culture*, 199–201. Consensual contracts were different in form but not in substance from literal contracts (recorded), real contracts (binding on delivery of goods), and verbal contracts (bound by ritual words).

3. Ibid., 194.

4. Ibid., 210–211 (notes omitted).

5. Edgar Bodenheimer, *Jurisprudence: The Philosophy and Method of the Law* (Cambridge, Mass.: Harvard University Press, 1962), 30.

6. For unknown reasons, mercantile law is referred to as "the law merchant." Regrettably, the term does not refer to a purveyor of laws.

7. Feudal law dealt with the rights and obligations of lords and their vassals and with land tenure systems. Manorial law dealt with the rights and obligations of lords and peasants and with agricultural production. It is interesting to note that the obligations, at least in the early days, went both ways.

8. One reason the Jews were expelled from England in the reign of Edward I (1272–1307) was to relieve the king of his enormous debt to them. See Winston Churchill, *The Birth of Britain* (New York: Dodd, Mead, 1958), pp. 289–291. Edward I was the same Edward Longshanks who executed the Scottish patriot William Wallace.

9. Wyndham Bewes, *The Romance of the Law Merchant* (London: n.p., 1923).

10. Bodenheimer, *Jurisprudence*, 33.

11. Ibid., 34.

> There is perhaps still an echo of this logic in the new notions of community which have arisen in egalitarian rhetoric in both the international environmental movements and in the Common Heritage of Mankind principle. Both suggest that individual needs or benefits should be foregone for the benefit of the global community. This new statism which places the community above the individual is found in astonishing places. Critical legal studies [CLS] offers an excellent example of egalitarian blame of the establishment: Offended by the hierarchical structures of domination that characterize modern society, CLS people work toward a world that is more just and egalitarian.

Alan C. Hutchinson, "Introduction," in *Critical Legal Studies*, ed. Alan C. Hutchinson (Totowa, N.J.: Rowman and Littlefield, 1989), 3. A more subversive approach to promote egalitarian structures was found in the "new public administration" espoused throughout the 1970s and 1980s. See Gary Wamsley et al., "The Public Administration and the Governance Process: Refocusing the American Dialogue," in *A Centennial History of the American Administrative State*, ed. Ralph Clark Chandler (New York: Free Press, 1987), 291–317.

12. The Magna Carta (1215) was an effort by the barons to halt this inexorable process. It protected the rights of the barons against the king by codifying feudal law and custom in contract form, complete with enforcement provisions. It was a "redress of feudal grievance extorted from an unwilling king by a discontented ruling class insisting on its privileges" (Churchill, *Birth of Britain*, 255–256). Despite its origins, the ultimate impact of the Magna Carta was to the benefit of all British citizens because it established for the first time that no one, not even the king, was above the law. Ibid., 252–257.

13. In 1056 the Customs of Genoa were recorded, and in 1095 the Amalfitan Table (a collection of Italian maritime law) was assembled.

14. See John M. Kelly, *A Short History of Western Legal Theory* (Oxford: Clarendon Press, 1992), and Harold Berman, *Law and Revolution: The For-*

mation of the Western Legal Tradition (Cambridge, Mass.: Harvard University Press, 1983).

15. See Michael Thompson, Richard Ellis, and Aaron Wildavsky, *Cultural Theory* (Boulder, Colo.: Westview Press, 1990), for a discussion of the policy implications of individualist, egalitarian, and hierarchical cultural preferences.

16. Hobbes's views of a state of nature were especially influential. See Huntington Cairns, *Legal Philosophy from Plato to Hegel* (Baltimore: Johns Hopkins University Press, 1949), 271. Morris Cohen and Felix Cohen note that social contract theory "was intended as an instrument of logical analysis rather than a theory of history (as most critics of the doctrine assume)" Morris Cohen and Felix Cohen, eds. *Readings in Jurisprudence and Legal Philosophy* (Boston: Little, Brown, 1951), 861.

17. Hedley Bull, "The Importance of Grotius in the Study of International Relations," in *Hugo Grotius and International Relations*, eds. Hedley Bull, Benedict Kingsbury, and Adam Roberts (Oxford: Oxford University Press, 1990), 71.

18. Bodenheimer, *Jurisprudence*, 32–33.

19. Bull, *Grotius and International Relations*, 78.

20. Bodenheimer, *Jurisprudence*, 30–31. This was the first Grotian moment in Western history; as noted in chapter 1, we are probably in the midst of a second.

21. See John Austin, "The Province of Jurisprudence Determined" (1832), in *The Province of Jurisprudence Determined and the Uses of the Study of Jurisprudence* (London: Wiedenfeld and Nicholson, 1955), 1–361.

22. This notion of sovereign and sanction extends to rights as well; in Austin's framework, a right is the power of a member of the community to draw down the sanction of the sovereign. Thus, according to Austin, a property right exists primarily in its enforcement. See Austin, "Province of Jurisprudence Determined"; John Austin, "The Uses of the Study of Jurisprudence" (1863), in *The Province of Jurisprudence Determined and the Uses of the Study of Jurisprudence* (London: Wiedenfeld and Nicholson, 1955), 363–393; and John Austin, *Lectures on Jurisprudence on the Philosophy of Positive Law*, 5th ed., ed. R. Campbell (London: John Murray, 1885).

23. Sir Henry Maine's admiration for the legal positivists was certainly tempered: "There is not the smallest necessity for accepting all the conclusions of [Bentham and Austin] with implicit deference but there is the strongest necessity for knowing what those conclusions are. They are indispensable, if for no other object, for the purpose of clearing the head." *Lectures on the Early History of Institutions* (London: John Murray, 1889), 343.

Later in the same work (p. 381) appears what is surely the first official reference to the "straight-face defense." Maine disagrees with Austin that it is "ridiculous" to call a father a sovereign and his wife and children his subjects, noting that in Roman law, a paterfamilias is precisely the sovereign of the family, but Maine says that the final appeal is to "a higher tribunal of which Austin allows the jurisdiction, our sense of the ridiculous."

24. See Kelly, *Western Legal Theory*, 402–407. There are even anomalies in national law. For example, some laws provide incentives but no sanctions (e.g., tax incentives), and some laws, such as certain environmental regulations, lack penalties for their violation. See Susan J. Buck and Edward Hathaway, "Designating State Natural Resource Trustees Under the Superfund Amendments," in *Regulatory Federalism, Natural Resources and Environmental Management*, ed. Michael Hamilton (Washington, D.C.: American Society for Public Administration: 1990), 83–94 for a discussion of the implementation of the state natural resource trustee provision of the Superfund Amendment and Reauthorization Act (SARA). A second example would be the American case in which a citizen wins a suit against the state. The state complies even though the citizen could not possibly enforce the decision. See Anthony D'Amato, "What 'Counts' as Law?," in *Law-Making in the Global Community*, ed. Nicholas Onuf (Durham, N.C.: Carolina Academic Press, 1982), 99–103. Some laws cannot even be "violated" in the Austinian sense—for example, laws governing marriage and divorce: unless the law is followed faithfully, neither the marriage nor its dissolution ever legally takes place.

25. These last two are frequently difficult to implement because they may lack clearly expressed goals and objectives or may fail to provide clear directions to the implementing agencies. However, application of general principles is often clarified by the rules that Elinor Ostrom, as discussed later in the chapter, identifies as critical to managing a common pool resource and by the national laws and regulations needed to comply with the international agreements. In addition, the unilateral declarations are accepted if no challenges to them arise. D'Amato, "What 'Counts' as Law?"

26. See Carol Rose, "Property as Storytelling: Perspectives from Game Theory, Narrative Theory, Feminist Theory," *Yale Journal of Law and the Humanities* 2 (1990): 27–57, for a provocative and entertaining discussion of the myths of property.

27. Ronald J. Coase, "The Nature of the Firm," *Economica* 4 (1937): 386–405. Coase won the Nobel Prize in economics for this article.

28. Francis S. Philbrick, "Changing Conceptions of Property in Law," *University of Pennsylvania Law Review* 86 (1938): 691ff at 708, in *Readings*

in Jurisprudence and Legal Philosophy, eds. Morris R. Cohen and Felix S. Cohen (Boston: Little, Brown, 1951), 40.

29. See Rose, "Property as Storytelling," (1990).

30. *The Federalist Papers* were written in the late eighteenth century to explain the proposed American Constitution to the voters of New York. Alexander Hamilton, James Madison, and John Jay, *The Federalist Papers* (1788) (New York: New American Free Library, 1961).

31. Martin Diamond, "Ethics and Politics: The American Way," in *Moral Foundations of the American Republic*, 3rd ed., ed. Robert Horwitz (Charlottesville: University of Virginia Press, 1986), 95.

32. Ibid., 99–100.

33. J. R. Commons, *Legal Foundations of Capitalism* (New York: Macmillan, 1924; Madison: University of Wisconsin Press, 1968), 6 (page citation is to the original and reprint edition). Commons's original meaning was "the Working Rules of Going Concerns, . . . such as the common law, statute law, shop rules, business ethics, business methods norms of conduct and so on, which these governing or regulating groups of associated individuals have laid down for the guidance of transactions." He compared the principle of working rules of going concerns with the principle of mechanism and the principle of scarcity. The term is now used more generally, as presented in the main text of this chapter.

34. Elinor Ostrom, Roy Gardner, and James Walker, *Rules, Games, and Common Pool Resources* (Ann Arbor: University of Michigan Press, 1994), 38–44.

35. Ostrom, Gardner, and Walker, *Rules, Games, and Common Pool Resources*.

36. See, for example, Fikret Berkes, ed., *Common Property Resources: Ecology and Community-Based Sustainable Development* (London: Belhaven Press, 1989), and Bonnie McCay and James Acheson, eds., *The Question of the Commons: The Culture and Ecology of Communal Resources* (Tucson: University of Arizona Press, 1987).

37. See, for example, Carol M. Rose, *Property and Persuasion: Essays on the History, Theory, and Rhetoric of Ownership* (Boulder, Colo.: Westview Press, 1994), and Douglas Baird, Robert Gertner, and Randal Picker, *Game Theory and the Law* (Cambridge, Mass.: Harvard University Press, 1994).

38. In 1890, the United States Bureau of the Census formally declared the closing of the American frontier: all the land from sea to sea was under some political jurisdiction. Some historians assert that this announcement precipitated the conservation movement in the United States. See Roderick Nash, ed., *American Environmentalism: Readings in Conservation History*, 3rd. ed.

(New York: McGraw-Hill, 1990), especially chapter 18. It is not surprising that citizens in the individualistic culture of the United States would react strongly to lost opportunities. It is little wonder, then, that governments of developing countries or nations emerging from repressive regimes are determined to preserve rights in their own resources and to obtain rights in the global commons.

39. David Downes, "Global Trade, Local Economies, and the Biodiversity Convention," in *Biodiversity and the Law*, ed. William Snape III (Washington, D.C.: Island Press, 1996), 202–216.

40. Henry Campbell Black, *Black's Law Dictionary: Definitions of the Terms and Phrases of American and English Jurisprudence, Ancient and Modern* (St. Paul, Minn.: West, 1990).

41. Stephen Krasner, "Sovereignty: An Institutional Perspective," *Comparative Political Studies* 21, 1 (1988): 86–87. See also "Multinationals: Back in Fashion," *The Economist*, 27 March 1993, 5–8 at 6.

42. D'Amato, "What 'Counts' as Law?" D'Amato recognizes that some people have tried to expand this notion of law to include nonhumans, citing Saint Francis of Assisi as one who tried to include animal rights (n. 21). Modern environmental ethicists can go much further; some even advocate abolishing vaccinations because they violate the rights of viruses. Probably the best-known twentieth-century proponent of an expanded natural law is Aldo Leopold, who proposed a "land ethic." Aldo Leopold, *Sand County Almanac* (Oxford: Oxford University Press, 1949, 1977).

43. Bull, *Grotius and International Relations*, 79; Benedict Kingsbury and Adam Roberts, "Introduction: Grotian Thought in International Relations," Ibid., 30.

44. George Kent, "Global Fisheries Management," in *The Global Predicament: Ecological Perspectives on World Order*, eds. David Orr and Marvin Soroos (Chapel Hill: University of North Carolina Press, 1979), 244.

45. *Note verble*, 17 August 1967, Permanent Mission of Malta to the U.N. Sec. General, U.N. Doc. A/6095.

46. Patricia Birnie and Alan Boyle, *International Law and the Environment* (Oxford: Clarendon Press, 1993), 120–122.

47. See Carl Q. Christol, *The Modern International Law of Outer Space* (Elmsford, N.Y.: Pergamon Press, 1982), 285–311, for a more complete discussion of the common heritage of mankind principle in space law.

48. Daniel Chiras, *Environmental Science: Action for a Sustainable Future*, 4th ed. (New York: Benjamin-Cummings, 1994), 71. For a fascinating discussion of convergent evolution, see Fiona Sunquist, "Two Species, One Design," *International Wildlife* 26, 5 (September–October 1996): 28–33.

49. Sunquist, "Two Species, One Design."

50. Oran Young, *International Cooperation: Building Regimes for Natural Resources and the Environment* (Ithaca, N.Y.: Cornell University Press, 1989), 12–13. Stephen Krasner defines *regimes* as "sets of implicit or explicit principles, norms, rules, and decisions-making procedures around which actor expectations converge in a given area of international relations." Stephen Krasner, "Structural Causes and Regime Consequences: Regimes as Intervening Variables," *International Organization* 36 (1982): 186. Robert O. Keohane, Peter Haas, and Marc A. Levy define *institutions* as "persistent and connected sets of rules and practices that prescribe behavioral roles, constrain activity, and shape expectations. They may take the form of bureaucratic organizations, regimes (rule-structures that do not necessarily have organizations attached), or conventions (informal practices)." Robert O. Keohane, Peter Haas, and Marc A. Levy, "The Effectiveness of International Environmental Institutions," in *Institutions for the Earth: Sources of Effective International Environmental Protection*, eds. Peter Haas, Robert O. Keohane, and Marc A. Levy (Cambridge, Mass.: MIT Press, 1993), 3–24.

51. Krasner, "Sovereignty," 55–94.

52. Young, *International Cooperation*, 15–18.

53. Ibid., 15.

54. Ibid., 20.

55. Mark W. Zacher, "Toward a Theory of International Regimes," in *The Evolution of Theory in International Relations: Essays in Honor of William T. R. Fox*, ed. Robert L. Rothstein (Columbia: University of South Carolina Press, 1991), 128.

56. Michael McGinnis and Elinor Ostrom, "Institutional Analysis and Global Climate Change: Design Principles for Robust International Regimes," in *Global Climate Change: Social and Economic Research Issues* (Chicago: Midwest Consortium for International Security Studies and Argonne National Laboratory, 1992), 45–85; Elinor Ostrom, *Governing the Commons: The Evolution of Institutions for Collective Action* (Cambridge: Cambridge University Press, 1990), especially chapter 6; Susan J. Buck, "Multijurisdictional Resources: Testing a Typology for Program Structuring," in *Common Property Resources: Ecology and Community-Based Sustainable Development*, ed. Fikret Berkes (London: Belhaven Press, 1989), 127–147; Ronald Oakerson, "A Model for the Analysis of Common Property Problems," in National Research Council, *Common Property Resource Management* (Washington, D.C.: National Academy Press, 1986), 13–30. See also Ronald Oakerson, "Analyzing the Commons: A Framework," in Daniel Bromley, ed. *Making the Commons Work: Theory, Practice, and Policy*

(San Francisco: ICS Press, 1992), 41–59. The 1992 publication is an updated version of the 1986 volume.

57. Ostrom, *Governing the Commons*, 51.

58. See Ostrom, *Governing the Commons*, 52–55, for a full discussion of levels of analysis and rules.

59. Ibid., 90. See also McGinnis and Ostrom, "Institutional Analysis," 55–58. Young's model of international regimes offers a remarkably similar set of concerns for regime analysis:

1. *institutional character*: the web of rights, rules, and collective choice rules;

2. *jurisdictional boundaries*: the functions, geographical area, and membership;

3. *conditions for operation*: e.g., economic efficiency, distributive justice;

4. *consequences of operation*: expected outcomes and evaluation methods; and

5. *regime dynamics*: history, future changes, and the transformation rules of the regime. Young, *International Cooperation*, 29.

60. McGinnis and Ostrom, "Institutional Analysis," 58. Of the eight principles, the seventh (rights to organize regimes are recognized by external authorities) is the least important in the global commons. Of course, at some threshold level, a nation-state must be accepted as legitimate by the rest of the international community before it can enter into treaties and other agreements, but that issue has not affected the regimes discussed in this book.

61. Ibid., 63.

62. Ibid., 65–69. See, for example, the eight categories of monitoring-sanctioning arrangements for international regimes.

63. *American Cetacean Society* v. *Baldridge*, 604 F. Supp. 1398 (D.C. 1985).

64. Victoria Edwards and Nathalie Steins, "Developing an Analytical Framework for Multiple-Use Commons" (paper presented at conference of the International Association for the Study of Common Property, Berkeley, Calif., 5–8 June 1996) (Department of Land and Construction Management, University of Portsmouth, Portsmouth, Hampshire PO1 2LF, United Kingdom); Ruth Meinzen-Dick and Lee Ann Jackson, "Multiple Uses, Multiple Users of Water Resources" (paper presented at conference of the International Association for the Study of Common Property, Berkeley, Calif., 5–8 June 1996) (International Food Policy Research Institute, 1200 17th St. NW, Washington, D.C. 20036); and Michael McGinnis, "Collective Action, Governance, and International Relations: The MAORCA Framework" (unpublished paper, November 1996) (Department of Political Sci-

ence, Indiana University, Bloomington, Ind. 47405). McGinnis's work in this paper applies to broadly defined international regimes rather than addressing common pool problems specifically. His analysis is rooted in rational choice theories of individual choice and collective action. This is a stimulating alternative to standard theories of international relations and when completed, it will be an essential component for analysis of international and global commons. I have not included this work directly in my discussion because (1) it is still a work in progress and I am fearful of misrepresenting McGinnis's arguments and (2) it is broader in its scope than is this volume.

65. See Meinzen-Dick and Jackson, "Multiple Uses, Multiple Users," for an analysis of this problem.

66. Morton Horwitz, "The Transformation in the Conception of Property in American Law, 1780–1860," *University of Chicago Law Review* 40 (1973): 248–290.

67. Edwards and Steins, "Developing an Analytical Framework."

Chapter 3

Antarctica

Great God! This is an awful place!

—Robert F. Scott (1912)

The "highest, driest, windiest, and coldest continent,"[1] Antarctica is so inhospitable that it has no native terrestrial mammals. The region was first explored and exploited in the late eighteenth century, but the development of a regime did not begin until late in the nineteenth century. Bound by fairly clear geographical limits and governed by a treaty system that originated with scientific exploration, Antarctica presents the most coherent regime of all the global commons.

There have been few practical demands on the continent itself; until recently, its principal value has been as a location for scientific research. In 1959, Antarctica was designated an international scientific reserve in the Antarctic Treaty by the twelve nations conducting scientific research on the continent (Argentina, Australia, Belgium, Chile, France, Great Britain, Japan, New Zealand, Norway, South Africa, the Soviet Union, and the United States). Recent discoveries that suggest the presence of substantial oil, gas, and mineral supplies on the Antarctic outer continental shelf have strained relations among the signatories, and a 1989 oil spill alerted environmentalists to the dangers of ecotourism. These new developments may bring substantial change to the existing treaty system.

This chapter begins with the history of the Antarctica region. Factors that discouraged the formation of a management regime before 1959 include conflicts over sovereignty, international tensions, internal bureaucratic conflicts, and a lack of American leadership. The next sections cover the origins of the International Geophysical Year (IGY) and its effect on the formation of the management regime. The formation of the Special Committee on Antarctic Research (SCAR) and the subsequent Antarctic Treaty are discussed next. The Antarctic Treaty System (ATS) and its administrative apparatus are described, as are the efforts of some developing nations to convert the treaty system into a United Nations regime. Finally, the rationale that underlies the treaty regime is discussed.

Early Exploration

Antarctica and the Arctic are literally poles apart, but the influence of Arctic policy has been felt from the earliest days of Antarctic discovery. The very name *Antarctic* derives from the area's contrast with the Arctic: the original name for the continent was *Antarktos* or "opposite the Bear," referring to Polaris, the North Pole indicator star, which lies in Ursa Major.[2]

The myth of a rich southern continent has existed since the time of the ancient Greeks, but exploration waited for the development of transoceanic ships. (See box 3.1, Antarctica: The Continent and box 3.2, Antarctica: Water.) In 1721, Jacob Roggevean was financed by the Dutch East India Company to seek the southern continent, and in 1739, Bouvet de Lozier made a similar journey for the French East India Company. After Captain James Cook circumnavigated the world between 1772 and 1775, crossing into the Antarctic region twice and finding his passage blocked everywhere by ice fields, the Western world accepted the fact that there were no habitable lands in the remote south.[3] However, this was no bar to extracting useful resources, and Cook reported plentiful fur seal colonies. Between 1793 and 1800, more than 3 million seals were killed at the Juan Fernández Islands, virtually exterminating the seal population there. Similar depredations occurred in other regions; between 1778 and 1822, about 1.2 million seals were taken from South Georgia.[4]

The primary impetus for exploration in the Antarctic regions in the early modern era was seal hunting and whaling, although scientific curiosity was certainly a close second. (See box 3.3 Antarctica: Terrestrial Life.) The British were the first to hunt there, in 1778, and the Americans followed suit between 1791 and 1794. They were followed by the Australians in 1813, the Argentines in 1819, and the French in 1825. After the accessible seals were gone (the ice pack having protected the Weddell, crabeater, leopard, and Ross seals), the harvesting emphasis shifted to whaling, with Germany in 1873 and New Zealand in 1880 joining the Antarctic fleets.[5] Certainly, the Antarctic hunting grounds were profitable.

Controversy still swirls about the first sighting of the Antarctic mainland. For years, American schoolchildren have been taught that Nathaniel Palmer made the first sighting in November 1820, but this is probably inaccurate.

Box 3.1 Antarctica: The Continent

Lying entirely within the Southern Polar region, Antarctica is roughly one and a half times the size of the United States. Ninety-eight percent of the continent is covered by an ice sheet 2,000–3,700 meters (6,500–12,000 feet) thick that contains approximately 90 percent of the world's freshwater. If melted, the ice sheet would raise mean sea level by 60 meters (200 feet). In addition to the ice sheet, nearly half of the continent is surrounded by ice shelves and pack ice. Bare rock can be found only on high mountain peaks or on scattered, sheltered patches on the coast; these are areas in which snow evaporates before it hits the ground.

The Transantarctic Mountains divide the continent into two regions. The land under the larger region, East Antarctica, is a plain 1,000 meters (3,300 feet) or higher in altitude that is covered by an ice dome, the top of which is more than 3,000 meters (9,900 feet) high. East Antarctica receives light snowfall and is blanketed by loose surface snow, although snow-free areas or dry valleys exist in there. In contrast, West Antarctica is an archipelago characterized by rugged mountains that protrude through the ice. The highest point in Antarctica is Vinson Massif, with an elevation of 5,140 meters (16,900 feet). Most of West Antarctica, however, has an average elevation of 1,700–2,000 meters (5,600–6,600 feet).

Sources: Auburn, *Antarctic Law and Politics*; Gow, "The Ice Sheet"; Hosking, *Antarctic Wildlife*; King, *The Antarctic*; Sugden, *Arctic and Antarctica*; Walton, *Antarctica Science*

Russian explorer Fabian Gottlieb von Bellingshausen sighted land on 28 January 1820, but since he apparently did not recognize what he had seen, the Russian claims of first sighting are suspect. The first reported discovery was made two days later by an Englishman, Edward Bransfield.[6]

From 1841 to 1899, little exploration was done. This hiatus had several

---

Box 3.2 Antarctica: Water

Antarctica receives only thirty to thirty-eight centimeters (twelve to fifteen inches) of precipitation per year, comparable to that received by the semiarid regions of the earth, and less than five centimeters (two inches) of snow falls annually at the South Pole. The climate is harsh, with temperatures persisting well below zero over 95 percent of the continent. The coldest terrestrial temperature ever recorded was -88° C, registered at Vostok.

Despite the lack of rain and the freezing temperatures, Antarctica does contain a few saline and freshwater lakes. The saline lakes, found in the dry valleys of Victoria Land, often have a greater salinity than the ocean. They are generally biologically sterile. The freshwater lakes, on the other hand, contain diverse life-forms such as algae, mosses, bacteria, rotifers, and fairy shrimp. In 1996, the largest subglacial lake ever discovered, measuring 48 by 240 kilometers (30 by 150 miles), was found under the ice cap. The only river on the continent, the Onyx, flows only in summer and, at 30 kilometers (19 miles) long, is too short to show up on most maps.

Sources: Auburn, Antarctic Law and Politics; Gow, "The Ice Sheet"; Hawkes, "Science Briefing"; Sugden, Arctic and Antarctica

---

Box 3.3 Antarctica: Terrestrial Life Forms

Due to its extreme temperatures, Antarctica is the only continent with no native terrestrial mammals. At least two types of insect (springtails and mites) are thought to be native to the continent; these insects live mostly near the coast, in mosses or lichen. The islands contain a few more of native insect species, including beetles, flies, and spiders, as well as two species of flowering plants. Fungi, which are largely responsible for decomposition of organic material in the Antarctic, are found in both organic and inorganic soils.

Sources: Sugden, Arctic and Antarctica; Walton, Antarctica Science.

Box 3.4 Antarctica: Ocean Life

Unlike the Antarctic Continent, the Antarctic Ocean is teeming with life. At the Antarctic convergence (the northern boundary of the Antarctic or Southern Ocean) the South Pacific, Atlantic, and Indian Oceans merge with the frigid Antarctic water, creating a turbulent barrier to marine life and defining the rich Antarctic ecosystem. Two-thirds of the fish in the Antarctic Ocean are of the group *Notothenioidei*. This group consists of four families of bottom, or deepwater, fish: dragon fish, plunderfish, cod, and icefish. Most of these fish are edible. They also possess special adaptations that enable them to survive the frigid water, such as an antifreeze-like compound that prevents their body fluids from freezing and an ability to maintain "neutral" buoyancy, or weightlessness. Krill, a subsistence food for other fish and marine birds and animals, are also found in these waters. It is believed that the annual sustainable yield of krill is between 91–136 million metric tons (100–150 million short tons), making krill potentially the world's largest source of protein. In addition to the fish, eight species of seals and a dozen species of whales, including the blue whale, migrate to the Antarctic region to feed. Six species of seals and forty-three species of birds actually breed within the Antarctic region. The emperor penguin is the only bird species that remains there during winter.

Sources: Eastman and Devries, "Antarctic Fishes"; Shapley, *Seventh Continent*; Stonehouse, "Birds and Mammals"

---

causes. First, British polar interests were focused on the Arctic, and most of Great Britain's resources available for exploration were devoted to Africa, which had clearer economic payoffs. Other European nations were striving to develop colonial empires, and American concerns were focused first on a bloody civil war and later on the Industrial Revolution and Western expansion.[7] It was not until the official closing of the American frontier in 1890 that Americans turned their national attention to other horizons.[8]

Toward the beginning of the twentieth century, scientific exploration of the polar regions captured the popular imagination. Starting in 1898, scientific expeditions wintered in the Antarctic; the first winter station was at Cape Adare, where Carsten Borchgrevink's *Southern Cross* Expedition conducted studies until 1900.[9] Other expeditions followed: in 1901 alone, the Germans, the Swedes, and the British all conducted scientific activity. In 1909, a party from the British Antarctic Expedition of 1907–1909 reached the South Magnetic Pole. Interest continued in the quest for the South Pole as Robert F. Scott and Roald Amundsen raced for the honor of being first, the Norwegian Amundsen winning by five weeks.[10]

The development of technology played a vital part in this new exploration. Comparatively efficient liquid fuel became available and portable stoves were produced, making the deadly cold less of an obstacle. Whaling became more profitable when the invention of harpoon guns with grenade heads increased hunting efficiency.[11] (See box 3.4, Antarctica: Ocean Life.) In 1904, large packs of great blue whales were discovered and whaling fleets converged on the southern continent. Within twenty years, factory ships with giant slipways for processing whale meat increased yields even further.

Military inventions of both world wars also affected Antarctic exploration. The development of airplanes and communications technology during World War I in particular had a tremendous impact. The invention in 1929 of the shortwave radio, which broadcast entertainment as well as direct messages, meant that for Antarctic residents, the "sense of total, prolonged isolation was gone forever."[12] Even the ancient explorers' curse of scurvy was eliminated; the cure for scurvy had been well known in Sir Francis Drake's time but forgotten in the intervening years. Research during World War I reestablished the value of vitamin C in preventing scurvy.[13] During World War II, military operations in extreme cold weather had prompted the development of cold-weather clothing; new forms of insulation reduced bulkiness and the dangers of hypothermia. All these advances made life in the Antarctic more bearable. The year 1943 was the last time that the Antarctic lacked a permanent human population.[14]

In the period between the world wars, the United States was the dominant presence in the Antarctic. Admiral Richard Byrd led privately financed expeditions in 1929–1931 and 1933–1935. Lincoln Ellsworth explored the Antarctic in 1935–1936, and the United States Antarctic Service, which had supported the explorations, survived until World War II. Several issues which were not directly connected to Antarctic policy itself pushed the U.S. government toward greater involvement. First, tensions between the British and the Argentine and Chilean governments were escalating. The South Americans invoked the terms of the Interamerican Treaty of Reciprocal Assistance (the Rio Pact) to induce the United States to support their fight against British territorial claims. A second issue was an increased Soviet interest in whaling. The Soviets had been whaling in the region since 1932, but after World War II, they expanded their southern fleet operations. This increased American concerns about possible Soviet–American confrontations on the high seas. The United States also needed a site for large-scale war games in a polar area, and the Arctic was too close to Soviet territory to be used in the tense atmosphere of the cold war.[15] The intensified international tension was partly responsible for the Antarctic Treaty negotiated in 1958.

Territorial Claims

Territorial claims in Antarctica complicated efforts to reach international consensus on access to the continent for research. Most claims were made in the period between the world wars. Until recently, the inaccessibility of the Antarctic made any territorial claims on its land "largely symbolic."[16] The conundrum of sovereignty in the Antarctic was not resolved by the Antarctic Treaty; indeed, it remains unresolved today.

In international law, nations may acquire recognized title to territory by several means: subjugation (taking by force), natural geographical accretion (i.e., continuation of land features such as mountain ranges), cession of territory by one country to another, prescription, and occupation of previously uninhabited land.[17] A mix of these methods is used by the various Antarctic claimant states; only subjugation and cession are not currently employed to justify claims. All the claimants to Antarctica except Norway invoke the sector theory: the claimant nations map out a wedge that originates at the far boundaries of their national land mass and converges at the South Pole. This procedure has been used in the Arctic, which has no land mass of its own, but it is more difficult to apply in the Antarctic, which not only is a separate continent but also is situated such that sector claims by several countries overlap.[18]

Seven nations claim territorial sovereignty over some portion of the Antarctic, but these claims vary in their forcefulness and credibility. Oddly, the first territorial claim in the Antarctic was made by France in January 1892 when it annexed the Îles de Désolation (Kerguelen Islands).[19] France's next claim was made in 1924, when Terre Adélie, discovered during an 1837–1840 expedition, was officially claimed.

British involvement in the region dates to 1775, when Captain Cook discovered the South Sandwich Islands. In 1908, during the heyday of the early whaling industry, the British claimed the territories in which they hunted[20] and tried to control the whale harvest by issuing permits to whaling ships within their territory. Whaling permits were first issued in 1910, and from then until 1931, the British maintained a stipendiary magistrate on Deception Island in the South Shetlands during the whaling season.[21] Part of the impetus for the developing factory ships to operate in the open ocean was an attempt to avoid the British permitting system.[22]

Extensive British scientific explorations enhanced British territorial claims, as did military activities following both world wars. After World War I, the first aircraft in the Antarctic were British.[23] In 1943–1944, the British launched Operation Tabarin, establishing permanent bases at Deception Island and Port Lockroy to strengthen claims in the region that might have been weakened by the wartime hiatus in activity.[24] The British base their claim on discovery and exploration sustained by effective occupation. British territorial claims overlap South American claims; the disputed territory covers one-fifth of the continent. Although the postwar crisis of 1947–1948 was resolved by an agreement not to sail warships south of 60° south latitude, the South Atlantic (Falklands) War in 1982 is evidence of the volatile nature of the dispute.

New Zealand asserts a territorial claim in the Antarctic based on a 1923 British order-in-council that established the Ross Dependency.[25] It has some record of exploration, but New Zealand has not been a strong advocate of territorial claims in the region; in fact, after World War II, New Zealand suggested internationalization of Antarctica.[26]

The Australian record in Antarctica is similar, but Australian adherence to territoriality is stronger. Australia began Antarctic exploration in 1911, but its first territorial claim was a British order-in-council in 1933 that laid claim to almost one-third of the continent. Australia has occupied the sector in three bases since the International Geophysical Year (IGY) in 1957–1958, with a fourth base acquired from the United States in 1959. This claim, like the British claim, rests on discovery and exploration perfected by occupation, but some shadow is cast by the difficulty of asserting effective occupation of such a large and generally hostile land mass.[27]

Argentina first claimed territory in 1927, although the Argentines had maintained a weather station in the South Orkneys since 1904. In 1942, an Argentine expedition claimed lands on the Antarctic Peninsula, and Argentina has maintained bases there since 1947. Ten years later, Argentina incorporated the sector into its metropolitan territory.[28] Like Chile, Argentina claims that under the papal bull *Inter Cætera* (1493) and the Treaty of Tordesillas (1494), it is the successor to Spanish claims in the region (see chapter 4). Argentina also contends that the western mountains of Antarctica are geological extensions of Argentina's own land mass. Despite the temporary agreement in the Antarctic Treaty to disregard sovereignty issues, Argentina continues to be the most active claimant in asserting sovereignty; Argentine maps show the Antarctica claim, the national cabinet has met regarding the claimed territory, and in 1978, a baby born at Esperanza Base at Hope Bay was declared an Argentine citizen.[29]

Chile has similar territorial claims dating to 1940. An interesting philatelic effort to claim sovereignty occurred in 1946, when Chile issued an Antarctic postage stamp, but this did not sway international opinion to its side.[30] In 1947, Chile established a permanent base on Greenwich Island in the South Shetlands. In 1955, Chile transferred administrative responsibility for the territory from its foreign ministry to a provincial governor, thus signaling that the Antarctic claim was part of Chilean metropolitan territory.[31] Because neither Chile nor Argentina has a colonial policy, both have labeled their Antarctic acquisitions as part of their national territories rather than as colonies or protectorates.[32] Both nations base their claims on similar arguments: (1) succession to Spanish rights established in 1494 under the Treaty of Tordesillas; (2) geographical proximity; (3) geological affinity (through extension of the Andean mountains); and (4) occupation.

Jeffrey Myhre notes that the first three bases for sovereignty are weak. Even if the Spanish succession were a generally valid legal argument for territoriality, the Spanish never discovered or occupied any portion of the Antarctic. Geographical proximity is difficult to justify, since Argentina is 700 miles from the Antarctic; the related claim of geological affinity rests on the dubious notion that Tierra del Fuego and the Antarctic Peninsula are connected by an underwater extension of the Andes. Only the fourth point, occupation, has some validity, although in Chile's case, the claimed territory overlaps territorial and occupied claims of both Britain and Argentina.[33]

The last country to make territorial claims was Norway. Norwegians had experience in fishing in Arctic waters and thus were in great demand in the developing Antarctic fisheries. Additionally, the credit for first reaching the South Pole is given to a Norwegian, Roald Amundsen. Norway's first claim was made in 1930, when it claimed sovereignty over Bouvet Island. The first mainland claim, however, was not made until 1939, and this claim was made primarily to block attempts by Nazi Germany to claim the same territory.

The United States has not made territorial claims in the Antarctic, even though the American presence there has been considerable. There are several reasons for this. Assertion of territorial sovereignty is not always advantageous, since such a claim could limit a country's activities to only the claimed territory and would require recognition of the claims of other nations as well. To claim territory might limit later access and exploitation of valuable resources. One main national objective of the United States in Antarctica has been to have full access to whatever resources exist, regardless of their location. Americans have also been somewhat constrained by the official position taken in 1924 by Secretary of State Charles Evans Hughes:

> [Discovery] of lands unknown to civilization, even when coupled
> with the formal taking of possession, does not support a valid claim
> of sovereignty unless the discovery is followed by an actual settle-
> ment of the discovered country.[34]

Given national economic goals and the Hughes doctrine, the United
States has neither made territorial claims nor accepted the claims of other
nations.

Toward the Antarctic Treaty System

The slow development of the Antarctic regime depended on several factors:
the status of national territorial claims previously discussed, bureaucratic
competition within national governments, the lack of policy leadership by
the United States in the critical years following World War II, and the cooperative institutions begun during the International Geophysical Year. (See
box 3.5, Chronology for Antarctica.)

Most of the interested states had established internal policy institutions or
networks to cope with Antarctic issues, but their administrative hierarchies
were usually divided among some mix of diplomatic, military, and scientific
bureaucracies. For example, in Argentina and Chile, the Antarctic agencies
were housed within the foreign ministries, but policies were largely implemented by the navies. In Argentina, the National Antarctic Commission was
an interdepartmental commission headed by a Foreign Ministry official;
Chile had a similar Chilean Antarctic Commission, although the Chilean
navy was less powerful and hence less involved in implementation of policy.

In the United Kingdom, responsibility was divided among the Foreign
Office, the Colonial Office (through the Falkland Islands Dependencies),
and Commonwealth channels that coordinated policy efforts with Australia
and New Zealand. France used a variety of bureaucracies in its Foreign Ministry, Ministry of Colonies, and navy, the latter with the leading role for
defense policy. Scientific activity was planned and supervised by the Ministry of Education, but actual implementation was done privately, through
Expéditions Polaires Françaises.[35]

This multiplicity of institutions complicated communications both
within the states and among them. Each internal bureaucracy had its own
clients to satisfy. Each needed to defend its policy territory, and, indeed, the
goals of the various agencies were often in conflict. Rivalry, lack of trust,
competing and often contradictory responsibilities, and changeable—at
times, unstable—political regimes made cooperation difficult. The very frag-

Box 3.5 Chronology for Antarctica

1820	Antarctic mainland first sighted
1882–1883	First International Polar Year
1898	First winter station (Cape Adare) established
1932–1933	Second International Polar Year
1957–1958	International Geophysical Year
1958	Special Committee on Antarctic Research (SCAR) formed
1959	Antarctic Treaty (in force 1961)
1959	Antarctica designated an international scientific reserve by Antarctic Treaty System (ATS) members
1961	SCAR renamed Scientific Committee on Antarctic Research
1964	Agreed Measures for the Conservation of Antarctic Fauna and Flora (in force 1982)
1972	Convention for the Conservation of an Antarctic Seals (Seal Convention) (in force 1978)
1980	Convention on the Conservation of Antarctic Marine Living Resources (CCAMLR) (in force 1985)
1982	South Atlantic (Falklands) War
1989	*Bahía Paráiso* oil spill
1991	Protocol (to Antarctic Treaty) on Environmental Protection (Environmental Protocol) (not in force)

mentation of these agencies is evidence that the national governments were not especially interested in the Antarctic: the Southern continent lacked resources, settlements, and apparently even the potential for profitability.

Another cause of the slow pace in reaching an international agreement in Antarctica may be laid at the door of American policy makers, who were expected to take the lead in Antarctic policy formation but were unable to formulate an acceptable policy.[36] In the late 1940s, the United States government initiated a policy study on the Antarctic. The military recommended staking a territorial claim;[37] however, this recommendation was rejected by the Department of State's policy planning staff, showing once again the disparity of goals among civilian and military bureaucracies. In June 1948, the State Department's policy planning staff released an Antarctic policy paper, PPS-31.[38] The main thrust of the paper was elimination of territorial disputes, preservation of the Antarctic for scientific study, and protection of American interests. The United States stood fast by its policy of no territorial claims and no recognition of others' claims. A draft agreement on Antarctica was attached to PPS-31 and circulated to the British for comment. The draft suggested a United Nations trusteeship, administered by the seven claimant nations and the United States, with a subordinate scientific organization. Following British comments, a new proposal was drafted that changed the trusteeship to an eight-nation condominium. Reaction among the claimant states was mixed, however, and the proposal was shelved.

In July 1948, Chile suggested a scientific exchange and a moratorium on all disputed claims,[39] partly to encourage scientific research but also to halt the British system of issuing whaling permits.[40] The United States began to see the virtue of the Chilean idea, especially as the Soviets were asserting their claims and interests with increasing vehemence. However, progress was impeded by American involvement in the Korean War, Chilean presidential elections, and numerous disputes over domestic policy. No one knows how the Chilean initiative might have played out. Before any final decision was made, the scientific community usurped national prerogatives and launched the International Geophysical Year.

The Impact of Scientific Communities

The two International Polar Years (IPY) in 1882–1883 and 1932–1933 had demonstrated that international scientific cooperation was possible.[41] The effect of the first IPY on the scientific community was immense. It was the first time that scientists of different nations and disciplines had merged their efforts to study global phenomena, and it was also the beginning of public funding for cooperative extranational scientific research.[42]

The focus of both International Polar Years was on the aurora, meteorology, and geomagnetism. Although none of these cooperative efforts had an Antarctic component, the IPY in 1932–1933 had demonstrated that permanent polar bases could be established and maintained. In 1957–1958, the International Geophysical Year (IGY) capitalized on the development of polar technology.[43]

The IGY was an ideal vehicle for delaying political decisions on Antarctica, partly because the Soviet Union could be included without entangling political implications. Indeed, from a scientific viewpoint, it could hardly be excluded.[44] The scientists were absolutely clear that their work should be free of the taint of politics; at the end of the first IGY planning session in July of 1955, they passed a resolution affirming the temporary and apolitical nature of their activities.[45]

The Soviet Union continued to affect the policy positions of the other nations with an interest in Antarctica. The Soviets conducted extensive photographic surveying and mapping, even though cartography had not been an official IGY discipline because of its political implications. They were eager for an extension of the scientific endeavors and announced plans to maintain an Antarctic research presence after the end of the IGY in 1958. Other states chose to follow suit.[46]

In August 1958, activities of the IGY were extended for an additional year, and the endeavor was labeled the International Geophysical Cooperation—1959 (IGC) to distinguish it from the IGY. This "extension" was not formally part of the IGY and represented a compromise between the Soviets, who wanted the IGY extended, and the American scientists, who were reluctant to ask their government for supplemental funding.[47] IGY participants stayed with the IGC for a number of reasons. They had a significant investment in the scientific studies, and, perhaps more important, they feared losing "territorial, political, or strategic advantage" if they withdrew.[48]

The Soviet launch of *Sputnik* in 1957 was an epiphany for the rest of the international community:

> *Sputnik* made the Southern Hemisphere allies nervous that the Soviets might install missiles in their Antarctic bases, putting their countries within range. Suddenly, their internecine disputes in Antarctica were dwarfed by the common fear of a Soviet military presence there. A formal accord among nations, including the Soviet Union, renouncing military activities [in Antarctica] seemed the only way to forestall a costly arms race.[49]

In 1958, the scientific community seized a unique opportunity. Clearly, the old bureaucratic and political disincentives to cooperation had been either reduced or eliminated, especially in comparison with the advantages of cooperation. This was not a matter of economic profit; the costs of cooperation were balanced by the mutual benefits of closing the Antarctic to a Soviet military presence while continuing to provide shared access to research for all participants. There was also the potential benefit of shelving the issue of territorial sovereignty, thereby avoiding political conflict and perhaps violence.

However, a less utilitarian view of the scientific community finds them seizing their opportunity to promote peaceful, scientific research in one of the last uncharted places on the planet. They were fortunate that the Antarctic was also virtually devoid of economic interest. No one foresaw the Antarctic tourism boom or the discovery of new, accessible sources of energy.

The scientists had the experience of the IGY behind them, public support generated by publicity about the IGY, and a triggering event in the launch of *Sputnik*.

The scientific community drew on national desires to protect the gains already made in the region to support the establishment of the Special (later Scientific) Committee on Antarctic Research (SCAR). SCAR was an important precursor to the Antarctic Treaty because in addition to its scientific functions, it provided a formal organization to coordinate national activities on the continent. Cooperation was justified as a mechanism to sustain the investments of the various national governments. A special Antarctic research organization had first been proposed during planning for the IGY when the United States National Committee recommended extending the Antarctic activities for another year. The committee made a proposal to the Special Committee in the Geophysical Year (CSAGI) in 1956. It was George Laclavère, chairman of CSAGI, who suggested the "gentlemen's agreement" that the IGY would be apolitical.[50] The proposal for SCAR was approved and recommended to the International Council of Scientific Unions (ICSU), an organization formed from the various national academies of science. The ICSU then formed a committee that in October 1958 became SCAR. All twelve of the original IGY participants were members of SCAR: Argentina, Australia, Belgium, Chile, France, Japan, New Zealand, Norway, South Africa, the United Kingdom, the United States, and the USSR. SCAR has one delegate from each country engaged in Antarctic research and representatives from the International Union of Geography (IUG), the International Union of Geodesy and Geophysics (IUGG), the International Union of Biological Sciences (IUBS), and the Union Radio Scientifique International (URSI).[51]

SCAR is a scientific rather than a government organization. It has its own constitution and governing rules, and its "territory" now includes the area out to the Antarctic convergence (where the cold Antarctic waters meet the warmer northern waters), thus extending beyond the initial area governed by the Antarctic Treaty System to include the area covered by the 1980 Convention on the Conservation of Antarctic Marine Living Resources, discussed in the following section. It was officially incorporated into the Antarctic Treaty System in 1961.

SCAR is headquartered at the Scott Polar Research Institute at Cambridge University and has had a permanent secretariat since 1972. The institute publishes the *SCAR Bulletin* as an appendix to its *Polar Record*. SCAR's constitution prohibits political activity except to provide technical advice to the nations involved. This prohibition has been scrupulously observed for the most part. Although SCAR itself provides only scientific advice, in practice many of the scientists involved with SCAR are also policy advisers for their governments. In theory, however, the roles are kept separate.[52]

The role of the Antarctic scientific community is unique in the annals of the international commons. These scientists were the policy entrepreneurs who had already invested financial, personal, and institutional resources in building a cooperative regime. Even more important, the scientific culture required the scientists to be politically impartial. As with the purity of Caesar's wife, it was not enough simply to be politically neutral; it was imperative to be seen as politically neutral as well. In fact, the appearance of neutrality might be an acceptable substitute for its reality.

The Antarctic Treaty System

In May 1958, representatives of twelve governments met to discuss a treaty for the Antarctic; attending were representatives of the seven nations with territorial claims (Argentina, Australia, Chile, France, New Zealand, Norway, and the United Kingdom) and five nations that had no claims but had joined the IGY (Belgium, Japan, South Africa, the United States, and the USSR). The treaty was possible for three reasons. First, the IGY had placed the Antarctic in the public and political eye, and the scientific community capitalized on this salience to push for a resolution of Antarctic issues. Second, issues of sovereignty could be left unresolved because there were no economic incentives to drive territorial claims. Third, the IGY had demonstrated that successful joint efforts were feasible.[53] The IGY had left an administrative legacy in SCAR and in the coordination of communications, rescue, operations, and weather forecasting through Antarctic Weather Central. This informal administrative structure provided a model for the Antarctic Treaty System.[54]

The Antarctic Treaty, signed on 1 December 1959 and in force on 23 June 1961, was the result of intense negotiations. The most difficult problem was the sovereignty issue. This was resolved in a Solomon-like fashion by Article IV of the Treaty.[55] No agreement was reached, but each signatory agreed to shelve the issue to deal with the other important Antarctic issues.

Article IV is masterful in its vagueness. By refusing to clarify the issue of ownership in Antarctica, it defused a volatile situation. A compromise would have been less successful and might even have led to the ultimate failure of the treaty. Instead of offering a compromise, the treaty stabilized a wide array of competing national interests. In the words of one commentator, this "preservation of the political balance, far more than its inspiring language, is the true reason it governs so successfully,"[56] although others suggest that the success of the Antarctic Treaty System may result more from the fact that it has yet to be fully tested under conditions of economic pressure.[57]

The current Antarctic Treaty System governs the area south of 60° south latitude. It includes the original 1959 treaty as well as the Scientific Committee on Antarctic Research (SCAR); recommendations agreed on by the consultative parties, such as the 1964 Agreed Measures for the Conservation of Antarctic Fauna and Flora (Agreed Measures); the 1972 Convention for the Conservation of Antarctic Seals (Seal Convention); and the 1980 Convention on the Conservation of Antarctic Marine Living Resources (CCAMLR or Southern Ocean Convention). The Protocol on Environmental Protection (Environmental Protocol) was added in 1991 but is not yet in force.

In 1964, the same year the Agreed Measures were adopted to ensure protection of native species, Norway began sealing in the Antarctic. Because there were no binding agreements concerning sealing, an additional convention was negotiated, and in 1972, the Seal Convention was signed. This convention banned pelagic sealing and set an optimum sustainable yield as an upper limit for harvesting on land.

The Seal Convention is noteworthy for two reasons. First, it represents the first application of the Antarctic Treaty System to the high seas. Second, it inaugurated a useful treaty mechanism that allowed nations not party to the Antarctic Treaty System to accede to a related resource management regime by joining the conventions.[58] It is characteristic of the Antarctic Treaty System that it encourages nonmember states to follow environmental policy directions that the member states find desirable. This mechanism has been used for subsequent agreements.

CCAMLR, adopted in 1980 and in effect in April 1982, was innovative, bringing an ecosystem perspective to resource management. Antarctica is one of the few places where some conservation and sustainability measures were put in place before damage was done. This has frequently led to regulatory strategies being planned prior to the regulated activity, although treaty members were unable to anticipate or control the sudden incursion of finfish fleets as they were pushed into the Antarctic after 200-mile fishing zones were adopted by the coastal states.[59]

Adoption of CCAMLR was motivated in part by concern for krill, a small crustacean that lives in the Southern Ocean and is fished extensively by Japanese and Soviet fishing fleets. In the 1980s, Polish and West German fleets were harvesting krill as well. Probably the most bitter dispute in the Antarctic prior to the 1989 oil spill from the *Bahía Paráiso* involved this abundant and inexpensive source of protein. Resource exploitation and scarcity had always been of interest to the Antarctic Treaty System members, but such concerns were largely speculative until 1968. In that year, during a SCAR symposium held at Cambridge, England, several Soviet papers on the small shrimplike species were presented. The Russians were harvesting krill for home consumption, and the potential market for the high-protein animal was large. Gradually, the treaty powers were beginning to see the economic potential of the Antarctic.

Political problems with large-scale harvesting arose immediately because krill is the staple diet of great blue whales, which are in danger of extinction, and for seals, penguins, and some fish. Political pressures became so intense that the Food and Agriculture Organization of the United Nations (FAO) withheld its scientific findings to avoid offending the krill-fishing nations. CCAMLR is intended to protect the marine ecosystem by requiring that nations harvesting krill consider the impact on other species when setting catch limits.

CCAMLR also expanded the territorial limits of the treaty system to the Antarctic convergence. This raised complicated related issues because part of the area covered by the convention overlaps the recognized territorial limits of several claimant states. Once again, Article IV of the Antarctic Treaty, with its vague agreements to set aside questions of sovereignty, was invoked.[60] As the text of CCAMLR makes clear, the extension of the convention to include the Antarctic convergence is in recognition of the scope of the Antarctic ecosystem. Where CCAMLR overlaps undisputed territorial claims, the states may impose stricter regulations than required by the commission and may themselves enforce the regulations within the 200-mile limit. CCAMLR establishes a separate commission to administer the convention, perhaps foreshadowing an increase in institutionalization for the regime. Although, the Commission has no powers of enforcement or sanctioning, it does have the responsibility to regulate conservation measures and to monitor compliance. Reports of noncompliance are supposed to trigger prosecution and sanctioning by the flag state involved. Other disputes are settled either by arbitration or by the International Court of Justice.

It is significant that the treaty powers chose to regulate krill fishing by convention rather than by additions to the Antarctic Treaty System. This allows nonmember states such as South Korea, which has an interest in krill but virtually no interest in Antarctica, to participate in the extended regime. Thus, in a quiet but nonetheless spectacular diplomatic coup, the treaty nations established themselves as the arbiter for resource regimes in the Antarctic.

The legal complexities raised by krill harvests, such as jurisdiction and access rights, were important in the exploitation of mineral resources as well. In 1973, trace hydrocarbons were found on the continental shelf of the Ross Sea, and this, coupled with the concurrent oil crisis, raised the stakes on Antarctic resources. The potential quantity of oil and gas in the region remains uncertain, but a 1974 report written for the U.S. Geological Survey (USGS) estimated 45 billion barrels of oil and 115 trillion cubic feet of natural gas.[61] When these figures were leaked to the press, public interest became intense. Even if the estimates were accurate, the recoverable oil and gas were significantly less, perhaps one-third of the potential, but the political implications were still substantial. Members of the Antarctic Treaty System were concerned about two issues: jurisdiction over mineral resources, an issue not covered by the treaty or by any subsequent agreements, and protection of the fragile Antarctic environment.[62] Further complications were raised by the demands of developing nations for a share in Antarctic resources. (See box 3.6 Antarctica: Minerals.)

The first hurdle to be passed by treaty members was the Law of the Sea (LOS) discussion over seabed mining. In exchange for a guarantee that the treaty powers would discuss Antarctic resources after the third United Nations Conference on the Law of the Sea (UNCLOS III), the Group of 77, a coalition of developing nations, agreed to exclude Antarctic resources from the LOS discussions.[63] Pressure for mineral exploitation on the Antarctic continent continues to increase, although a 1988 draft convention dealing with minerals was rejected by two members of the Consultative Meeting largely because of concerted opposition led by the environmental NGOs, particularly the Antarctic and Southern Ocean Coalition (ASOC). On 5

Box 3.6 Antarctica: Minerals

Mineral wealth in Antarctica is mostly untouched. Coal, iron ore, oil, and natural gas have all been found on the continent. It is estimated that iron ore deposits in the Prince Charles Mountains may be extensive enough to satisfy world demand for two hundred years. However, Australia and Canada contain vast resources of iron that are more accessible and economically feasible to mine. Natural gas has been discovered under Antarctica's Ross, Weddell, and Bellingshausen Seas; the estimates of oil and gas reserves there are in the tens of billions of barrels. Currently, however, the costs of extraction and transportation of these minerals make mining unprofitable.

Source: Sugden, *Arctic and Antarctica*

October 1991, the Protocol on Environmental Protection (Environmental Protocol) was added to the Antarctic Treaty; as of this writing, it had not entered into force. The protocol bans mineral and oil exploration in Antarctica for at least fifty years and contains stronger provisions to protect the marine ecosystem from pollution and overharvesting of living resources. The Environmental Protocol establishes Antarctica as a "natural reserve," following the world park concept formally proposed by New Zealand in 1975.[64]

Administration

The Scientific Committee on Antarctic Research (SCAR) first became part of the Antarctic Treaty System at the 1961 Canberra Meeting. At issue was the institutional role SCAR would fill. The British proposed a formal role, giving SCAR responsibility for implementing the scientific program under Article III of the treaty; however, SCAR's existing status as a nongovernmental body related to the International Council of Scientific Unions (ICSU) made this proposal problematic. In 1960, Great Britain proposed a formal administrative organization;[65] this would have achieved that end through the back door by using SCAR as a substitute for an earlier proposed bureau that was rejected. The United States opposed the idea of a formal, independent bureaucracy, and American counterproposals finally led to SCAR remaining both independent and nongovernmental.[66]

SCAR has become increasingly important, and it now has two primary areas of responsibility. First, it coordinates the scientific research on the continent, and second, it provides expert support services for members of the Antarctic Treaty System. SCAR is also given legal status CCAMLR. Under the Seal Convention and under the Convention on the Conservation of Antarctic Marine Living Resources, SCAR is the formal scientific advisory body for breeding, research, and hunting; it is charged with collecting statistical information on seal hunting within the convention zone as well as recording information on proposed seal-hunting expeditions. SCAR is no longer the sole source of information for the Antarctic Treaty System, however. For example, CCAMLR has its own Scientific and Technical Committee, and the Consultative Meetings draw on the resources of the World Conservation Union (IUCN) and the World Meteorological Organization (WMO).[67]

Despite British efforts to incorporate a bureaucratic management component into SCAR's scientific mission, no formal administrative institution supervises the Antarctic Treaty System. No formal archive is kept, and no individual group or state speaks for the consultative parties in the international sphere.

Prior to the 1961 Canberra Meeting, Australia proposed a permanent sec-retariat in Canberra with Australian Foreign Office staff. This proposal was energetically opposed by the United States. A compromise position evolved: the government hosting each meeting agreed to send certified conference documents and to supply information to all Meeting participants; the sub-sequent host would select the date and next agenda in consultation with the other parties; standard diplomatic channels would be used for consultations between meetings; consultative parties would be notified by the United States government (as the depository government) of approvals of recom-mendations (Recommendation I–XIV).[68] Although flawed, this system operated without formal discussion until 1963, when a Preparatory Meeting was held in Brussels. From that point on, treaty administration has been a recurring agenda item, although no permanent secretariat has yet been estab-lished.[69]

Chile and Argentina were opposed to a permanent, international secre-tariat, probably because it would undermine the value of their territorial claims. The USSR was reluctant to participate in another international orga-nization in which it had little control.[70] The Commonwealth consultative parties were in favor of a secretariat because it would act as a check on Amer-ican tendencies to control the treaty regime. It is also probable that the high prestige of the civil service in Commonwealth countries increased the will-ingness of Australia to house and staff the secretariat without fear of creating a self-perpetuating bureaucratic monster. France apparently was opposed on principle, arguing that bureaucratic organizations become self-serving and expansionist—surely a peculiar argument for a nation with a highly profes-sionalized public bureaucracy.[71]

North–South Issues

Some arguments have been made that the notion of the common heritage of mankind should apply to the Antarctic. Although developing countries have successfully included the common heritage concept in the Law of the Sea and in outer space treaties, all developing countries are not in accord with its applicability to the Antarctic. For example, L.F. Macedo de Soares Guimaraes of Brazil (a consultative party) suggests that the consultative par-ties created a management framework in a legal vacuum, quite properly using the treaty mechanism to resolve disputes and to promote economic and social advancement. He notes: "[The] common heritage of humankind . . . is not a concept to be applied automatically to any area not tradition-ally subject to national sovereignty. For instance, it should not be applied to Antarctica."[72] He describes the seabed issues of the Law of the Sea as a questions of resource access and exploitation, distinct from the management issues of the Antarctic, which are questions of regulation of scientific activities.[73]

The North–South coalitions do not hold together over the Antarctic because some developing nations (e.g., India) are already strong parties in the treaty system. They therefore have status and access to lose if the CHM principle were to apply to the Antarctic. In the Antarctic, the consultative parties, which do not see themselves as an exclusive group, have resisted any application of the CHM principle. They assert, quite logically, that numerous claims of territorial sovereignty have already been made in the resource domain. The treaty has merely set the disputes aside while scientific research continues. In contrast, the other CHM domains have no outstanding territorial claims, and the dispute is between advocates of *res nullius* and *res communes*. That is not the case in the Antarctic, where territorial claims not only exist for the entire continent but also overlap.

Although issues regarding resource access and exploitation are now arising, they must be resolved within the existing Antarctic Treaty System. This may not be as exclusionary as it seems at first glance; the number of nations seeking to accede to the Antarctic Treaty System has increased. As of 1992, twenty-seven nations in addition to the original twelve had acceded to the treaty; twelve of these are now consultative parties, for a total of twenty-four consultative parties. Seven of the new consultative parties are developing countries: Argentina, Chile, Brazil, India, the People's Republic of China, South Korea, and Uruguay. Six of the countries that have only acceded are also developing countries: Colombia, Cuba, Ecuador, North Korea, Papua New Guinea, and Peru.[74] The treaty requires any nation seeking consultative status to engage in "substantial scientific activity" (Article IX [2]). Eligibility for membership in SCAR is also related to status in the Antarctic Treaty System: SCAR's constitution requires member states to be "actively engaged in Antarctic research."[75]

This requirement has been applied more stringently to developed nations seeking consultative status. For example, in 1977, Poland spent $3 million to build Arctowski Station, a year-round scientific research station, and in 1981, West Germany invested $100 million in Antarctic-related activities.[76] In contrast, in 1983 neither Brazil nor India was required to establish a permanent research station as a condition to becoming consultative parties.[77] M. J. Peterson writes that "the contrast with what was asked of Poland and West Germany is clear, and represents a conscious effort to broaden the coalition of consultative parties by including more Third World states."[78]

SCAR has continued the trend by allowing nonconsultative parties (those countries that have acceded to the treaty but are not consultative parties) to send observers to consultative meetings.[79] This has effected a sharp increase in the impact of nonconsultative parties (NCPs):

> Though [the NCPs] are not included in meetings of the heads of delegations . . . , they have tabled papers and taken an active part in all other debate. Since the consultative parties make no decisions until discussion reveals unanimity on some proposition, participation in debate can mean real influence.[80]

The Role of Interest Groups

Environmental interest groups have also increased their role in the Antarctic Treaty System. For example, in the 1980s, Greenpeace established a research base in Antarctica. Not only is the Antarctic and Southern Ocean Coalition (ASOC) a formal observer at ATS meetings, but its members also serve as representatives on several national ATS delegations. ASOC also publishes *ECO*, a broadsheet produced daily at major international environmental conferences to provide up-to-date information on negotiations.

The role of NGOs in the Antarctic regime should not be underestimated. For example, ASOC and others kept alive the concept of world park status for Antarctica throughout negotiations for the 1988 Convention on the Regulation of Antarctic Mineral Resource Activity (CRAMRA). In 1989, Australia refused to ratify CRAMRA; eventually, all ATS members refused to ratify it, and the 1991 Environmental Protocol, which designated Antarctica as a nature reserve, was enacted in its place.[81]

ASOC also monitors compliance with environmental agreements. Although in 1983 it was unable to stop France from destroying several small islands in order to construct an airstrip in Terre Adélie, ASOC publicized the French violation to ATS members and to the United Nations. ASOC and other environmental NGOs continue to monitor waste disposal projects on the continent.[82] Their position was considerably strengthened when, in January 1989, the *Bahía Paráiso* ran aground and leaked 170,000 gallons of fuel oil. The ship had deliberately entered dangerous waters, an action taken in part to entertain the eighty-one tourists on board.[83]

A recent source of conflict on the Antarctic continent is the new tourism industry, a development the framers of the Antarctic Treaty System apparently did not anticipate. The burden for tourism-related problems has fallen by default on local research stations, but their resources are sufficient only for station personnel, and no station is prepared to cope with or to repair environmental harm caused by tourists and the tourism agencies. In 1991, the International Association of Antarctic Tour Operators (IAATO) was formed. Some nations, such as the United Kingdom, require any tour groups visiting their stations to be members of IAATO, but the impact of such regulations is unclear at present.[84]

Discussion

The preamble to the Antarctic Treaty states that Antarctica should be used only for peaceful purposes and the advancement of scientific knowledge. M. J. Peterson suggests a third, implicit principle: "There is an Antarctic community that should share the continent and its governance."[85] Thus, the basis of the treaty rests on the central idea of open access for members of the Antarctic Treaty System to conduct scientific research with no overt military activities. Military bases and fortifications, military maneuvers, and weapons testing are explicitly prohibited (Article I). However, Antarctica is not an open-access regime in that any nation with the technical ability to do so may set up research stations on the continent or its surrounding ice; it is an international commons because membership in the governing system is restricted to nations with a substantial research presence. As discussed in chapter 1, Antarctica is usually included in the group of global rather than international commons because its community of users is not based on regional or geographical considerations, it is not subject to national sovereignty, and the Antarctic Treaty System is explicitly linked to some United Nations treaties that do have global applications.

It is no surprise that the Antarctic regime should prove so stable. All levels of institutional choice, from constitutional choice decisions about membership to collective choice decisions to forgo a permanent secretariat to operational choice rules on nuclear waste and sled dogs, are given full legitimacy by both regime participants and external actors. The boundaries of the resource domain are clearly defined. The user pool is doubly clear. First, the matter of which countries and organizations may participate is beyond dispute. Second, the actual users (i.e., the scientists and government officials who come to Antarctica—the epistemic community) also form a community that is recognized both internally and in the international arena.

The brutal physical conditions on Antarctica have a great deal to do with the success of the regime. They limit physical participation in the regime, they encourage congruence between operational rules and "local conditions" because local conditions do not allow much flexibility, and they ease monitoring. Sanctioning has not been much of an issue on Antarctica, in part because it is so difficult to break the rules. The community is generally self-disciplined, so any sanctioning that does occur is usually informal.

Potential problems have been identified, however, with the discovery of large oil and gas reserves and with the advent of the tourism industry. If the region's energy reserves should become profitable and technologically feasible to extract, conflict among user groups would erupt. The comfortable research communities would find their resource threatened, and the policy actors interested in energy extraction would inject an entirely new factor into the resource domain. Some of these problems have already been seen, although to a lesser extent, in the region's growing tourism industry. The domain is unable to support tourism at the rate some tour operators seem to want, and tour operators are not represented in the regime at any level (except as they can lobby national governments). Redesigning operational rules for users who are not land based and who have no interest in participating in research will not occur without the participation of the tour groups, in the regime, so the operators are likely to violate existing rules. Even without their formal participation, operating rules and mechanisms for monitoring may need to be modified to accommodate their presence.

The Antarctic regime is saved, in part, by the continent itself, since tourism is limited to the warmer months and extraction of mineral and energy resources would be difficult under Antarctic conditions. However, some modification will be necessary in the coming years if the regime is to remain sustainable.

Suggested Reading

Peterson, M. J. *Managing the Frozen South: The Creation and Evolution of the Antarctic Treaty System*. Berkeley: University of California Press, 1988. A very detailed description and analysis of the Antarctic Treaty System. An essential book for readers interested in international regimes in general and Antarctica in particular.

Shapley, Deborah. *The Seventh Continent: Antarctica in a Resource Age*. Washington, D.C.: Resources for the Future, 1985. This is a splendid book. It is, of course, no longer current but its discussions of Antarctic history and politics up to 1985 are cogent. It is not an academic tome (a virtue rather than a flaw!), but it is thorough and provides an excellent introduction.

Notes

---

1. D. W. H. Walton, *Antarctica Science* (Cambridge: Cambridge University Press, 1987), 153.

2. Trevor Hatherton, "Antarctica Prior to the Antarctic Treaty—A Historical Perspective," in Polar Research Board, *Antarctic Treaty System: An Assessment* (Washington, D.C.: National Academy Press, 1986), 15.

3. V. E. Fuchs, "Antarctica: Its History and Development," in *Antarctic Resources Policy: Scientific, Legal, and Political Issues*, ed. Francisco Orrego Vicuña (Cambridge: Cambridge University Press, 1983), 13; Hatherton, "Antarctica Prior to the Antarctic Treaty," 17–19.

4. Fuchs, "Antarctica: Its History and Development," 13; Hatherton, "Antarctica Prior to the Antarctic Treaty," 21.

5. Fuchs, "Antarctica: Its History and Development," 13.

6. Ibid., 14.

7. Hatherton, "Antarctica Prior to the Antarctic Treaty," 25.

8. For a more complete discussion of the closing of the American frontier following the 1890 census, see Roderick Nash, *Wilderness and the American Mind*, 3rd ed. (New Haven, Conn.: Yale University Press, 1982).

9. Fuchs, "Antarctica: Its History and Development," 14. Borchgrevink's expedition was the first to winter intentionally; members of a Belgian expedition led by Adrien de Gerlache de Gomery wintered inadvertently when their ship was icebound during their 1898–1900 expedition. See also F. M. Auburn, *Antarctic Law and Politics* (Bloomington: Indiana University Press, 1982), 2.

10. Fuchs, "Antartica: Its History and Development," 15; Hatherton, "Antarctica Prior to the Antarctic Treaty," 23–25.

11. Hatherton, "Antarctica Prior to the Antarctic Treaty," 28. Although Hatherton writes that harpoon guns were invented in the 1860s, others give the date of the invention as 1904. See Josyane Couratier, "The Regime for the Conservation of Antarctica's Living Resources," in *Antarctic Resources Policy: Scientific, Legal and Political Issues*, ed. Francisco Orrego Vicuña. (Cambridge: Cambridge University Press, 1983), 139–148 at 139. See also J. N. Tonnessen and O. A. Johnsen, *A History of Modern Whaling*, abridged English ed. (Berkeley: University of California Press, 1982).

12. Philip Quigg, *A Pole Apart: The Emerging Issue of Antarctica* (New York: McGraw-Hill, 1983), 30.

13. Hatherton, "Antarctica Prior to the Antarctic Treaty," 29.

14. Ibid., 29.

15. Walter Sullivan, "Antarctica in a Two-Power World," *Foreign Affairs* 36, 1 (1957): 160.

16. Lynton Caldwell, *International Environmental Policy* (Durham, N.C.: Duke University Press, 1984), 254.

17. R. Y. Jennings, *The Acquisition of Territory in International Law* (Manchester, England: University of Manchester Press, 1963): 6–7. Cited in Jeffrey D. Myhre, *The Antarctic Treaty: Politics, Laws, and Diplomacy* (Boulder, Colo.: Westview Press, 1986), 8, and in Auburn, *Antarctic Laws and Politics*, 5. See also Andrew Haley, *Space Law and Government* (New York: Appleton-Century-Crofts, 1963), 119–127.

18. Deborah Shapley, *The Seventh Continent: Antarctica in a Resource Age* (Washington, D.C.: Resources for the Future, 1985), 67–68.

19. Fuchs, "Antarctica: Its History and Development," 15–16.

20. The claimed territory included all islands south of 50° south latitude between longitudes 20° and 80° west as well as Graham Land (the territory called the Palmer Peninsula by the United States). Letters patent of 21 July 1908, text in *British and Foreign State Papers* 101 (1912): 76–77. Cited in M. J. Peterson, *Managing the Frozen South: The Creation and Evolution of the Antarctic Treaty System* (Berkeley: University of California Press, 1988), 33, n. 6.

21. Fuchs, "Antarctica": Its History and Development," 16.

22. Auburn, "Antarctic Laws and Politics," 3.

23. Myhre, *Antarctic Treaty System*, 14.

24. Sullivan, "Antarctica in a Two-Power World," 159.

25. Shapley, *Seventh Continent*, 72.

26. Myhre, *Antarctic Treaty System*, 15.

27. Ibid., 14.

28. Ibid., 12–13.

29. Shapley, *Seventh Continent*, 76.

30. "'Chilean Antarctica' Stamp," *New York Times*, 5 December 1946, 43.

31. Myhre, *Antarctic Treaty System*, 13.

32. Peterson, *Managing the Frozen South*, 60.

33. Myhre, *Antarctic Treaty System*, 13.

34. Charles Evans Hughes, letter to A. W. Prescott, in G. H. Hackworth, *Digest of International Law*, vol. 1 (Washington, D.C.: Government Printing Office, 1963), 1,245, cited in Myhre, *Antarctic Treaty System*, 24.

35. Peterson, *Managing the Frozen South*, 59–60.

36. Ibid., 65; Auburn, *Antarctic Law and Politics*, 74.

37. U.S., Department of State, *Foreign Relations of the United States, 1948*

vol. 1, part 2 (National Security Council paper of 18 July 1948, H.920.5) (Bethesda, Md.: Congressional Information Service 1980) passim, cited in Myhre, *Antarctic Treaty System*, 27.

38. Ibid., 977–987.

39. Enrique Gajardo Villarroel, "Apuntes para un libro sobre la historia diplomática del Tratado Antártico y de la participación chilena en su elaboración," *Revista de difusión INACH* 10 (1977): 46–47. Cited in Auburn, *Antartic Laws and Politics*, 86.

40. Peterson, *Managing the Frozen South: The Creation and Evolution of the Antarctic Treaty System*, 37.

41. Twelve nations were involved in the first International Polar Year, establishing forty-odd research stations in the Arctic, but the second year involved a smaller effort because of political unrest in Europe and the worldwide economic depression. Shapley, *Seventh Continent*, 83.

42. E. Fred Roots, "The Role of Science in the Antarctic Treaty System," in Polar Research Board, *Antarctic Treaty System*, 171–172. Twelve nations participated: Austria/Hungary, Canada, Denmark, Finland, France, Germany, the Netherlands, Norway, Russia, Sweden, the United Kingdom, and the United States.

43. Robert Rutford, "Summary of Science in Antarctica Prior to and Including the International Geophysical Year," in Polar Research Board, *Antarctic Treaty System*, 99.

44. Sixty-four nations were involved in the International Geophysical Year: Argentina, Australia, Austria, Belgium, Bolivia, Brazil, Bulgaria, Burma, Canada, Ceylon, Chile, China (Taiwan), Colombia, Cuba, Czechoslovakia, Denmark, the Dominican Republic, East Africa, Ecuador, Egypt, Ethiopia, Finland, France, Germany, Ghana, Greece, Guatemala, Hungary, Iceland, India, Indonesia, Iran, Ireland, Israel, Italy, Japan, the Democratic Republic of Korea, the Federation of Malaya, Mexico, the Mongolian People's Republic, the Netherlands, New Zealand, Norway, Pakistan, Panama, Peru, the Philippines, Poland, Portugal, Southern Rhodesia, Romania, Spain, Sweden, Switzerland, Tunisia, the Union of South Africa, the Union of Soviet Socialist Republics, the United Kingdom, the United States, Uruguay, Venezuela, the Vietnam Democratic Republic, the Republic of Vietnam, and Yugoslavia. The People's Republic of China was involved but withdrew formal participation after Taiwan was recognized as a participant.

45. Peterson, *Managing the Frozen South*, 39.

46. Myhre, *Antarctic Treaty System*, 26–27; Peterson, *Managing the Frozen South*, 39; Auburn, *Antarctic Law and Politics*, 88–89.

47. Auburn, *Antarctic Law and Politics*, 92.

48. Hatherton, "Antarctica Prior to the Antarctic Treaty," 31.

49. Shapley, *Seventh Continent*, 90.

50. Ibid., 84.

51. Hatherton, "Antarctica Prior to the Antarctic Treaty," 31–32.

52. Unless otherwise noted, this material is from James Zumberge, "The Antarctic Treaty as a Scientific Mechanism—The Scientific Committee on Antarctic Research and the Antarctic Treaty System," in Polar Research Board, *Antarctic Treaty System*, 153–184.

53. For a full discussion, see Peterson, *Managing the Frozen South*, especially chapter 5, "Successful Regime Creation in 1959."

54. Shapley, *Seventh Continent*, 88.

55. Antarctic Treaty (1959), Article IV reads as follows:

> 1. Nothing contained in the present Treaty shall be interpreted as: (a) a renunciation by any Contracting Party of previously asserted rights or claims to territorial sovereignty in Antarctica; (b) a renunciation or diminution by any Contracting Party of any basis of claim to territorial sovereignty in Antarctica which it may have whether as a result of its activities or those of its nationals in Antarctica, or otherwise; (c) prejudicing the position of any Contracting Party as regards its recognition or non-recognition of any other State's right of or claim or basis of claim to territorial sovereignty in Antarctica.

> 2. No acts or activities taking place while the present Treaty is in force shall constitute a basis for asserting, supporting or denying a claim to territorial sovereignty in Antarctica or create any rights of sovereignty in Antarctica. No new claim, or enlargement of an existing claim to territorial sovereignty in Antarctica shall be asserted while the present Treaty is in force.

56. Shapley, *Seventh Continent*, 94.

57. John A. Heap and Martin Holdgate, "The Antarctic Treaty System as an Environmental Mechanism—An Approach to Environmental Issues," in Polar Research Board, *Antarctic Treaty System*, 207.

58. Peterson, *Managing the Frozen South*, 104.

59. Heap and Holdgate, "Antarctic Treaty System," 203–207.

60. Shapley, *Seventh Continent*, 153.

61. N. A. Wright and P. L. Williams, *Mineral Resources of Antarctica*, U.S. Geological Survey Circular No. 705 (Reston, Va.: U.S. Geological Survey, 1974).

62. Shapley, *Seventh Continent*, 125.

63. Ibid., 149.

64. Gareth Porter and Janet Welsh Brown present an interesting discus-

sion of the evolution of the Environmental Protocol in *Global Environmental Politics*, 2nd ed. (Boulder, Colo.: Westview Press, 1996), 88–92.

65. Lord Lansdown, speech to the House of Lords, 18 February 1960, *Parliamentary Debates*, vol. 221 cols. 188–191, cited in Peterson, *Managing the Frozen South*, 75.

66. Myhre, *Antarctic Treaty System*, 78. In general, see chapter 7, "Role of SCAR."

67. David Drewry, "Conflict of Interest in the Use of Antarctica," in *Antarctic Science: Global Concerns*, ed. Gotthilf Hempel (New York: Springer-Verlag, 1994), 22.

68. In citations of recommendations, the first Roman numeral designates the Consultative Meeting at which the recommendation was adopted, and the second number, whether Roman or Arabic, designates the sequence number assigned at that meeting to the particular recommendation.

69. See Myhre, *Antarctic Treaty System*, chapter 9: "Administrative Arrangements," 93–98.

70. Ibid., 97.

71. Ibid., 97.

72. L. F. Macedo de Soares Guimaraes, "The Antarctic Treaty System from the Perspective of a New Consultative Party," in Polar Research Board, *Antarctic Treaty System*, 342. See also S. Z. Qasim and H. P. Rajan: "[It] is doubtful where the [common heritage of mankind] concept, however relevant in the context of the law of the sea [sic], is appropriate or workable if applied to [sic] antarctic resources." S. Z. Qasim and H. P. Rajan, "The Antarctic Treaty System from the Perspective of a New Member," in Polar Research Board, *Antarctic Treaty System*, 369.

73. De Soares Guimaraes, "Antarctic Treaty System," 342. See also Richard A. Woolcott, "The Interaction Between the Antarctic Treaty System and the United Nations System," in Polar Research Board, *Antarctic Treaty System*, 386.

74. Robert J. Griffiths, "From the Ocean Floor to Outer Space: The Third World and Global Commons Negotiations," *Journal of Third World Studies* 9, 2 (1992): 380–381.

75. SCAR Constitution, 367 *SCAR Circular* (16 December 1976), cited in Auburn, *Antarctic Law and Politics*, 173.

76. Peterson, *Managing the Frozen South*, 101. Poland was admitted to SCAR in 1976 based on its intent to build the station. Auburn, *Antarctic Law and Politics*, 173.

77. Peterson, *Managing the Frozen South*, 101.

78. Ibid., 103.

79. Meetings of SCAR are closed, and the deliberations and results are

not made public. Thus, by nonvoting acceding parties gaining access to the meetings, they are also gaining access to the discussions and information generated there. This is a considerable concession on the part of the consultative parties.

80. Peterson, *Managing the Frozen South*, 102 (notes omitted).

81. Paul Wapner, *Environmental Activism and World Civic Politics* (Albany, N.Y.: State University of New York Press, 1996), 136.

82. Ibid., 137.

83. Mort Rosenblum, "Plan to Develop Antarctica Leaves Environmentalists Cold," *Greensboro News and Record*, 8 October 1989, A16, col. 1.

84. Drewry, "Conflict of Interest," 14–18.

85. Peterson, *Managing the Frozen South*, 41.

Chapter 4

The Oceans

Ocean, *n.* A body of water occupying about two-thirds of a world
made for man—who has no gills.

—Ambrose Bierce, *The Devil's Dictionary* (1906)

The earliest written records of ocean law proclaim the freedom of the seas.
Asian and Arab nations followed the general principles of freedom of navigation and trade.[1] However, in the Middle Ages, European hunger for
colonies led European princes to assert sovereignty over faraway oceans as
well as coastal waters nearer to home. This inevitably led to conflict, and
from the fifteenth century on, jurists and governments struggled to define
ownership of the ocean waters and their resources.

The ocean regime is the most complex of all the global commons regimes,
and its historical roots extend at least to Roman times. Every nation with a
coastline is concerned with the regime, and nations have gone to war to gain
access to critical seas. The oceans contain an elaborate array of resources, and
even in this day of air and space travel, they are the premier international
highways. For millennia, the oceans have been a dump for waste, and they
are critical in maintaining weather patterns and atmospheric quality. Given
this complexity—and the complete story of the oceans is vastly more complex than portrayed here—it is impossible to outline the development of the
entire ocean regime. Unlike the evolution of the Antarctic regime, which is
coherent, modern, and relatively stable, the ocean regime has evolved over
centuries and is based on a patchwork of customs and multilateral treaties.

This chapter is organized into six sections. The first discusses the evolution of laws concerning ownership of the oceans and the range of the territorial seas. The second describes the purposes and results of the three United

Nations Conferences on the Law of the Sea (UNCLOS). The third section addresses the deep seabed mineral regime first proposed at UNCLOS III and its subsequent modification. The fourth section focuses on living marine resources; the fifth section describes international efforts to control marine pollution, and the sixth section provides an analysis of the evolution of the ocean regime using the analytic model developed in chapter 2.

History of the Oceans and Territorial Seas

Of all the global commons discussed in this book, the oceans and territorial seas have the longest and most complex histories. Every nation in the world has a vital interest in ocean policy because of its effect on international commerce and national security.

The Oceans

As early as the second century, the Romans had declared that the seas were *communes omnium naturali jure*, or common to all humankind. Drawing on the second-century works of the Roman jurist Marcianus, the Digest of Justinian, written by Roman emperor Justinian I (483–565), was the first recorded statement on the law of the sea.[2] The Digest declared that the sea and its fish were available to all and no state could extend its jurisdiction beyond the shore, which was defined as the high-water mark. This generous approach to ocean ownership was possible in part because the Romans were the undisputed lords of the Mediterranean Sea, the only sea of importance to them. However, as the mercantile city-states of the Middle Ages grew in power and commerce, control of territorial waters assumed more importance. By 1269, Venice was charging tolls from all vessels in the Adriatic Sea, and Venetian control continued until the seventeenth century.[3]

Not only in the Mediterranean were states laying claim to the oceans. The Baltic Sea was under competing claims from Denmark, Sweden, and Poland, and the British were making extravagant claims to the English Sea.[4] Even when England and other seafaring nations were asserting extensive claims to territorial seas, custom provided that coastal states were entitled to claim some portion of the contiguous seas. Even later advocates of the freedom of the seas such as Grotius acknowledged these national rights. However, there was no agreement among the nations about the distances to which nations might lay claim, and there were certainly no expectations that a landlocked nation would have any rights to oceanic resources.

Early Italian jurists proposed coastal jurisdictions based on the range a ship could travel in a relatively short period of time. Bartolo of Saxoferrato (1314–1357) proclaimed a distance of 100 miles, or slightly less than two days' travel. His pupil, Baldus Ubaldus (1327–1400), compressed this "imperium" to one day's travel, or 60 miles. The probable basis for these pronouncements was the control of piracy, although the hundred-mile distance proposed by Bartolo also had the effect of turning the Adriatic into an Italian sea. There is, however, no indication that either Bartolus or Baldus affected the international perceptions of limits to territorial seas.[5]

The usual explanations for the desire to assert sovereignty over the world's oceans are based on some mix of the commercial aspects of the claims, national security, protection of fisheries, and collection of tariffs. The historical context for these explanations begins with the collapse of the Roman Empire, when true anarchy ruled on the seaways. Merchants were constantly in danger of pirates, who would steal cargo, crew, and vessel. There were no rights on the oceans, only a common vulnerability to danger. Just as land merchants traveled in caravans with mercenaries as guards, seafaring merchants combined forces for mutual safety. Gradually, the maritime governments assumed this chore; it did, after all, ensure the collection of taxes and tariffs and provide yet another arena in which to assert power. By the thirteenth century, the police function became a national prerogative, and from this a national right to jurisdiction was derived.[6]

As noted in the discussion of the sovereignty claims in the Antarctic, the competition between Spain and Portugal over new lands was intense. Throughout the fifteenth and sixteenth centuries, the two nations struggled over which was to have control over the New World. In 1455, Pope Nicholas V (pope 1447–1455) ceded permanent rights to the Portuguese for all of Africa and beyond, ostensibly to encourage them to bring Catholicism to the unconverted. Of course, the pope was also concerned with the development of trade and commerce. The Portuguese king believed that under the papal decree, the discoveries made by Christopher Columbus and sponsored by Ferdinand V and Isabella I of Spain were within his territories. When the Spanish rulers learned he was preparing an armada to take possession of the lands discovered by Columbus, they appealed to Pope Alexander VI (pope 1492–1503), a native of Spain.[7] In 1493, Alexander issued a papal bull, *Inter cætera*, in which he awarded all territory beyond longitude 35° west to Spain. A series of papal bulls continued to grant new lands to Spain.

The Portuguese protested, and a compromise was reached. The Portuguese recognized Spanish claims in the New World, and in return, the Spanish agreed to a new dividing line between the two national spheres of influence. In June 1494, Portugal and Spain agreed to the Treaty of Torde-sillas, which in effect divided the earth into two equal hemispheres, one under Portuguese control and the other belonging to Spain.[8] Spain now "owned" the western Atlantic Ocean, the Pacific Ocean, and the Gulf of Mexico, and Portugal had the southern Atlantic and the Indian Oceans. This division was not achieved without controversy. The main opponent was the distinguished jurist and Spanish Dominican Francisco de Vitoria (ca. 1486–1546), who in 1532 took the surprisingly modern view that the Pope had no authority to grant lands to Spain or Portugal that were already inhab-ited by the Indians and presumably belonged to them.

This happy allocation of the world's oceans lasted for less than a century. The political division of the oceans primarily benefited the most powerful seafaring nations. As the English, Dutch, and French expanded their ocean empires, the Spanish and Portuguese found enforcement of their preposter-ous claims increasingly difficult. The great controversies regarding closed seas (*mare clausum*) and freedom of the seas (*mare liberum*), which form the basis of modern international law, began with these Portuguese and Spanish claims. The allocation of the world's oceans into two dominions was so ques-tionable that even legitimate governments saw fit to ignore the division. Some adventurers sailed under letters of marque, which gave them permis-sion from their sovereigns to capture merchant vessels of other nations. Oth-ers sailed with the unofficial blessing of their sovereigns, disavowed if cap-tured but welcomed home with their booty as long as a percentage went into the royal coffers. Early in the sixteenth century, France, England, and Hol-land began to challenge Spanish domination of the oceans. The French especially were a thorn in the side of the Spanish, establishing colonies in the Americas and attacking Spanish treasure ships. They refused to recognize the authority of the papal bulls dividing the world's oceans, claiming that the seas were *res communes*, or common property, free for all to use. French jurists such as Jean Bodin (1530–1596) protested Spanish claims to the oceans, citing Baldus's view that sixty miles from the coastline was} as much as any nation could fairly claim.[9] By the sixteenth century, the Scan-dinavian countries, in particular the Atlantic-focused countries of Norway and Sweden, were propelled by their fishing interests into the controversies over territorial seas. In May 1598, the Danes ordered the capture of any English vessel in the waters they considered part of their territorial domain.[10] The Dutch were also involved, having begun a protracted revolt against Spain in 1567 that was finally resolved with the Treaty of Westphalia in 1648.

The Territorial Seas

The year 1588, which saw the defeat of the Spanish Armada, was a watershed year for the British. Their ascendancy in world maritime affairs was ensured with the destruction of the Spanish fleet. Throughout this period, there was no definitive agreement as to the extent of the Sea of England. Although the British navy frequently petitioned the government for formal boundaries, the requests remained unsatisfied. This was not so much from official ignorance as from official policy: vague boundaries could be enforced vigorously when England was strong but treated more cavalierly when national power or interests were otherwise engaged. After 1588, England worked with France and Holland to colonize the newly discovered lands to the west. Some of Elizabeth I's counselors were opposed to close treaty ties with Holland, correctly foreseeing Dutch competition and economic pressures, but the queen rejected their advice.

Because enforcement of territorial claims on the high seas was virtually impossible, nations abandoned active pursuit of this territorialism and focused on coastal waters, where enforcement was more feasible. In 1602, the recently founded Dutch East India Company seized a Portuguese galleon in the Strait of Malacca in retaliation for Portuguese resistance to Dutch trade in the East Indies. The company commissioned Hugo Grotius (1583–1645) to write a legal brief defending the action.

Freedom of the Seas (*Mare liberum*) is part of a larger work, *On the Law of Spoils* (*De jure praedae*), written in 1604–1605. The more famous *Freedom of the Seas* is a chapter excerpted at the request of the Dutch during truce negotiations with Spain in 1608.[11] In this work, Grotius argued that the sea, like the air, cannot be appropriated, in part because the sea cannot be occupied, since the passage of a ship leaves no permanent traces. He also argued that the pope had no authority over the oceans for two reasons. First, because the oceans are unpopulated, there were no human beings in them over whom the pope could exercise spiritual authority. Second, Grotius argued, because Jesus renounced temporal authority and the pope is God's earthly representative, the pope cannot have power that God himself has renounced;[12] thus, the pope lacked the temporal authority to allocate sovereignty over the oceans.[13]

Just as Grotius had prepared *On the Law of Spoils* as an advocate for the Dutch East India Company, so did John Selden (1584–1654), an English jurist, respond to a request from James I of England to prepare a rebuttal to Grotius in defense of the British seizure of Dutch cargoes off the coast of

Greenland. Selden's great work, *Mare clausum* (*The right and dominion of the sea*), has been eclipsed by the reputation of Grotius, although it seems that Selden may have the last word as modern states continue to increase their claims to territorial seas.[14]

Grotius did not reject the notion of territorial seas. In 1625, he published *De jure belli ac Pacis* (On the law of war and peace), in which he acknowledged that "lordship" over some ocean territory was possible if a fleet were in place to enforce the claims and that coastal waters close enough to shore to be protected from land could be considered sovereign territory as much as was the land itself. One significant idea suggested by Grotius in this work was the old one of control: a nation could claim sovereignty over the amount of territory it could control. In the seventeenth century, that distance was defined by the length of a cannon shot.

The cannon-shot rule was first advocated by the Dutch in 1610, when they protested to the English that a nation could claim territorial waters only as far as a cannon shot would reach.[15] Soon the Belgians and the French were also advocates of the rule, which was used to determine territoriality only for security purposes such as neutrality and for prizes, not for simple commercial purposes such as fishing.[16] The problem, of course, was that cannon-shot distances changed with advances in technology. In the fourteenth, fifteenth, and sixteenth centuries, cannons could throw iron balls 4,200 feet (about 0.8 statute miles) and stone balls more than a mile and a half. Spain claimed to have built cannons in the sixteenth century that could fire shot more than three miles, but even if this were true, firing over such a distance was of doubtful accuracy, and the cannons of the day were notoriously unsafe. During the eighteenth century, the cannon-shot rule was accepted by England, the Italian states, Spain, Portugal, the United States, and Russia. At the end of the eighteenth century, the king of Spain repudiated the cannon-shot rule as an appropriate measure, instead proclaiming two miles as the limit of his domain.

Other methods to measure territorial seas were proposed: the Scandinavian league (approximately four nautical miles), suggested in 1598 by the Danes as the territorial limit for the Danish–Norwegian fishing fleets; the midchannel principle, which uses the center of a river as demarcation for national boundaries, a concept that has given rise to much dispute, since rivers are notorious for changing their paths; and the line-of-sight principle, suggested because it was only within the sight of humans stationed on the coast that hostile or encroaching vessels could be observed. None of these ever achieved widespread acceptance.[17] An even less practical principle evolved from fishing rights, suggesting that the size of the territorial sea should be determined by the extent of national dependence on fishing. Rich agricultural nations thus would have small seas, and poorer nations that depended on fisheries would have larger territories.[18]

None of these various principles attracted universal acceptance. During the seventeenth and eighteenth centuries, the principle that finally became accepted was that national jurisdiction extended only as far as a nation could enforce its control from shore. Beyond artillery range, the high seas were open to all.[19] This principle rested more on practical considerations than on elegant expositions of legal principles. The boundary of territorial seas eventually evolved into one marine league, or three miles. This was the distance used by the United States in 1793 when it defined its neutral coastal area during the war between Great Britain and France.[20]

The first treaty to recognize the three-mile limit was the Fishing Convention of 1818.[21] A long-standing dispute between Britain and the United States over fishing in Canadian waters was exacerbated by the Treaty of Ghent, which resolved the War of 1812. Americans insisted that the treaty did not change fisheries agreements reached before the war, but the British claimed that all earlier agreements between the two nations were annulled by the treaty. The convention recognized the British rights to a three-mile territorial limit off the coast of the British possessions in North America. Between 1876 and 1883, Great Britain formally limited itself to a three-mile limit for all purposes with the passage of the Customs Consolidation Act of 1876, the Territorial Waters Jurisdiction Act of 1878, and the Sea Fisheries Act of 1883.[22]

As the preeminent sea power, Great Britain set the standard in international maritime law. Throughout the nineteenth century, British treaties, conventions, and domestic legislation and the British courts affirmed the three-mile limit. In each of five treaties with France signed between 1839 and 1882, Britain established a limit for fisheries set at three nautical miles, measured from the low-water mark.[23] By 1853, laws were passed establishing the three-mile limit for British possessions in North America; in 1877, a similar limit was imposed for the Pacific islands. In 1881, Cyprus was placed under a three-mile limit for neutrality; the same year, a one-league (three-nautical-mile) limit for fisheries for New South Wales, Australia, was established.[24]

Several legal cases also affirmed the three-mile limit. The first British case dealing with the three-mile limit was *Twee Gebroeders* (3 C. Robinson 162 [1800]). In this case, the British High Court of Admiralty ordered four seized Dutch ships returned because they had been improperly seized in Prussian territorial waters within the three-mile limit. The second case, *The*

Anna (5 C. Robinson 373 [1805]), involved an American vessel captured by the British that was also ordered returned because it had been seized improperly. In 1808, a French prize court confirmed the capture of several American ships because they had been taken outside the three-mile limit of the Prussian coast. American law followed the arguments, if not the exact precedents. In *The Brig Ann* (1 Gallison 62 [1812]), Justice Storey of Massachusetts held that the said brig had been within American waters when seized.

As expected, the rest of Europe followed the lead set by Great Britain: Spain (1828), Belgium (1832), Greece (1869), the Netherlands (1882), Denmark (1882), Italy (1888), and the Ottoman Empire (1893). Spain soon reneged on this limit, however, and in 1830 adopted a six-mile zone.[25] By this time, France had acceded to the three-mile limit, however, for fishing. In 1855 and again in 1888, the French promulgated laws setting territorial limits at three nautical miles from the low-water mark. Austria and Prussia also accepted the three-nautical-mile standard, although Austria had a marine border only on the Adriatic.[26] Independent Oriental countries also used the three-mile limit: in 1879, Japan proclaimed a three-mile limit, as did Hawaii.

Russia was a different story. Fearing the depletion of Russian seal fisheries by foreign fleets, in 1821 Tsar Alexander I declared a territorial limit of 100 miles. Vessels found within these limits were subject to confiscation. He drew the boundary to include the Bering Sea, the Gulf of Alaska, and the Sea of Okhotsk. The Americans and the British (who had fishing interests in western Canada) were incensed, and when in 1822, the Russians seized the American brig *Pearl*, intense negotiations began between Russia, Great British, and the United States. In separate conventions with the United States (1824) and Britain (1825), Russia retreated to the three-mile rule, although the *Pearl* was not released until 1829.[27]

In Latin America, Chile set a standard that differed from the European norm. In 1855, Chile claimed territorial waters out to a marine league (three miles) but claimed four leagues for national security and customs. In 1870, Chile asserted a 150-mile neutrality zone during the Franco-Prussian War.[28] Other Latin American countries followed Chile's lead: Ecuador (1857), El Salvador (1860), Argentina (1869), and Honduras (1880).[29]

After World War I, the League of Nations began a program of legal reform to codify international law. One of the topics discussed was the territorial limit of three miles, long accepted in western Europe but not the norm in the new countries carved out of the former colonies. The subcommittee in charge of the issue of territorial seas contained some jurists who were not enamored with the three-mile limit, having been advocates of larger limits throughout their professional careers. The committee circulated a lengthy questionnaire to the various governments. By the simple expedient of *raising* the issue of the three-mile limit, its continued usefulness was questioned. When the Hague Conference for the Progressive Codification of International Law (1930) convened, it was unable to reach a consensus over the range of the territorial seas.[30]

In the following years, the limit of territorial seas was regularly disputed. Although regulation of fisheries often was the source of the disputes, it was not the only one. The right of innocent passage was at issue in *The Corfu Channel Case*, heard in the International Court of Justice in 1949.[31] In 1946, Albania had mined the northern Corfu Straits, and the United Kingdom claimed damages for loss of lives and the damages to British Royal Navy ships that had collided with the mines. Albania's contention that the right of passage did not apply to the northern Corfu Straits was rejected, and the British claim that the straits were international waters was accepted. Although this case decided the status of international straits, it left undecided the issue of territorial seas in general.[32] That issue remained unresolved until the third Law of the Sea Conference in 1982 (UNCLOS III), when a separate regime for international straits was adopted at the insistence of the major seafaring nations. They refused to accept Article 3 of the convention, which allowed a twelve-mile limit in territorial seas and could lead to disputes over international straits. Articles 34–45 of the convention addressed these concerns by providing a comparatively liberal right of passage for surface ships and submerged submarines; the only justification for halting a ship in transit was violation of international regulations for protection of the marine environment.[33]

During UNCLOS III, a consensus was reached in which the nations agreed on a range of territorial seas. A 12-mile limit for the right of innocent passage was set, but straits less than 24 miles wide were to be governed not as territorial waters but by a new regime of "transit passage."[34] Beyond this 12-mile limit, coastal states had a monopoly on fish and living resources to the 200-mile limit and on energy sources and minerals to 350 miles.[35] This enclosed 36 percent of the world's oceans, including 90 percent of commercially exploitable fish and 87 percent of projected offshore oil reserves.[36]

United Nations Conferences on the Law of the Sea

The three United Nations Conferences on the Law of the Sea (1958, 1960, and 1982) codified existing international law in a treaty regime that entered into force in 1994 (See box 4.1, Chronology for the Law of the Sea.) UNC-LOS I was the starting point, and the resulting ocean regime, excluding the deep seabed mining provisions, was a classic case of enclosure.[37]

UNCLOS I

Spurred by the discovery of huge reserves of oil and natural gas off the coast of the United States, in September 1945 President Harry Truman issued two proclamations in which the United States claimed jurisdiction over the nat-

---

Box 4.1 Chronology for the Law of the Sea

1493	Papal bull *Inter cætera*
1494	Treaty of Tordesillas
1588	British defeat of the Spanish Armada
1608	*Freedom of the Seas* (Grotius)
1635	*Mare clausum (The right and dominion of the sea)* (Selden)
1818	Fishing Convention of 1818 (three-mile limit)
1954	International Convention for the Prevention of Pollution of the Sea by Oil (in force 1958)
1958	First United Nations Conference on the Law of the Sea (UNCLOS I)
1958	Convention on the High Seas (Conservation Convention) (in force 1962)
1958	Convention on the Continental Shelf (in force 1964)
1958	Convention on the Territorial Sea and the Contiguous Zone (Territorial Seas Convention) (in force 1964)
1958	Convention on Fishing and Conservation of the Living Resources of the High Seas (Conservation Convention) (in force 1966)
1960	Second United Nations Conference on the Law of the Sea (UNCLOS II)
1972	Convention on the Prevention of Marine Pollution by Dumping of Wastes and Other Matter (London Convention) (in force 1975)
1972	Convention for the Prevention of Marine Pollution by Dumping from Ships and Aircraft (Oslo Convention) (in force 1974)
1973	International Convention for the Prevention of Pollution from Ships (MARPOL) (in force 1983)
1982	United Nations Third Convention on the Law of the Sea Treaty (UNCLOS III) (in force 1994)

ural resources found on the continental shelf and indicated an inclination to claim extended fishing zones on the high seas. These claims were a dramatic indication that the tradition of open oceans was under challenge, yet they were met with little fanfare or outcry. Despite language in the proclamations that recognized the freedom of the seas as an enduring principle, it was clear that at least for the United States, offshore development was a primary goal of ocean policy.[38] Several Latin American states followed suit. Then in 1951, the International Court of Justice undermined the concept of the three-mile limit in the *Anglo-Norwegian Fisheries* case. The decision accepted a 1935 Norwegian royal decree that established Norway's territorial fishery limit at four miles, with a baseline drawn from coastal islands rather than the more usual low-water mark. This technique involves drawing territorial boundaries across the mouths of bays, harbors, rivers, and fjords. The baseline then becomes the starting point from which to measure the territorial seas.[39] This is of great advantage for countries with wide gaps in their shoreline that extend deep into the interior of the country. Clearly, the time had come to change the rules. In 1950, the International Law Commission established a committee to codify existing customary ocean law, giving special attention to the territorial seas.[40] This led to the first United Nations conference on ocean law.

At the time of the first United Nations Law of the Sea Conference (UNCLOS I), most states accepted the minimal three-mile territorial limit. However, national and international events were pointing toward changes in the ocean regime. Many states were striving to extend their territorial limits for reasons other than nationalism; they wanted to control their coastal resources, to halt foreign research off the coasts, to prevent spills and pollution, and to protect national security.[41] At this conference, the Communist bloc nations advocated the position that each nation should set its own territorial limit; even landlocked Czechoslovakia and Hungary agreed.

UNCLOS I met in Geneva in 1958 and passed four conventions based on the findings of the International Law Commission: the Convention on the High Seas, the Convention on the Continental Shelf, the Convention on the Territorial Sea and the Contiguous Zone (Territorial Seas Convention), and the Convention on Fishing and Conservation of the Living Resources of the High Seas (Conservation Convention). Although these conventions were binding only on the nations that ratified or acceded to them, many of their provisions are, in effect, codifications of customary law and are therefore binding even against states that are not parties to them. No consensus was reached at UNCLOS I, and international conflicts over territorial seas escalated.

UNCLOS II

UNCLOS II was prompted by the "cod war" between Iceland and Great Britain. In 1948, Iceland had proclaimed sovereignty over the fishing rights on the continental shelf, and in 1952, it in effect extended its territorial sea by adopting the measuring technique of straight baselines in use by Norway and accepted by the International Court of Justice. This new method of determining territorial seas excluded the British fishing fleet from some of its traditional fishing grounds. The British boycotted Icelandic fish, but following UNCLOS I in 1958, the conflict escalated. With the failure of UNCLOS I to codify the width of the territorial sea, Iceland asserted a twelve-mile fishing limit. Following UNCLOS II, a compromise was reached in 1961 in which Great Britain accepted the twelve-mile limit and Iceland agreed to allow British fishermen within six miles of shore.[42] The British sent armed vessels to escort their far-distance fishing fleet that was harvesting inside the twelve-mile limit. Eventually, Great Britain and Iceland agreed to a gradual phasing in of the Icelandic claims. Iceland's position was strengthened in this dispute by two factors: first, the strategic importance of Iceland as an observation post for naval operations originating in the Soviet Union, and second, Iceland's firm belief that its internal fisheries were crucial to national economic well-being.[43]

Little was accomplished at UNCLOS II, although a compromise on the question of fishing zones and the limits of the territorial seas was almost reached. However, the Arab states and the Communist bloc countries joined forces to defeat the compromise proposal, and in the end nothing was achieved.[44]

The East–West confrontation was a crucial factor in discussions of territorial limits during UNCLOS I and II, as was the confrontation between the major maritime states and states with primarily coastal interests. By the mid-1970s, economic considerations had become paramount. Fisheries claims and their attendant issues of territoriality became prominent as the movement to extend national sovereignty gained power.

UNCLOS III

The negotiations that preceded UNCLOS III began in 1973, with twelve sessions taking place over a period of nine years. The task was to design a new legal regime for the oceans.[45] The developing countries had an additional mission: to operationalize the idea of the common heritage of mankind, first proposed as a principle of ocean management in 1967 by the United Nations ambassador from Malta, Arvid Pardo.[46]

The seabed regime was a major consideration at UNCLOS III. On 17 December 1970, the United Nations General Assembly unanimously adopted a Declaration of Principles that declared the seabed to be the "common heritage of mankind" that must be "exploited for the benefits of mankind as a whole, and taking into particular consideration the interests and needs of the developing countries."[47] Most participants agreed that arrangements for this and other emerging ocean issues had to be resolved through a joint effort. Increasingly wide claims for fishing territories and concerns about the possibility of underwater nuclear or military installations enlarged international concerns. Existing law was clearly inadequate, and a new Conference was called.

Many countries—not just the developing countries—saw economic advantages in following the common heritage regime for the oceans and in particular for the seabed minerals. Supervision by the United Nations would allow both small and large states access to the benefits of exploitation, and the "one country, one vote" norm in the United Nations gave the developing countries the majority necessary to protect their interests. The call for a seabed regime was in part a response to the possibility that coastal states would divide up the deep seabed among themselves on the basis of proximity. Countries that lacked coastlines or adequate ports were guaranteed representation. Countries with land-based mining investments that might be affected by ocean mining saw the common heritage of mankind (CHM) principle as a mechanism to keep prices artificially high. Still others saw the potential revenue for the United Nations as a way to reduce dependence on funding from the Western countries. Even the superpowers offered a qualified endorsement, driven in part by a concern for political stability in the wake of a scramble for newly available resources should the common heritage idea fail. All in all, the common heritage concept had widespread support from some surprising quarters, even if all supporters did not agree on interpretation of the term.[48]

Collective action rules were developed to promote as much mutual agreement as possible without allowing one nation to block decisions completely. In its convening resolution, the conference was instructed to produce a single treaty governing all aspects of the Law of the Sea, a mandate that required substantial compromise from all participants.

The Conference was organized into three committees: Committee I, for the seabed; Committee II, for maritime law dealing with "territorial seas, straits, islands, archipelagoes, the high seas, and economic zones to include living and nonliving resources within 200 miles of coastlines, the continental shelf, and access to the sea, especially by landlocked nations"; and Committee III, which dealt with issues of ocean pollution, scientific research, and technology transfer.[49] A separate group considered issues of dispute resolution.

The next three sections of this chapter discuss the regimes for deep seabed minerals, marine living resources, and marine pollution. The sections provide the historical background leading up to UNCLOS III for each regime and then describe the regimes that emerged.

The Deep Seabed Mineral Regime

Although the problem was not apparent at first, the design of UNCLOS III was flawed because it tried to reach agreement on two completely different resource domains: the sea and the deep seabed.[50] The United States had hoped to limit the Conference to seabed issues, but these hopes were quickly dashed. The various actors in the international arena, especially the United States and the other major industrialized nations, were watching the arrangements carefully, concerned that whatever was decided for deep sea mining might set a precedent for other global commons such as the Antarctic, outer space, the moon, and the electromagnetic and geostationary orbits. Resolution of the seabed issue was almost impossible, and by linking the two, issues of the ocean regime were dragged under as well.

Two major questions at this conference revolved around the issue of deep seabed mining: who would actually do the mining, and how were the arrangements to be financed? In deciding on the deep seabed regime, developed and developing nations were, as usual, concerned with different issues, and this particular issue was complicated by concerns of the Communist bloc nations and of countries with substantial land-based mining enterprises. The seabed regime that was finally adopted satisfied no one.

As the countries most likely to engage in mining in the near future, the developed nations were interested in establishing an international authority that would function primarily as a claims registry. Their greatest concerns were access to the minerals and the associated economic benefits. The developing countries wanted the international organization in charge of mining (the Enterprise) to be the actual mining operator on their behalf. They wanted equitable shares of the revenues from mining, and they wanted control over the Enterprise.

Complicating matters further, the Communist bloc nations were caught in the middle. They were technically mining countries because they "owned" seabeds, but they lacked resources to begin mining. The result was that the Communist bloc nations catered to the interests of the developing nations while trying to protect their future mining interests, on the chance that their technology and economy would eventually support mining. Finally, the land-based mining interests opposed any orderly regime for the seabed at all, fearing that new mineral sources would at best undercut their profits and at worst collapse the minerals market altogether.

By 1976, a "parallel" system had begun to emerge, with two major components. First, private and state-sponsored organizations would be permitted to mine the seabed. Second, the Enterprise would be permitted to mine for the international community; it would have access to minerals, technology, personnel, and money. To ensure an equitable allocation of sites, states or private companies wanting to mine were to apply for two sites, and the International Seabed Authority (ISA), the claims registry of the United Nations, would grant one application and keep the second for the Enterprise. This would save the United Nations the cost of exploration and pass on the costs to the technologically developed nations.

This seemed to be a suitably balanced solution to the allocation problem, but it did not address the ever-present problems of uncertain data (investment costs, operating costs, and world market stability). The financial problems of deep seabed mining are enormous, and lack of information only exacerbates the difficulties. Mining firms that would pay royalties to the Enterprise had to worry about extraction costs and the opportunity costs of tying up capital, which increased corporate risks.

The initial seabed-mining regime was problematic. It was designed to be a combination of private property regime and cooperative property regime, but the developing nations failed to recognize that manganese nodules are unlikely prospects for community management. (See box 4.2, Deep Seabed Minerals.) In negotiating financial arrangements, the various policy actors took different approaches in their estimations of success and risk. The developing countries anticipated high returns from deep seabed mining and were more willing to accept risk because both risk and cost were practically nonexistent for them. The developed countries were more conservative in their estimates of profits and, because of the high capital investment needed, were assuming a higher risk. The developed countries correctly saw very high opportunity costs, and they failed to support the treaty.

Although the United States played a major role in UNCLOS III and had accepted the parallel system, after the election of Ronald Reagan as president, the United States refused to accede to the treaty. This change came about for a number of reasons. First, tensions over rights of passage that would have been resolved under the Law of the Sea had diminished, and the United States no longer was under pressure to negotiate new navigation

---

Box 4.2 Deep Seabed Minerals

The HMS *Challenger*, a British survey ship, discovered manganese nodules in the 1870s while surveying the Pacific Ocean. These are brown or black potato-shaped mineral aggregates, granular and spongy on the underside, smooth on the upper side, and 5–10 centimeters (2–4 inches) in diameter. Manganese nodules are composed of thirty-seven elements, four of which are commercially valuable: manganese, iron, copper, and cobalt.

Manganese nodules are not found in very deep ocean trenches or along the continental shelves. They generally occur in single layers in horizontal deposits at a depth of 3.2–6.4 kilometers (2–4 miles) and in water that is rich in oxygen and contains little sedimentation. Forming concentric rings around a nucleus, they grow slowly, at a rate of 2–4 millimeters per million years.

The eastern, central, and western regions of the Pacific Ocean have been singled out for their uniform nodule content. It is estimated that together these regions contain an average of 31.9 kilograms (70 pounds) per square mile of manganese nodules, with the highest-grade nodules thought to exist southeast of Hawaii. However, since only a small percentage of the ocean floor has been surveyed in any detail, these estimates could be misleading.

Sources: Barkenbus, *Deep Seabed Resources*; Borgese, *The Mines of Neptune*; Chiras, *Environmental Science*; Congressional Research Service, *Ocean Manganese Nodules*; Dubs, "Minerals of the Deep Sea"; Jones, "Manganese"; Marx, *The Oceans*

---

agreements that might have come at the price of accepting the seabed regime.[51] Second, the Americans believed that the seabed-mining arrangements set dangerous precedents, especially regarding technology transfer, the Enterprise (a completely new type of international organization), and the mission of the Seabed Authority.[52] Finally, the Reagan administration saw better alternatives to the treaty; for example, both the United States and Germany passed domestic legislation to govern deep seabed mining.[53] This domestic legislation opened the possibility that the seabed-mining states could develop a regime outside the United Nations framework, similar to the Antarctic Treaty System.[54]

Starting in July 1990, United Nations Secretary-General Javier Pérez de Cuéllar initiated informal consultations in the international community to restructure the seabed regime. There were several reasons why he was eager to bring the developed nations into the Law of the Sea Treaty before it came into force in November 1994. First, it would be much more difficult to amend the treaty after that date. Second, commercial mining in the deep seabed would not be a viable option until well into the next century, so the various negotiation positions had softened since UNCLOS III. Third, international policy was increasingly reliant on market principles and incentives; the common heritage of mankind principle was fading from the world of practical politics. Finally, the design for the Enterprise was seriously dated; the newer approach to institutional design was in the market tradition, emphasizing decentralization and deregulation.[55]

Over the next four years, a series of fifteen meetings was held, first under the auspices of Pérez de Cuéllar and later under his successor, Boutros Boutros-Ghali. On 28 July 1994, the final text of the Agreement Relating to the Implementation of Part XI of the United Nations Convention on the Law of the Sea of 10 December 1982 was adopted. It contains six main changes from the original Part XI of the Convention. First, initial mining operations by the Enterprise will be joint ventures between the Enterprise and the mining states. Second, technologically advanced countries will have more control over formal decisions. Third, technology transfer is no longer a requirement. Fourth, production limitations have been removed. Fifth, the principle of the common heritage of mankind is preserved in the treaty, and the International Seabed Authority, although modified, is retained. Finally, the new agreement establishes an economic assistance fund for developing nations with land-based mining operations that find themselves in direct competition with seabed mining.[56]

Living Resources

Protection of the living resources of the high seas was largely outside the purview of the earliest Law of the Sea negotiations, although the issues of territoriality were certainly related questions. Attempts to introduce an international fisheries regime through the League of Nations were unsuccessful; despite a clear need for some international fisheries agreements, the league's 1930 Convention on the Law of the Sea could not reach agreement on a draft convention.[57] However, after UNCLOS I in 1958, four conventions were adopted that affected the international fisheries: the Convention on the High Seas Convention, the Convention on the Continental Shelf, the Convention on the Territorial Sea and the Contiguous Zone (Territorial Seas Convention), and the Convention on Fishing and Conservation of the Living Resources of the High Seas (Conservation Convention). These conventions did not have a substantial effect on high seas fisheries because they were essentially codifications of existing practices.

The primary effect on fisheries came with the Convention on the Continental Shelf, which differentiated sedentary species such as oysters from free-swimming species and assigned the sedentary species to the coastal states' jurisdiction. Several of these conventions expressed conservation ideals, but none provided any serious measure to implement conservation practices. Although all four conventions were in force by 1966, several of the major fishing nations (e.g., Japan and the USSR) did not join the Conservation Convention. As noted by Patricia Birnie and Alan Boyler, efforts to promote conservation of the marine fisheries were ineffective:

> Scientific findings were modified for political and economic reasons; enforcement was poor and international inspection [was] both rare and limited to reporting offenders to the flag states without follow-up; dispute settlement procedures, if the conventions provided for them at all, were seldom activated; developing countries involved in particular fisheries, as in the tuna fisheries, considered that their food and developmental needs entitled them to higher catches and that developed states should bear the brunt of any cuts in catch required for conservation. The latter mostly regarded the [Conservation] Convention as a moral code that they preferred not to violate but which they were none the less prepared to ignore in certain circumstances, in the view of many.[58]

Throughout the 1960s and 1970s, conservation of marine living resources continued to be an unresolved problem. Although various multinational treaties addressed the issue,[59] a broader ecological approach failed to materialize, and concerns for habitat protection and marine pollution were not integrated into fishery conservation needs. The 1972 United Nations Conference on the Human Environment (UNCHE or Stockholm Conference) adopted a Declaration of Principles that addressed conservation concerns (Principles 2–5) but did not have an explicit fisheries component.[60] It was not until UNCLOS III that conservation and fisheries became a direct concern. While preparations for UNCLOS III were under way, several treaties relating to conservation were negotiated. The most important of these were the 1973 Convention on International Trade in Endangered Species of Wild Fauna and Flora (CITES), the 1979 Convention on the Conservation of Migratory Species of Wild Animals (Bonn), the 1979 Convention on the Conservation of European Wildlife and Natural Habitats (Bern), and the 1980 Convention on the Conservation of Antarctic Marine Living Resources (Canberra) (CCAMLR or the Southern Ocean Convention). These four, along with the 1980 World Conservation Strategy and the 1982

World Charter for Nature, set the stage for the fisheries concerns reflected in the UNCLOS III negotiations.

The issues of conservation and territorial seas are closely linked, and they were finally addressed at UNCLOS III. One impetus behind the developing countries' desire for larger territorial seas was fear of the harvest capabilities of the developed countries' fleets; a key factor was the availability of factory ships to process large catches practically on-site. For example, Iceland, Ecuador, and Korea wished to exclude the fleets of Great Britain, the United States, and Japan, respectively, from their coastal waters.[61] Fishermen from the United States were employing large seine nets that captured and killed tons of unwanted fish, which were then discarded into the ocean. Even though this often contravened local fishing regulations, the 1954 American Fishermen's Protective Act, which reimburses American fishermen for fines and losses, shielded the vessel operates from the fines.[62] Conservation of the fisheries was a real concern, as the larger, technologically sophisticated vessels could move on to other lucrative fisheries, leaving the local fishermen with depleted resources. (See box 4.3, Ocean Fisheries.)

Unfortunately, the coastal fisheries do not inhabit geologically similar territories, and it is difficult to design treaties around the behavior of such a mobile resource as fish. Arguments based on the biological and economic efficiencies of harvesting fish from the continental shelf supported the territorial claims of nations such as Iceland and Korea, which have continental shelves. However, several major fishing nations, such as Chile, Ecuador, and Peru, do not have a continental shelf on which to base a territorial claim. These nations advanced an alternative ecosystem claim; in the 1950s, when this explanation was first offered, the idea of ecosystems and their biomass was an innovation.[63] The Pacific coast states of Latin America developed the rather startling *bioma theory*, which argues that native fishermen are part of the coastal ecosystem but foreign fishermen are not. Therefore, allowing foreigners to fish in coastal waters violates ecological principles.[64] The United States rejected this theory in 1955, noting that numerous fish stocks migrate through several ecosystems and claiming that the more logical approach would be to manage the entire fishery throughout its range.[65]

Independent of the logic of the situation, the Latin American nations continued to exert their extended territorial claims. In 1952, Chile, Ecuador, and Peru (the CEP states) declared a 200-mile territorial limit. The Latin American states continued to defend the 200-mile limit; in 1965, the First Latin American Parliament adopted a resolution proclaiming the 200-mile limit for all coastal states.[66] Individual nations soon passed new constitutions or legislation formalizing the resolution.[67]

Box 4.3 Ocean Fisheries

The world catch of fish peaked in 1970–1971 and has been in decline ever since. Although most countries engage in some form of commercial fishing, fish are not distributed evenly throughout the world: 90 percent of the world's fish come from only 3 percent of the world's oceans. The majority of these fish species are found within 200 miles of shore, in the Exclusive Economic Zone (EEZ). The best fishing areas tend to be located where the continental shelf is shallow and wide or where mineral upwellings occur.

Nearshore and offshore demersals (fish on or near the ocean floor) account for one-third of the ocean's harvestable biomass and include cods, hakes, pollacks, crustaceans, and mollusks. Pelagic fish and squid live higher in the water column and nearer to the surface. They make up two-thirds of harvestable biomass, half of which comes from clupeid fish, members of a large family (Clupeidae) of soft-finned bony fish that feed on plankton. Small clupeids such as sardines, herrings, and anchovies are the primary food source for larger fish and are the most economically useful in the production of fish meal and oil.

Sources: Bardach, "Sustainable Development of Fisheries"; Chapman, "Food from the Sea"; Crutchfield, "Resources from the Sea"; Eckert, Enclosure of Ocean Resources; Lerman, Marine Biology; Marx, The Oceans; Satchell, "Rape of the Oceans"

Other nations were also at odds over territorial limits. In 1963, Canada adopted a 12-mile fishing limit, and in 1970, over American objections, Canada extended its jurisdiction for the purposes of pollution control to 100 miles.[68] Other disputes erupted between Sweden and the Soviet Union, Norway and Great Britain, Iceland and Great Britain, and Korea and Japan. These concerns were brought to UNCLOS III.

One of the most useful accomplishments of UNCLOS III was the clarification of territorial limits: the 12-mile limit for the territorial sea; the contiguous zone extended to 24 nautical miles; the continental shelf to its natural margin or 200 nautical miles, whichever is farther; and an Exclusive Economic Zone (EEZ) not to exceed 200 nautical miles.[69] The EEZ is subject to the control of the littoral (coastal) states; thus, its waters are no longer an open-access regime.

Although UNCLOS gives the rights of conservation and management in the EEZ to the coastal states, this has clearly not been sufficient to achieve effective conservation. For example, in May 1992, the northern cod fishery off the coast of Newfoundland was closed because of depletion of its fisheries stock. Observers apportion blame generously: inshore fishers blame offshore trawlers for indiscriminate overfishing, and offshore fishermen accuse inshore fishers of cheating on quotas. Canadians blame Europeans for taking migratory fish in international waters in violation of regulations of the Northwest Atlantic Fisheries Organization, but Canada has also contributed to the problem by subsidizing its fleet and processing plants since 1977.[70]

In July 1993, a United Nations conference on global fisheries management agreed on the problem but not on the solution. The Food and Agriculture Organization of the United States (FAO) reported worldwide depletion of stocks.[71] FAO data from 1989 showed the value of the world catch at $72 billion and the cost of the catch at $92 billion.[72] It is not only the cod fisheries off the northeastern coast of North America that are in trouble; in 1993, Russia proposed a three-year moratorium on fishing in its Pacific waters.[73] At the United Nations conference, tensions between the coastal fishing nations (e.g., Argentina, Canada, Chile, Iceland, New Zealand, and Peru) and the distant-water nations (e.g., China, Japan, Poland, Russia, Spain, and the United States) were high. The coastal nations proposed binding regulations for high seas fisheries, even threatening to seize erring vessels in international waters. Such regulations would signal the end of the high seas as an open-access resource domain. Resource scarcity and the increasing costs of exploitation have apparently made the costs of regulation politically feasible. Clearly, if the fisheries are to survive at all, an effective regime must be devised.

Currently, the only restrictions on the high seas fisheries are those deriving from treaty obligations and the rights of coastal states to protect the fishery stocks that migrate between the EEZ and the high seas.[74] Part VII of the United Nations Convention on the Law of the Sea establishes the states' duty to cooperate in managing and conserving these migratory stocks, but the lack of monitoring, enforcement mechanisms, or sanctions in the treaty removes much of the incentive for states to comply once the treaty is in force.

The convention contains some innovative provisions, such as the species-specific approach for highly migratory species, marine mammals, and anadromous and catadromous species. Anadromous species, such as salmon, which spawn in freshwater, live at sea, and return to their origins to reproduce and die, are largely the responsibility of the coastal states in which they originate; other states are charged with the responsibility of cooperating with the state of origin. The intent of this section of the treaty is to discourage high seas harvesting of these species.[75] Catadromous species, such as some eels, which spawn at sea but live in freshwater rivers and lakes, are also the

responsibility of the coastal states in whose waters they live. Effective cooperation has so far been minimal; however, in light of the current state of the
world's fisheries, effective enforcement may move up on the international
agenda.

As the United Nations fisheries conference in the summer of 1993
emphasized, global fisheries are in a perilous state. The fleets are overcapital-
ized; in 1991, *The Times* (London) reported that a 40-percent reduction in
the fleet of the European Community (European Union) was necessary to
protect the fisheries in the North Sea and Baltic Sea.[76] This figure reflects the
optimistic assumption that the remaining 60 percent of the fleet would not
simply increase its fishing efforts to make up the difference. Efforts to reduce
coastal harvests may simply displace the fleets to international waters. The
costs associated with monitoring these fleets are substantial; the European
Union relies on a computer system that is prohibitively expensive for developing countries to adopt.[77]

Management of sustainable fisheries may prove to be an elusive dream.
Scientific data on fisheries stocks are often incomplete or inconclusive. To
make matters worse, fishermen frequently choose to ignore management
recommendations, whether because they disbelieve the data, or they cannot
afford to alter their activities, or short-term economic gains are more important to them than long-range stock preservation. Some fishery policies are
designed to protect nontarget species (e.g., the use of turtle excluder
devices), and fishermen see compliance with these policies as having little
economic benefit and high economic cost. Developing nations often depend
on catches for both internal consumption and export. Overlapping political
jurisdictions and the highly migratory habits of some species only exacerbate
the problems.

Marine Pollution

Although the primary focus of this book is the development of regimes to
manage exploitable resources, the control of marine pollution is a significant
part of the ocean regime. Marine pollution stems from several sources: land-
based discharges and discharges from ships, waste disposal, and oil drilling.
Land-based discharges include sewage, radioactive waste, industrial waste,
and agricultural pollutants (e.g., herbicides, pesticides, and fertilizers). Discharges from ships include contaminants from ballast, invasive species,
garbage, sewage, and spills of fuel, oil, and other cargoes. Some marine pollution is the result of official policies that allow ocean dumping or ocean-

based incineration for disposal of various wastes. Seepage of natural oil from the ocean floor contributes 15 percent of oil pollution, whereas offshore oil production is responsible for only 5 percent.[78] Scientists estimate that in the North Sea and the North Atlantic Ocean alone, as many as 450,000 marine birds die each year from ongoing oil pollution.[79]

Because ocean currents are found throughout the water column, these pollutants are distributed not only across the surface of the oceans but also from the surface to unmeasured depths. The immediate impact of these pollutants ranges from unsafe and unsightly waste-strewn beaches to fishing stocks that are depleted or unfit for consumption. Over the past century, it has become clear that the ocean is not an inexhaustible sink for waste disposal or pollution.

Because these pollutants arise from so many sources, international control has been troublesome to establish. Some, such as agricultural runoff, are nonpoint-source pollutants that cannot be easily reduced even on a national level, and others, such as spills from offshore oil drilling or industrial waste disposal, originate from activities with such high economic value that strong regulatory statutes are difficult to enact. As with most pollution, the costs are often borne by ecosystems far from the point of origin, and penalties for generating negative externalities are hard to impose, especially across international boundaries.

However, the many treaties and conventions agreed on over the past thirty years have made significant progress in controlling marine pollution. Many scholars accept the argument that UNCLOS III has incorporated the 1972 Convention on the Prevention of Marine Pollution by Dumping of Wastes and Other Matter (Dumping Convention) and the 1973 International Convention for the Prevention of Pollution from Ships (MARPOL) (both are discussed in the following paragraph) into the Law of the Sea, and nations are under an international obligation to protect the ocean environment.[80]

Early efforts to contain marine pollution failed; draft conventions negotiated in 1926 and 1935 never entered into force. The first major international treaty on this issue entered into force in 1958; the International Convention for the Prevention of Pollution of the Sea by Oil (London) focused on pollution from oil tankers. Even with amendments in 1962 and 1969, the Convention was not very successful. States had little incentive to enforce its provisions, and costs of monitoring were extremely high. The benefits within each state's coastal waters were uncertain, and states were reluctant to assume costs to protect other nations' waters. Shipping companies could avoid compliance almost completely by registering with flag states that had not signed the convention. Although the 1958 Convention on the High Seas and the report of the 1972 Stockholm Conference encouraged closer compliance, they offered no incentives for ratification or sanctions for noncompliance.

In October 1983, the London Convention was superseded when the International Convention for the Prevention of Pollution from Ships (MARPOL) entered into force. MARPOL was first adopted in 1973 and was amended in 1978, partly to expedite its ratification.[81] Although many nations that were party to the London Convention have not ratified MARPOL, few of these nations are heavily invested in large-scale tanker operations, so the negative impact on the marine environment is not substantial.[82] More than 85 percent of the world's shipping fleet has become party to MARPOL.[83] It follows the London Convention's focus of technological solutions to the problems associated with discharge of oil into the marine environment, but it also covers other discharges, such as the dumping of garbage from cruise ships, and its enforcement provisions are more effective. Inspection and enforcement are strengthened, for example, by requiring each flag state to inspect ships and to issue "international oil pollution prevention certificates," which may be verified at other port states. Port states that find a ship with an invalid certificate may refuse to allow the ship to sail, and port states cooperate to ensure that foreign vessels are checked systematically. Under the 1982 Paris Memorandum of Understanding on Port State Control, fourteen European states agreed to inspect at least one-fourth of the foreign vessels entering their ports annually. This has resulted in more than 70 percent of ships in these ports being inspected for compliance with MARPOL and other International Maritime Organization (IMO) agreements.[84]

In the late 1960s, several major coastal spills led to the International Legal Conference on Marine Pollution (1969). From this conference two treaties emerged, both ratified in 1975: the International Convention Relating to Intervention on the High Seas in Cases of Oil Pollution Casualties (Brussels) and the International Convention on Civil Liability for Oil Pollution Damage (Brussels). The International Fund for Compensation of Oil Pollution Damage became effective in 1978. Political scientist Lynton Caldwell writes that from the slow pace of ratification,

[the] conclusion follows that although there is international recognition of the harmfulness of ocean pollution, national economic interests have remained powerful enough to handicap or delay

action that would impose cost, inconvenience, or responsibility upon shipping interests.[85]

Dumping of hazardous waste at sea is also controlled by treaty. The 1972 Convention on the Prevention of Marine Pollution by Dumping of Wastes and Other Matter (London Convention) and the 1972 Convention for the Prevention of Marine Pollution by Dumping from Ships and Aircraft (Oslo Convention) apply to the high seas and the northeastern Atlantic, respectively. The London Convention distinguishes some harmful wastes (those on the so-called black list, such as organohalogenic compounds and mercury), which are absolutely prohibited, from other less harmful products (those on the grey list, such as lead, arsenic, copper, and pesticides), which may be dumped if the appropriate permit is obtained.[86] A third category of waste requires only a general permit. The Oslo Convention has a similar structure. The London Convention is widely ratified and applies to all marine areas not considered territorial waters, so the regime it establishes has been a global regime.[87]

Neither convention prohibits dumping absolutely, but the continued acceptance of ocean dumping is doubtful. For centuries, water has been an economical medium for waste disposal, and free-flowing rivers will indeed cleanse themselves of some natural waste products. However, the development of large volumes of wastes that are not biodegradable has eliminated the utility of disposal of waste into water bodies. Scientific uncertainty regarding cumulative and latent effects of wastes; an increasing awareness of how social, economic, and environmental costs shift from polluters to second parties; and the strengthening voices of developing countries that are unwilling to accept these costs have all changed the international focus on ocean dumping. In 1990, the parties to the London Convention decided to ban all ocean dumping of industrial waste by 1995.[88]

Other agreements that control ocean dumping apply to particular geographical regions, such as the 1974 Convention on the Protection of the Marine Environment of the Baltic Sea Area (Helsinki) and the 1980 Protocol for the Protection of the Mediterranean Sea against Pollution from Land-Based Sources (Athens). These agreements are focused on land-based sources of pollution such as agricultural runoff and urban sewage.

Incineration of wastes at sea is not addressed through a separate convention. Instead, the International Commission under the Oslo Convention has begun to incorporate rules on incineration into the convention. An annex opened for signature on 2 March 1983 and in force on 1 September 1989 set limits on material that can be incinerated and established proper mechanisms for incineration.[89]

Discussion

The changes brought about by the Law of the Sea negotiations, and the very topics of negotiation, have fundamentally altered the international view of the oceans. No longer are the oceans seen as a resource domain that contains an infinite supply of renewable resources or has an infinite capacity to absorb environmental harm. The old freedom of the seas has given way to a new perspective based on scarcity, which in turn encourages the evolution of property rights.

Legal and economic issues change with the location of the waters: internal, contiguous, continental shelf, territorial, or high seas. Inshore, a nation's interest is in exclusivity, whereas the farther one gets from the coast, the more nations seek to be inclusive in order to maximize their own access.[90] The desire to increase territorial seas does not arise solely because nations are interested in immediate resource exploitation. There are also strong concerns for national security, international prestige, and the protection of resources for future exploitation.

The temptation to shirk and to allow spillovers is extremely high. Changes in technology and products have vastly increased the amount of money to be made while diminishing the risk to capital and personnel. Still, the same advances in technology, in the form of radar and satellite overflights, make it easier to monitor and enforce regulations, although the costs of doing so are enormous and often affect other policy areas. Technological advances have also simplified the expansion of national territories. In effect, the nations now have *very* long cannons.

Application of the analytic framework developed in chapter 2 emphasizes the strategies behind expansions of territorial seas and the emerging regime for deep seabed minerals. The progression from UNCLOS I to UNCLOS III was in part an effort to define the boundaries of the resource domain. Although the working rules of customary law had been adequate in the past, technological advances in both fishing and resource extraction, discoveries of valuable reserves of oil and natural gas, and decreasing supplies of living ocean resources made open-access domains undesirable. The flexibility of customary law was no longer an advantage.

Correspondence between local conditions and operational rules has been elusive, in part because good information about local conditions is difficult to find. Monitoring and sanctioning are difficult, in part because international cooperation is inhibited by the economic and political demands of interest groups within each country. However, control of marine pollution, which certainly has an enormous impact on other facets of ocean policy, has been more successful, in part because monitoring and sanctioning are simpler for pollution than for fishing, and the associated economic gains are not as large, visible, or widespread. The value of these design principles (congruence, monitoring, and sanctioning) has, unfortunately, been demonstrated convincingly by the loss of sustainable fisheries stocks.

The principle that a multiple-use commons must be able to support all uses provides some explanation of why support for pollution control is relatively high; the ability of the resource domain to continue to provide any of the living resources depends in part on lowered levels of pollution. Therefore, the many users of the living resources are likely to unite to support antipollution policies while the comparatively few domain users who benefit from lax marine pollution policies find it difficult to oppose new pollution policies openly.

The deep seabed mineral regime is a different story. Although the Law of the Sea Treaty seemed to provide a clear regime, it was not sustainable. The group of nations most likely to be actively involved in the regime was unwilling to accept the participation of the developed nations and its notion of common heritage. In this case, it was not so much that all users were not represented but rather that many of the represented groups were not accepted as legitimate users. One might say that their right to organize the regime was not recognized or that the constitutional-level choices made in establishing the regime were not accepted. The latest arrangement has yet to be tested, since deep seabed mining is not yet a profitable activity, but application of the design principles for sustainable regimes suggests that this regime will need considerable modification before it can be implemented successfully.

Suggested Reading

Grotius, Hugo. *Freedom of the Seas, or The Right Which Belongs to the Dutch to Take Part in the East Indian Trade (Mare Liberum)* (1608), trans. Ralph Van Deman Magoffin. New York: Oxford University Press, 1916. Reprinted, New York: Arno Press, 1972. Everyone *talks* about this book, but hardly anyone *reads* it. It is a pleasure to read Magoffin's elegant translation, and the ideas are fresh and stimulating.

Guberlet, Muriel. *Explorers of the Sea: Famous Oceanographic Expeditions.* New York: Ronald Press, 1964. Although this book was written for older children, adult readers will enjoy the personalized stories of great ocean explorers and their scientific discoveries. It's a great read.

Oxman, Bernard, David Caron, and Charles Buderi, eds. *The Law of the Sea: U.S. Policy Dilemma.* San Francisco: ICS Press, 1983. A good introduction to the issues leading up to UNCLOS III, with an appendix summarizing the third Law of the Sea Conference.

Peterson, M. J. "International Fisheries Management," in *Institutions for the Earth: Sources of Effective International Environmental Protection,* eds. Peter Haas, Robert O. Keohane, and Marc A. Levy, 249–305. Cambridge, Mass.: MIT Press, 1993. A concise and current account of international fisheries management, with a focus on the economic aspects.

Notes

1. R. P. Anand, *Origin and Development of the Law of the Sea* (The Hague: Martinus Nijhoff, 1983), 82–83.

2. Robert Jay Wilder, "The Three-Mile Territorial Sea: Its Origins and Implications for Contemporary Offshore Federalism," *Virginia Journal of International Law,* 32, 3 (spring 1992): 689.

3. Sayre A. Swarztrauber, *The Three-Mile Limit of Territorial Seas* (Anapolis, Md.: Naval Institute Press, 1972), 11.

4. Thomas Wemyss Fulton, *The Sovereignty of the Sea* (Edinburgh and London: Blackwood, 1911; Millwood, N.Y.: Kraus Reprint, 1976), 7–15 (page citations are to the reprint edition). In the thirteenth century, the English customarily required all vessels to lower their sails when challenged by a British military vessel. In 1609, James I issued a proclamation requiring all foreign fishermen to obtain a British license, and by the time of the reign of his son, Charles I (1625–1649), any foreign ship meeting a king's ship in the Sea of England (which encompassed all the water between England and the Continent) was required to lower its topsails and strike its flag. Following the Restoration (1660), the ceremony was slowly relegated to a token, and after the battle of Trafalgar in 1805, which established British supremacy at sea, the requirement was quietly removed from admiralty instructions.

5. Fulton, *Sovereignty of the Sea,* 541–593; Swarztrauber, *Three-Mile Limit,* 11 (notes omitted). However, in the seventeenth century, the Supreme Court of Piedmont relied on Bartolo and Baldus in approving the interception of a Spanish ship only fifty miles from Monaco.

6. Fulton, *Sovereignty of the Sea*, 6 (notes omitted).

7. This pope was the father of Cesare and Lucrezia Borgia, a fact that should either reduce our wonder at his behavior or explain theirs.

8. The Treaty of Tordesillas contains one of the earliest expressions of the right of innocent passage: Spanish ships, when crossing through Portuguese oceans to reach their own territories, were permitted

> to sail in either direction, freely, securely, and peacefully, over the said seas of the said King of Portugal, and within the said line....They shall take their courses direct to the desired region and for any purpose desired therein and shall not leave their course, unless compelled to do so by contrary weather.

Swarztrauber, *Three-Mile Limit*, 13 (notes omitted).

9. Swarztrauber, 15. In note 16, Swarztrauber discusses the disagreement among scholars as to the actual distance advocated by Bodin, which apparently arose because it is not clear whether he intended sixty *miles* or thirty *leagues*. In Bodin's time, a league could be two to four miles, so the difference is considerable. The problem is in the translation of Bodin's Latin and French versions of *Les six livres de république de J. Bodin Anquein* (*De république*) (Paris: Chez I. du Puis, 1583), both of which appeared at the same time. However, as he was apparently citing Baldus, who advocated sixty miles, the Latin version would appear more likely to be correct.

10. Swarztrauber, *Three-Mile Limit*, 16.

11. The full document was not published until 1868. *Freedom of the Seas* is chapter 12 of this manuscript.

12. See, for example, John 18:46 ("My kingship is not of this world").

13. Swarztrauber, *Three-Mile Limit*, 19.

14. Scott Allen, "National Interest and Collective Security in the Ocean Regime," in *Ocean Governance: Strategies and Approaches for the 21st Century*, ed. Thomas Mensah (Honolulu: Law of the Sea Institute, 1996), 23.

15. Schwarztrauber, *Three-Mile Limit*, 25. He cites a note given by the Dutch to the English, reputedly written by Grotius: "For that it is by law of nations, no prince can challenge further into the sea than he can command with a cannon except gulfs within their land from one point to another." See also Fulton, *Sovereignty of the Sea*, 156.

16. Swarztrauber, *Three-Mile Limit*, 30–35. Cannons first became common weapons of war in the fourteenth century, beginning with the Hundred Years War between France and England (1337–1453).

17. Wilder, "Three-Mile Territorial Sea," 697–699; Fulton, *Sovereignty of*

the Sea, 541–545. See also Swarztrauber, *Three-Mile Limit*, especially chapters 2, 3, and 4.

18. Fulton, *Sovereignty of the Sea*, 547.

19. Ibid., 549.

20. Ibid., Fulton, 573.

21. Great Britain and the United States, "Convention Respecting Fisheries, Boundary, and the Restoration of Slaves, October 20, 1818," in *Public Statutes at Large*, vol. 8, ed. Richard Peters (Boston: Little, Brown, 1850). Currently *United States Statutes at Large*.

22. Swarztrauber, *Three-Mile Limit*, 70–71.

23. The treaties are the Convention of 1839, the Convention of 1857, the Convention of 1859 (not ratified by France), the Convention of 1867 (terms similar to the 1859 convention), and the multilateral North Sea Fisheries Convention of 1882. Ibid., 65.

24. Ibid., 66, nn. 6–12.

25. Herbert A. Smith, ed., *Great Britain and the Law of Nations: A Selection of Documents Illustrating the Views of the Government in the United Kingdom upon Matters of International Law*, 2 vols. (London: P. S. King, 1932–1935), 183–184. Cited in Swarztrauber, *Three-Mile Limit*, 75–76.

26. Swarztrauber, *Three-Mile Limit*, 72–73.

27. Thomas Baty, "The Three-Mile Limit," *American Journal of International Law* 22 (July 1928): 520, cited in Swarztrauber, *Three-Mile Limit*, 73–74. Apparently, damages were paid by Russia.

28. Swarztrauber, *Three-Mile Limit*, 77.

29. Ibid., 77 and n. 68.

30. Ibid., 131–140.

31. *The Corfu Channel Case* (United Kingdom–Albania), 1949 I.C.J. 4ff.

32. Michael Akehurst, *A Modern Introduction to International Law*, 6th ed. (London: Unwin Hyman, 1987), 172.

33. Bernard H. Oxman, "Summary of the Law of the Sea Convention," in *The Law of the Sea: U.S. Policy Dilemma*, ed. Bernard Oxman, David Caron, and Charles Buderi (San Francisco: ICS Press, 1983), 151.

34. James Sebenius, *Negotiating the Law of the Sea* (Cambridge, Mass.: Harvard University Press, 1984), 79.

35. Ibid., 74. One of the side effects of this was a change in the rules governing ships traveling through territorial waters; for example, submarines were required to travel on the surface rather than submerged, and airplanes needed permission to fly off the coastal waters.

36. Jeremy Rifkin, *Biosphere Politics* (New York: Crown, 1991), 55.

37. Eckert calls this enclosure a novel use of the term for those familiar

with the enclosure movement in British history. In earlier times, *enclosure* referred to an individual asserting individual property rights over land he owned that had traditionally been managed as *res communes*. The high seas were traditionally open access. See Ross Eckert, *The Enclosure of Ocean Resources: Economics and the Law of the Sea* (Stanford, Calif.: Hoover Institution Press, 1979).

38. The critical portion of the Proclamation on the Continental Shelf read as follows:

> Having concern for the urgency of conserving and prudently utilizing its natural resources, the Government of the United States regards the natural resources of the subsoil and sea bed of the continental shelf beneath the high seas but contiguous to the coasts of the United States as appertaining to the United States subject to its jurisdiction and control. In cases where the continental shelf extends to the shores of another State, or is shared with an adjacent State, the boundary shall be determined by the United States and the State concerned in accordance with equitable principles. *The character as high seas of the waters above the continental shelf and the right to their free and unimpeded navigation are in no way thus affected* [emphasis added].

Truman Proclamation on the Continental Shelf (Proclamation 2667), September 1945. *Department of State Bulletin* 13, 327 (30 September 1945: 485.

39. *Fisheries Case* (*United Kingdom* v. *Norway*), 1951 I.C.J. 116. Clyde Sanger, *Ordering the Oceans: The Making of the Law of the Sea* (Toronto: University of Toronto Press, 1987), 14–15; Henry Steiner and Detlev F. Vagts, *Transnational Legal Problems: Materials and Texts* (Mineola, N.Y.: Foundation Press, 1986), 302–310. This case established the rule that constant objection to an evolving custom could block the development of customary law and that new customs that encroach on old rights must be formally accepted by the involved nations. Patricia Birnie and Alan Boyle, *International Law and the Environment* (Oxford: Clarendon Press, 1993), 24–25.

40. Marvin Soroos, *Beyond Sovereignty* (Columbia: University of South Carolina Press, 1986), 268.

41. James Sebenius, *Negotiating the Law of the Sea*, 74; Sanger, *Ordering the Oceans*, 14–17.

42. Gerhard von Glahn, *Law Among Nations*, 6th ed. (New York: Macmillan, 1992), 497. However, in 1971, Iceland asserted a fifty-mile con-

servation zone. Despite findings in Great Britain's favor by the International Court of Justice (*Fisheries Jurisdiction Case* [*United Kingdom* v. *Iceland*], [Merits] 1974, I.C.J., 3, 23–29, text in 13 I.L.M 1049 [1974]), Iceland persisted in its claim, leading to armed confrontations and extreme tension between the two countries.

43. Iceland played these two cards again during confrontations with the International Whaling Commission, blandly announcing that compliance with restrictions on whaling would require it to issue permits for inshore fishing to Russian trawlers (a notorious intelligence-gathering ruse of the Russians). The Western allies quickly backed down from their demands. Milton M. R. Freeman, personal communication, August 1986.

44. Sanger, *Ordering the Oceans*, 17–18.

45. See Marcel Berlins, "A Sea of Troubles for International Law Makers," *The Times* (London), 12 June 1974, 16(a). In November 1993, Guyana became the sixtieth nation to ratify the treaty, which entered into force in November 1994. "Milestone for Law of Sea Treaty," *The InterDependent* 19, 4 (winter 1993–1994): 4.

46. 22 U.N. GAOR C.1 (1515th mtg.) at I, U.N. Doc. A/C.1/PV.1525 (1967). Cited in Sebenius, *Negotiating the Law of the Seas*, 7.

47. G.A. Res. 2749, 25 U.N. GAOR Supp. (No. 280) 24, U.N. Doc. A/8028 (1970).

48. Eckert, *Enclosure of Ocean Resources*, 41–42.

49. Sebenius, *Negotiating the Law of the Sea*, 13.

50. Robert A. Goldwin, "Common Sense vs. 'The Common Heritage,'" in Oxman, Caron, and Buderi, *Law of the Sea*, 60.

51. John Lehman (Secretary of the Navy), "The Navy and the Law of the Sea," letter to the editor, *Washington Post*, 30 July 1982.

52. Richard Darman, "The Law of the Sea: Rethinking U.S. Interests," *Foreign Affairs* 56 (1978): 373–395.

53. "Deep Seabed Hard Mineral Resources Act of 1980, Pub. L. No. 96-283; "Act of Interim Regulation of Deep Seabed Mining," *Bundesgesetzblatt*, part 1, 9080 (22 August 1980). Both cited in Sebenius, *Negotiating the Law of the Sea*, 82.

54. This possibility became reality in 1982 when France, Germany, the United Kingdom, and the United States signed the Agreement Concerning Interim Arrangements Relating to Polymetallic Nodules of the Deep Sea Bed. These nations agreed to inform one another of the location of mining claims. In 1984, these same nations, joined by Belgium, Italy, Japan, and the Netherlands, signed the Provisional Understanding Regarding Deep Seabed Mining, which bound the signatories to refuse to authorize mining in an

area already claimed by a company from another state. Clearly, they were sending a message to the United Nations that they intended to mine outside the UNCLOS regime. Yuwen Li, *Transfer of Technology for Deep Sea-Bed Mining: The 1982 Law of the Sea Convention and Beyond* (Boston: Martinus Nijhoff, 1994), 89–90.

55. Ibid., 241; L. D. M. Nelson, "Some Observations on the Agreement Implementing Part XI of the 1982 Convention on the Law of the Sea," in *Ocean Governance: Strategies and Approaches for the 21st Century*, ed. Thomas Mensah (Honolulu: Law of the Sea Institute, 1996), 204.

56. Li, *Transfer of Technology*, 253; Nelson, 212–213. Germany, Japan, the United Kingdom, and the United States have signed the new mineral regime, although of those four, only Germany is also party to the Law of the Sea Convention.

57. Birnie and Boyle, *International Law and the Environment*, 502.

58. Ibid., 506.

59. For example, in 1964, a European Fishery Convention was negotiated (581 U.N.T.S. 57), but was aimed primarily at restricting the access of foreign states to coastal fisheries. Ibid., 506.

60. *Report of the United Nations Conference on the Human Environment (UNCHE), Stockholm, 5–16 June 1972*, U.N. Doc. A/CONF.48/14/Rev. 1 (1973). The Declaration of Principles was adopted in the United Nations General Assembly (G.A. Res. 2997, 27 U.N. CAOR [1972]).

61. United Nations *Conference on the Law of the Sea* (1958) at 59 (remarks of Mr. Anderson, delegate from Iceland), 62 (remarks of Mr. Ponce y Carbo, delegate from Ecuador). Cited in Swarztrauber, *Three-Mile Limit*, 181.

62. U.S.C. 22, §1971 et seq. (1982).

63. See F. V. Garcia Amado, *The Exploitation and Conservation of the Resources of the Sea: A Study of Contemporary International Law* (Leiden: A. W. Sijthoff, 1963), especially 73–79.

64. Swarztrauber, *Three-Mile Limit*, 183.

65. Susan J. Buck, "Multijurisdictional Resources: Testing a Typology for Program Structuring," in *Common Property Resources: Ecology and Community-Based Sustainable Development*, ed. Fikret Berkes (London: Belhaven Press, 1989), 127–147. See also Henry Reiff, *The United States and the Treaty Law of the Sea* (Minneapolis: University of Minnesota Press, 1959), 307–308, cited in Swarztrauber, *Three-Mile Limit*, 183.

66. "Latins Ask Widening of Offshore Limits," *New York Times*, 20 July 1965, cited in Swarztrauber, *Three-Mile Limit*, 187.

67. Nicaragua included the limit in its new constitution (1965); legislation was passed by Panama (1967) and Uruguay (1969). Uruguay also

claimed air space above the oceans out to the 200-mile limit. Swarztrauber, *Three-Mile Limit*, 187.

68. Ibid., 187. This extension followed an oil spill by an American tanker.

69. Fisheries law within the new contiguous zone is not mentioned in the new Law of the Sea Treaty; under the Territorial Seas Convention, these waters are on the high seas and therefore are open-access fisheries. However, the 200-nautical-mile Exclusive Economic Zone, also established under the treaty, seems to remove that confusion. Birnie and Boyle, *International Law and the Environment*, 518.

70. "Leaving the Feeding Grounds," *The Economist*, 7 August 1993, 40.

71. In 1990, the FAO reported the total world catch at 95.2 million metric tons (104.9 million short tons), in contrast to the 1989 catch of 99.6 million metric tons (109.7 million short tons). This was the first decline in total fish catch in thirteen years. Jacqueline Vaughn Switzer, *Environmental Politics: Domestic and Global Dimensions* (New York: St. Martin's Press, 1994), 249–250.

72. David Pitt, "Talks at U.N. Combat Threat to Oceans' Species from Overfishing," *New York Times*, 25 July 1993, 7.

73. "Collective Action Needed to Protect Fish Stocks," *Greensboro News and Record*, 7 August 1993, A20.

74. Birnie and Boyle, *International Law and the Environment*, 525.

75. Switzer, *Environmental Politics*, 267.

76. *The Times* (London), 24 January 1991, 14, cited in Birnie and Boyle, *International Law and the Environment*, 539.

77. Birnie and Boyle, *International Law and the Environment*, 540.

78. Penelope ReVelle and Charles ReVelle, *The Environment: Issues and Choices for Society* (Boston: Jones and Bartlett, 1988), 429.

79. G. Tyler Miller Jr., *Living in the Environment*, 5th ed. (Belmont, Calif.: Wadsworth, 1988), 473.

80. Birnie and Boyle, *International Law and the Environment*, 254–257.

81. Ibid., 267.

82. Ibid., 266.

83. Ibid., 267 (notes omitted).

84. Ibid., 270.

85. Lynton Caldwell, *International Environmental Law and Policy*, 2nd ed. (Durham, N.C.: Duke University Press, 1990), 295.

86. Alexandre Kiss and Dinah Shelton, *International Environmental Law* (Ardsley-on-Hudson, N.Y.: Transnational, 1991), 182.

87. Birnie and Boyle, *International Law and the Environment*, 320.

88. Ibid., 322, citing L.D.C. Res. 43/13; UNCED. U.N. Doc. A/CONF.151/PC/31 at 4–6 (1991).

89. Protocol Amending the Oslo Convention for the Prevention of Marine Pollution by Dumping from Ships and Aircraft, 972 Int'l Envtl. L. 12/A (1983).

90. Myres S. McDougal, "International Law and the Law of the Sea," in *The Law of the Sea: Offshore Boundaries and Zones*, ed. Lewis Alexander (Columbus: Ohio State University Press, 1967), 16.

Chapter 5

The Atmosphere

This most excellent canopy, the air, look you, this brave o'er-
hanging firmament, this majestical root fretted with golden fire,
why, it appears no other thing to me but a foul and pestilent con-
gregation of vapours.

—*Hamlet*, Act II, Scene II

The atmosphere is the envelope of gases that surrounds our planet. Held in
by gravity, propelled outward by centrifugal force, it shields us from the vacuum of space and the sun's radiation. It provides water and oxygen to sustain life on Earth. It is a highway for commerce and recreation and a canvas
for heart-stopping displays of beauty. Our contribution to this wonder,
when we think about it at all, is pollution.

This chapter is divided into two sections. The first provides a brief
description of the airspace regime, which had the potential of becoming a
global commons regime but did not. This material provides the background
explaining why resolution of issues involving atmospheric pollution is so
dependent on national legislation and compliance. The second section
examines atmospheric pollution in three critical areas: acid deposition,
global climate change, and stratospheric ozone depletion.

The Airspace Regime

Just as Antarctica is the resource domain for research stations (chapter 3),
and outer space is the domain for geostationary orbits (chapter 6), airspace
provides the domain for flight, research, and telecommunications. (See box
5.1, The Atmosphere.) The regime that now governs airspace is only partly
a global commons regime because most of the world's airspace is subject to

Box 5.1 The Atmosphere

Earth's atmosphere has five layers. The *troposphere*, closest to the Earth, extends 10 kilometers (6.2 miles) above Earth's surface and contains 75 percent of the planet's air mass. Most weather and air pollution occur here. The troposphere's upper limit (tropopause) marks the upper limit of wide-scale turbulence. The *stratosphere*, characterized by slowly increasing temperatures, is found from 10 to 50 kilometers (6.2 to 31 miles) above Earth's surface. Strong, steady winds blow in the stratosphere, and the ozone layer is contained in upper limits, where the absorption of radiation causes an increase in temperature. The *mesosphere* reaches from 50 to 80 kilometers (31 to 50 miles) above Earth; its temperature decreases with altitude. Below the mesosphere's upper limits lies 99.99 percent of Earth's atmosphere. Beyond this lies the *thermosphere*; its electrified layers reflect high-frequency radio waves and other waves, allowing long-distance radio communications on Earth. In the thermosphere, temperatures continue to rise with altitude as the gases absorb x-rays and shortwave ultraviolet radiation; temperatures there can reach 1,000° C. The final layer is the *exosphere*, in which gradually diminishing evidence of Earth's atmosphere is found. Traces have been detected as far as 96,540 kilometers (60,000 miles) from Earth's surface.

Sources: Lay and Taubenfeld, *Activities of Man in Space*; Hendersen-Sellars, *Pollution of Our Atmosphere*; Oliver and Hidore, *Climatology*; Walker, *Cambridge Air and Space Dictionary*

national sovereignty. This arrangement, however, did not evolve without considerable debate over the nature of airspace, and the debate is not yet finished. The history of the airspace regime provides an intriguing contrast to the emerging space regime (discussed in the next chapter), especially since the airspace regime model was not followed in developing the outer space regime.

Sovereignty in outer space is undergirded by sovereignty issues in airspace. Even in Roman times, the right of a landowner to the use of his property above and below ground level was recognized,[1] and when any discussion of the remote airspace was mooted (which was not often, the likelihood of manned flight being slight), parallels with the freedom of the seas were drawn.[2] However, once the military uses of the balloon and, soon afterward, of the airplane became clear, scholars and politicians alike began to call for national sovereignty of the airspace, limited perhaps by the right of "innocent passage" that was obtained on the high seas.[3] Their call was not heeded at first: in 1910, the International Conference on Air Navigation still allowed free overflight.

In 1913, the first law to claim national control over air travel was enacted by Great Britain. Among other things, this law asserted British jurisdiction over almost the entire English Channel, which, given the history of the British in asserting sovereignty over large portions of the sea, was probably no surprise to Britain's European neighbors. France and Germany soon passed similar laws, no doubt in partial anticipation of aerial combat to come.[4]

The Netherlands was especially adamant in asserting its rights, probably because it was under the air corridor between Germany and England. In 1914, the Netherlands interned a German hydroplane forced down off its coast, rejecting the German claim that the hydroplane was a ship rather than a plane and therefore was governed by the international law for belligerent vessels.[5] In 1915, the Netherlands interned a German pilot who had become lost during a training flight, and in 1916, it fired on a German zeppelin over its territory. Finally convinced that the Dutch were serious about protecting their airspace, the Germans agreed to a system of distress signals and acknowledged the rights of the Dutch to intern vessels and crews that violated their territory.[6]

Perhaps if the airspace regime had developed in a more peaceful era, it might have been more international in character. However, by 1919, the military advantage of the airplane was clear, and this, coupled with the exciting economic potential of commercial air travel, led to demands for national control of airspace. Nations could now negotiate access to their facilities and protect their domestic airlines. In October 1919, the Paris Convention Relating to the Regulation of Aerial Navigation was signed, giving each signatory exclusive sovereignty in the airspace above its territory. This convention set certain standards of conduct, such as rights of innocent passage (subject to regulation), equal treatment of all nations, and rights of nations to establish protected zones though which no aircraft might fly.[7] Although the United States did not accede to the Paris Convention,[8] it did observe the conditions of the convention on an informal basis, and several national statutes reflected the convention's policy decisions.[9] In 1928, the United States signed the Pan American Convention (Havana), which contained the same policy provisions as the 1919 Paris Convention and was signed by nations of the Western Hemisphere and Spain.[10] By 1944, the international consensus was expressed in the Chicago Convention on Civil Aviation, which recognized "that every State has complete and exclusive sovereignty over the airspace above its territory."[11] Although in theory the convention granted limited rights of innocent passage, in practice most states insisted on prior consent to entry.[12]

In the 1950s, several proposals were offered to define the limits of national airspace. One was that sovereign airspace was *usable* airspace, that portion of the atmosphere above a nation in which aircraft could operate. This was an extension of the Roman law of private property, which recognized the right of a property owner to protection from, for example, projecting eaves or trees overhanging his property.[13] Another proposal, known as "zones of control," was based on the notion of contiguous zones in the customary law of the sea. The initial suggestion of a 300-mile zone over which the subjacent state could claim control (subject to the same rights of peaceful passage as the oceans) soon changed to 600 miles, which seemed beyond the realm of practicality and usefulness. By the time *Sputnik* was launched, of course, this theory had collapsed.[14]

International treaties, conventions, and "soft-law" options have proliferated.[15] International concern with these issues has even generated proposals for a Law of the Air treaty. In March 1989, France, the Netherlands, and Norway cosponsored a conference in The Hague to discuss such a treaty. The twenty-four conference participants proposed strengthening international authority over the air by either enhancing current institutions or creating new ones.[16] The issue of territorial airspace was not easily resolved, especially as the problems of satellite reentry, space debris, and liability became prominent. As the exploration of outer space becomes commonplace, national and international concerns about sovereignty above land have been extended to the realm of space. This issue is taken up again in chapter 6, in the discussion of the evolution of the outer space program.

Atmospheric Pollution

Resolution of the problems associated with atmospheric quality can be addressed only by international agreements because pollutants do not remain in the political jurisdiction in which they are produced. The receiving country has no authority over the polluter and must rely on international understandings for regulation. These issues have achieved international prominence as acid deposition, changing climate and weather patterns, and declining stratospheric ozone disrupt the biosphere in numerous ways.

Acid deposition is noted for its impact on aquatic systems, but its effect is not limited to lakes and the life-forms they support. The acid leaches out metals found in the soils, increasing contamination of the food chain. Birds that nest in affected areas have low nesting success, in part because high acidity interferes with eggshell formation. Forests and crops fail to grow to their full potential if exposed to acid deposition.[17] Damage to the built environment (e.g., buildings, monuments, statues) is also extensive.[18]

The potential harm from global climate change is even more devastating for humans. The United Nations Intergovernmental Panel on Climate Change (IPCC) predicts a rise in sea level of 30–109 centimeters (12–43 inches) by the year 2010; even at the low end of the range, that is enough to cause permanent flooding of substantial portions of many developing countries, such as Bangladesh. In addition, if predictions of global warming are accurate, precipitation patterns will change. This will alter agricultural productivity and crop distribution and is likely to increase desertification.

Of the three topics discussed in this section (acid deposition, global climate change, and depletion of stratospheric ozone), stratospheric ozone depletion has the most immediate effect on the human population. Medical researchers predict with a fair amount of certainty that a 1 percent decrease in stratospheric ozone will cause a corresponding 2 to 4 percent increase in human malignant melanoma, one of the most deadly forms of cancer.[19]

Acid Deposition

Air pollution became an international issue in the late 1960s, although acid deposition had been linked to the burning of fossil fuels as early as 1872 with the publication of a British book titled *Air and Rain*.[20] (See box 5.2, Acid Deposition.) The first modern warning signs appeared in Sweden and Norway in the late 1960s, when some lakes no longer could support normal biological processes, including plant and animal life.[21] Scientists determined that the acid precipitation affecting these lakes had originated in Europe and in other parts of Scandinavia. Sweden offered to host the 1972 United Nations Conference on the Human Environment (UNCHE) partly to publicize the threat of acid deposition.[22] Alarmed by these scientific findings, the Nordic states convinced the Organization for Economic Cooperation and Development (OECD) to monitor transboundary air pollution between 1972 and 1977; the results confirmed that air pollution was indeed a transboundary problem and could be controlled only by international cooperation.[23] Over the next twenty years, evidence showed similar and increasing problems with acid deposition throughout the European continent and North America.

In August 1980, the United States and Canada signed a memorandum of intent indicating that each would reduce the sulfur and nitrogen emissions from coal-fired furnaces, which are the major source of acid deposition.[24] However, the Reagan administration immediately backed away from the agreement and advocated more study to confirm the connection between coal-fired furnaces and acid deposition. This was a difficult position for the White House to maintain, given several reports from the American scientific community that confirmed the connection.[25]

Sweden, Finland, and Norway were practically alone in their drive to establish international controls on sulfur dioxide and nitrous oxides, the major causes of acid deposition. Industrialized nations that were heavily dependent on coal-fired utilities, such as the United States and the United Kingdom, vetoed any agreements that might force their energy costs up. A small step was made in 1979, when the Convention on Long-Range Transboundary Air Pollution (Geneva Convention) was signed.[26] However, the convention was widely viewed as a "toothless agreement" that did not regulate acid deposition adequately.[27] It is so general that, for example, the United States's continued pollution in Canada is not a violation of the convention.[28]

Discouraged by the slow pace of international programs, some nations have taken the unusual step of committing to additional restrictions outside the larger treaty systems. In Ottawa in 1984, ten nations formed the Thirty-Percent Club and pledged that they would reduce 1980 sulfur dioxide emission levels by 30 percent by 1993. The group then provided a forum for negotiations, which led to the 1985 Protocol on the Reduction of Sulphur Emissions or Their Transboundary Fluxes by at Least 30 Percent (Helsinki

---

Box 5.2 Acid Deposition

Acid deposition occurs when sulfur dioxide (SO_2) and various nitrous oxides (NO_x) combine in the atmosphere with water (H_2O) and oxygen (O_2) to form sulfuric acid (H_2SO_4) and nitric acid (HNO_3). The acids then fall to Earth as *wet deposition* (rain, snow, hail, fog, clouds, or *dry deposition* (primarily sulfates of calcium and magnesium). Unpolluted rain is slightly acidic because of naturally occurring carbon dioxide in the atmosphere, usually with a pH of 5.6 or higher (a pH of 7.0 is neutral), although it can have a pH as low as 5.0. About 40 percent of the sulfur dioxide in Earth's atmosphere is from anthropogenic sources (i.e., caused by human activities). Regional levels of anthropocentric pollution vary; for example, in the northeastern United States, where high-sulfur coal is burned, anthropogenic sources account for more than 90 percent of emissions.

Sources: Chiras, *Environmental Science*; Forster, *Acid Rain Debate*; Revelle and ReVelle, *Global Environment*; Seitz, *Global Issues*; Switzer, *Environmental Politics*

Protocol). Unfortunately, the United States, Poland, and the United Kingdom, all major sources of transboundary sulfur dioxide pollution, were not parties to this convention.

The United States was unwilling to accede to substantial reductions in nitrogen oxide emissions, claiming that unilateral reductions had already fulfilled any American obligations. In 1988, a second protocol was added to the Geneva Convention: the Sofia Protocol Concerning the Control of Emissions of Nitrogen Oxides or Their Transboundary Fluxes (Sofia Protocol). The Sofia Protocol mandated an emissions freeze at 1987 levels but allowed many countries, such as the United States, to delay compliance until 1994 to compensate for earlier reductions.[29] However, not all nations that signed the Geneva Convention are parties to these protocols, and even those that are parties often do not fully implement protocol provisions.[30]

Since then, international evidence of the impact of transboundary pollution has mounted. Forests in the eastern United States are endangered, and more than half of the trees in Germany are damaged from acid deposition. Eastern Europe is also plagued with damaged areas, the extent of which has only recently become apparent as political regimes have changed.

One stumbling block for international cooperation to stem acid deposition is the great difficulty nations have had in reaching internal agreement on their own remedies. For example, in the United States, conflicts between industry and environmentalists, among coal-producing regions, and between coal-burning and acid deposition–receiving regions complicate any legislative attempts to deal with the problem.[31]

These problems are exacerbated on the international scale. For example, the effects of continuing carbon dioxide emissions may benefit some countries by lengthening their growing seasons or increasing rainfall, and the economic cost of substantial reductions in fossil fuel use is unacceptable in many developing countries.[32]

International concern over potential climate change due to human activities goes back at least thirty years. It culminated in the Framework Convention on Climate Change, which was opened for signature in Rio de Janeiro in 1992. At the time of this writing, negotiations for a new convention that would allow trading of emissions across nations were taking place in Bonn.

Climate Change

Climate change (global warming) is an anticipated increase in average planetary temperature caused by three major sources: increased atmospheric concentrations of carbon dioxide and nitrous oxides (by-products of fossil fuel combustion); methane, originating primarily in agricultural processes, especially animal wastes and paddy farming; and chlorofluorocarbons (CFCs), which are also implicated in the loss of stratospheric ozone.[33] Increased carbon dioxide levels are also a product of destruction of rain forests (where trees absorb carbon dioxide) and the reduced capacity of the world's oceans to absorb more carbon dioxide.

The scientific community still has not reached consensus over the causes of global climate change,[34] although scientists now generally agree that a warming trend is occurring.[35] Earth's temperature appeared to stabilize in the late 1980s, but many scientists attribute this to the cooling effect of the eruptions of Mount St. Helens (United States, 1980), El Chichón (Mexico, 1982), and, later, Mount Pinatubo (Philippines, 1991). Danish scientists have even discovered a correlation between sunspot activity and temperature fluctuation.[36] Some scientists assert that Earth moves through warming and cooling cycles independent of human activity and that the current warming trend is simply part of the planet's natural cycle. Recent research points toward a complex relationship between climate and massive oscillations in ocean currents in the North Atlantic and Pacific Oceans. If the global warming trend continues despite cooler ocean currents, the likelihood that human activities are the main culprit is increased.[37] Although the cumulative impact of climate change is uncertain, changes in patterns of agriculture and in sea level seem likely; the problem comes not from climate change alone but from the *rate* of change.

The greenhouse effect was first noted in 1827 by French mathematician Baron Jean-Baptiste-Joseph Fourier, although he did not draw an explicit connection between human activity and climate change.[38] In 1853, Lt. Matthew Maury (U.S. Navy) organized the First International Meteorological Conference, which standardized meteorological data collection from on board seafaring vessels; by 1873, when the International Meteorological Organization was established, weather data from land stations were standardized as well.[39]

In 1908, Swedish physicist and chemist Svante Arrhenius was the first scholar to connect human industrial processes, carbon dioxide emissions, and world temperatures.[40] However, climate change remained a minor item on the world's environmental agenda until well after World War II. Collection of weather data had become more sophisticated in order to provide information for military and commercial aviation, and cold war fears of a possible "nuclear winter" led scientists to examine climate data carefully. Concurrent research on oceans suggested that they were not an inexhaustible carbon dioxide sink,[41] and in 1957 the first permanent monitoring station for carbon dioxide was established at Mauna Loa, Hawaii.

The Global Atmospheric Research Programme (GARP) was created in 1967 by the World Meteorological Organization (WMO) and the International Council of Scientific Unions (ICSU); GARP and the World Weather Watch (WWW, 1968) formed the institutional foundation for weather monitoring and scientific study, but their mandate was *weather* rather than *climate*. However, departures from weather norms, such as severe droughts in the Sahel, the Soviet Union, and Europe, made the world community aware of its dependence on climate and on the likelihood of catastrophic social and economic change if the climate were not protected.[42]

By 1979, a scientific consensus was emerging that carbon dioxide and other greenhouse gases were inclining to dangerous levels. In 1985, an international conference at Villach, Austria, concluded that climate warming appeared inevitable, and participants began to talk of a climate convention.

After the Villach Conference, the pace of policy formation picked up considerably. The same year, British scientists discovered a large "hole" in the stratospheric ozone layer over the Antarctic, an event that dramatically underscored the idea that human activities could damage Earth's atmosphere. In 1987, the United Nations Environment Programme (UNEP) and the WMO created the Intergovernmental Panel on Climate Change (IPCC) to study global warming.

Politicians jumped on the bandwagon: U.S. president Ronald Reagan signed the Global Climate Protection Act (January 1988), British prime minister Margaret Thatcher discussed global warming in a public speech (September 1988), and U.S. presidential candidate George Bush made global warming a campaign issue. Once elected, however, Bush proved less enthusiastic, and in an example of spectacular political misjudgment, his administration ordered National Aeronautics and Space Administration (NASA) scientist James Hansen to alter his testimony to Congress to suggest scientific uncertainty about the effect of greenhouse gases on global climate. Hansen went public with the issue, and the ensuing media attention brought global warming to the political forefront. Despite increasing international pressures, the United States continued to oppose a climate change convention.

In December 1988, the United Nations General Assembly passed the Resolution on Protection of the Global Climate.[43] Three months later, an international panel of legal and policy experts on atmospheric protection met in Toronto and supported an international convention on climate change. In 1990, the final report from the IPCC's first working group presented a relatively united front from the world's atmospheric scientists affirming that increasing levels of carbon dioxide were having a deleterious effect on Earth's climate. Many nations took this conclusion very seriously: between May and

December, a majority of the OECD member states had begun to curb green-house emissions.[44] (See box 5.3, Chronology for Atmospheric Pollution.)

In the same year, the Second World Climate Conference met in Geneva to address global climate change issues.[45] Representatives from more than 130 nations called for an international convention on global warming; this call eventually resulted in the 1992 Earth Summit (UNCED) in Rio de Janeiro, where the Framework Convention on Climate Change was opened for signature. Parties to this convention agreed to limit and mitigate carbon dioxide emissions and to provide technology transfer and financial assistance to developing nations. As a concession to American policy, the convention contains no quantified emissions targets.

Movement toward a climate change convention was extraordinarily susceptible to domestic politics.[46] The climate change conversations were essentially an extension of the acid deposition and ozone debates, shrouded in scientific uncertainty. The same coalitions that had opposed acid deposition policies were also opposed to climate change programs because the same domestic economic interests were threatened. For example, nations that were members of the Organization of Petroleum Exporting Countries (OPEC) did not support the convention because they feared the development of

---

Box 5.3 Chronology for Atmospheric Pollution

1972	United Nations Conference on the Human Environment (UNCHE)
1979	Convention on Long-Range Transboundary Air Pollution (Geneva Convention) (in force 1983)
1985	Protocol (to 1979 Geneva Convention) on the Reduction of Sulphur Emissions or Their Transboundary Fluxes by at Least 30 Percent (Helsinki Protocol) (in force 1987)
1985	"Hole" in stratospheric ozone layer discovered over Antarctica
1985	Convention for the Protection of the Ozone Layer (Vienna Convention) (in force 1988)
1987	Protocol (to 1985 Vienna Convention) on Substances That Deplete the Ozone Layer (Montreal Protocol) (in force 1989)
1988	United Nations Resolution on Protection of the Global Climate
1988	Protocol (to 1979 Geneva Convention) Concerning the Control of Emissions of Nitrogen Oxides or Their Transboundary Fluxes (Sofia Protocol) (in force 1991)
1992	Framework Convention on Climate Change (in force 1994)

alternative energy sources (especially nuclear power), which would cut into their exports. The United States relies heavily on cheap fossil fuels, and for America, the potential economic costs of the convention were high. Nor did the other developed nations present a united front. The newly industrialized countries were willing to accept emissions limits only in exchange for the most current technology, and some smaller countries, especially members of the Alliance of Small Island States (AOSIS), wanted strict international controls at any price because they are so vulnerable to even the smallest elevation in sea level.

Ozone Depletion

Another air pollution issue with global implications is the diminishing level of stratospheric ozone. Ozone shields Earth's surface from ultraviolet radiation and affects temperature gradients and weather patterns across the planet. Depletion levels vary by location. (See box 5.4, Chlorofluorocarbons and Stratospheric Ozone.) For example, in 1993, ozone levels above the United States were 13 percent lower than 1981 levels, and levels above Canada were 17 percent lower; Siberia recorded a decline of 20 percent.[47] Scientists estimate that a 10 percent decrease in ozone levels will cause 12,000 additional deaths from skin cancer and 1.6 million additional cataracts per year.[48]

American action to curtail ozone loss predated international efforts by several years. In 1974, two scientific studies hypothesized a dangerous connection between release of chlorine from chlorofluorocarbons (CFCs) and reduction of stratospheric ozone.[49] In 1977, the United States amended the Clean Air Act to reinforce regulations announced by the Environmental Protection Agency (EPA) and the Food and Drug Administration (FDA) to ban the use of nonessential CFCs.[50] The EPA was authorized to regulate "any substance . . . [which] . . . may reasonably be anticipated to affect the stratosphere, especially ozone in the stratosphere, . . . [if] such an effect may *reasonably be anticipated* to endanger public health or welfare" (emphasis added).[51] Federal regulations limited the use of CFCs in aerosols in 1978, and Canada, Norway, and Sweden soon followed suit.[52] The European Community was slow to join the effort, proposing a slower reduction extended over a longer period; several observers attribute this reluctance to industry pressures and a lack of public interest.[53]

In 1982, the United Nations Environment Programme (UNEP) convened the Ad Hoc Working Group of Legal and Technical Experts for the Preparation of a Global Framework Convention for the Protection of the

---

Box 5.4 Chlorofluorocarbons and Stratospheric Ozone

Ultraviolet radiation from the sun is both mutagenic and carcinogenic, and stratospheric ozone prevents 99 percent of ultraviolet radiation from reaching Earth. Why is the ozone layer so susceptible to loss? The answer lies in the peculiar chemical properties of chlorine free radicals, a breakdown product of chlorofluorocarbons (CFCs). CFCs are nonpoisonous and relatively inert chemicals used in refrigerants and as aerosol propellants, which are extremely stable and can remain in the atmosphere for decades or longer. Chlorine free radicals combine with ozone to produce chloride oxide and oxygen. The chloride oxide then combines with oxygen free radicals to form chlorine and oxygen, thus producing another chlorine free radical. Chloride oxide can also combine with ozone directly.

$Cl + O_3 \rightarrow ClO + O_2$ (chlorine and ozone produce chloride oxide and oxygen)

$ClO + O \rightarrow Cl + O_2$ (chloride oxide and free oxygen produce chlorine and oxygen)

$ClO + O_3 \rightarrow ClO_2 + O_2$ (chloride oxide and ozone produce chlorine dioxide and oxygen)

A single CFC molecule can destroy 100,000 ozone molecules.

Source: Chiras, *Environmental Science,* 377–378

Ozone Layer. In 1983, the Toronto Group (Canada, Finland, Norway, Sweden, and Switzerland) met for the first time. As a result of this meeting, the group brought a proposal to limit CFC emissions to the Ad Hoc Working Group. The United States joined the Toronto Group later in the year. The proposal to limit CFC emissions was violently opposed by the European Community (EC). These two coalitions—the Toronto Group and the EC—continued to oppose each other throughout the negotiations.[54]

In 1985, compromise was reached when the Convention for the Protection of the Ozone Layer (Vienna Convention) was negotiated. The convention called for an economic workshop, information exchange, and further research.[55] As in the Transboundary Air Pollution Convention, serious questions of economic equity between developing and developed nations were at issue during the negotiations because no practical substitutes for CFCs were available and their use in industrial processes and refrigeration was critical in technology transfers to developing countries. The Vienna Convention is another typical framework convention, which was nonetheless important for two reasons: its ecosystem approach, which implies that the natural environment has intrinsic worth, and its emphasis on preventing future harm rather than merely providing remedies for current problems.[56]

Scientific data indicating a dramatic decrease in stratospheric ozone continued to accumulate. The world environmental community was shocked at the 1985 reports of an enormous ozone hole over the Antarctic.[57] The hole was so extensive that the scientists who discovered it had delayed publication while they rechecked the data: American satellite measurements had not observed the dissipation because computers in the United States had been programmed to ignore losses of such magnitude as anomalies.[58] The ozone hole is more severe over the Antarctic because the air there is the coldest on Earth, and the chemical reaction that removes ozone from the stratosphere is accelerated in cold temperatures and at the polar vortex.[59] As of 1997, the exposed area was equal to the size of the continental United States,[60] and a similar but smaller hole existed over the Arctic.

In 1986, a landmark research report was published by the World Meteorological Organization (WMO) and the United Nations Environment Programme (UNEP).[61] The study reported the results of a remarkable cooperative research effort by scientists sponsored by the U.S. National Aeronautic and Space Administration (NASA), the U.S. National Oceanic and Atmospheric Administration (NOAA), the U.S. Federal Aviation Administration (FAA), UNEP, WMO, the West German Ministry for Research and Technology, and the Commission of the European Community.[62] The study confirmed what had been feared: even though the use of CFCs was not increasing, CFC levels in the atmosphere were continuing to rise.[63] The models predicted dangerous reductions in stratospheric ozone in the coming years and warned that the contributions of CFCs to global warming were much higher than originally anticipated.[64]

In September 1987, twenty-four nations (including the major CFC-producing countries) and the Commission of the European Community signed the Protocol on Substances That Deplete the Ozone Layer (Montreal Protocol).[65] This was the first time the international community had agreed to control a valuable commodity in the present in order to prevent environmental damage in the future.[66] The protocol imposed substantial reductions in the use of CFCs when no replacement chemical was available, mandating reductions of CFCs to 50 percent of 1986 levels by 1998 and reductions of halons[67] to 1986 levels by 1992. This bypassed the customary "best available technology" approach in favor of a standard that recognized the urgency of the ozone problem.[68] By the beginning of 1990, fifty-one countries, including twenty-three developing countries, had ratified the Montreal Protocol.[69] This general acceptance was induced in part by the use of selective incentives built into the protocol; for example, the Soviet Union was "grandfathered" for factories under construction, and developing countries were allowed to delay compliance for ten years.[70]

The Montreal Protocol represented a major shift in the relationship between scientific certainty and public policy decision making. The political and economic pressures in much of the world to resist establishing policies to reduce CFCs and related compounds were intense. Richard Benedick, chief U.S. negotiator for the ozone protection treaties, attributes the success of the negotiations to several factors, among which are close relationships between atmospheric scientists and government officials, use of education and public opinion to sway politicians, leadership by the United Nations Environmental Programme and by financially influential countries such as the United States, and consideration of the needs of developing countries.[71] Another significant factor was the ability of leading chemical manufacturers to produce chemical substitutes for CFCs. E. I. du Pont de Nemours and Company, the world's leading CFC manufacturer, had initially opposed CFC regulation but invested millions of dollars in research and development of substitute chemicals while the legitimate CFC market was collapsing. Executives decided to view the protocol deadlines as an opportunity to market the more expensive substitutes while making a considerable public relations coup, and they switched sides, announcing corporate plans to phase out CFCs ahead of the deadlines.[72]

Although support for the Montreal Protocol was substantial, the international community soon realized that more stringent deadlines were required. In March 1989, the EC states decided to reduce the production of CFCs by 85 percent with the goal of complete elimination by 2000. This decision exceeded the demands of the Montreal Protocol; a change in the position of the British was the major impetus behind the change.[73] In May 1989, eighty-one nations adopted the nonbinding Helsinki Declaration on the Protection of the Ozone Layer,[74] which urged ratification of the Montreal Protocol and accelerated phaseouts of CFCs, halons, and other ozone-depleting substances.[75] The 1990 amendments to the protocol shortened the timetable further: industrialized countries agreed to total elimination of CFCs and halons by 2000, and developing countries were allowed a ten-year extension. The parties also established a temporary Multilateral Fund to provide assistance to developing countries—the first time such a fund had been created for implementation of an environmental policy—and although all contributing parties have not yet met their obligations fully, more than $450 million had been disbursed by early 1997.[76] The Copenhagen meeting of parties to the Montreal Protocol in late 1992 again moved the timetable up because stratospheric ozone had continued to decline. The Multilateral Fund became permanent in the amendments agreed to in Copenhagen.

The ultimate effectiveness of the ozone regime is still in doubt. Seasonal loss of ozone over the Antarctic in 1992 and 1993 was near total at some altitudes,[77] and the long-term impact on the Antarctic food chain is troubling. In November 1991, marine scientists working in Antarctica announced that the Antarctic ozone hole was harming the single-celled organisms that form the bottom link of the oceanic food chain by allowing ultraviolet radiation to penetrate more deeply into the ocean, not only reducing the productivity of the phytoplankton but also increasing genetic damage in the organisms.[78] Recent scientific reports indicate that the damage is not limited to phytoplankton. In 1997, scientists found extensive genetic damage in the eggs and larvae of Antarctic icefish that correlated with exposure to ultraviolet light. This was the first direct indication that reductions in stratospheric ozone could cause genetic damage to higher animals.[79] CFC smuggling has become a major industry, and the usefulness of the Multilateral Fund is unclear. Still, as Gareth Porter and Janet Welsh Brown write:

> [The] Montreal Protocol is the best example so far of a regime that has been continually strengthened in response to new scientific evidence and technological innovations. If these implementation problems can be overcome, it can actually reverse in future decades the damage to the ozone layer which has occurred since the 1960s.[80]

Discussion

International controls for atmospheric problems have been extremely difficult to negotiate. Issues of sovereignty have plagued the policy arena from the start, and scientific data have been both conflicting and confusing. Developed and developing countries have disagreed on the proper balance between economic development and pollution abatement. Control technology has been expensive, and the costs of monitoring compliance and enforcing regulations are high. At the national level in many industrialized countries, businesses with strong political influence have successfully blocked regulatory efforts. The multijurisdictional nature of air pollution and other atmospheric problems has exacerbated the difficulties, and the lack of established international organizations charged with the coordination of transboundary air policy has delayed progress toward resolution of the problem.[81]

It is not clear whether the atmosphere is truly a commons. Although it has some characteristics of a common pool resource domain, international and domestic policies which have evolved to address pollution issues in the atmosphere may also be considered protective regulatory policies intended to mitigate negative externalities.[82]

Writers who view the atmosphere as a global commons make the following argument.[83] Clean air is the resource found in the atmosphere; although it is not extracted, it does become scarce as pollutants are added. For example, if carbon emissions are viewed as "using up" the carbon absorption capacity of the air, then one country's emissions reduce the absorptive capacity available to another country.[84] Obviously it is almost impossible to exclude anyone from access to the atmospheric absorptive capacity. Thus, these writers argue, the resource has both high subtractability and difficult exclusion (see table 1.1) and thus is a common pool resource.

There is a seductive logic to this argument, but it has analytic flaws. Atmospheric absorptive capacity is not a resource in the same sense as are, for example, ocean fisheries. There is no resource flow to any appropriator; fish are taken by fishermen, but pollution diffuses throughout the available airspace. One might argue that there is no resource flow in geostationary orbits either (see chapter 6). However, the orbital slots are definable units, and it is clear when a slot is appropriated and when it is not because the right to occupy the orbital slot and its associated frequencies is limited to the engineering lifetime of the satellite.[85]

If we accept the argument, what should we make of stratospheric ozone, a resource we do *not* want to extract? In fact, extraction of this resource is harmful. We might argue that like geostationary orbital slots and Antarctic research stations, it is a spatial-extension resource, except that we are indifferent to the specific location of any ozone molecule so long as it remains in the stratosphere. Certainly ozone is subtractable, and once it is gone, it is unavailable to others, but that characteristic alone does not make it either a natural resource or a spatial-extension resource.

Some writers suggest that gases circulating in the atmosphere are analogous to water resources flowing in a transboundary stream. A better analogy, however, would be sunlight, which may be blocked or diminished by human activity but which, to my knowledge, has never been labeled a common pool resource. Another analogy that is sometimes made is that use of the atmosphere as a pollution sink equates the atmosphere to a municipal dump, where waste products are deposited in a domain that has a limited carrying capacity and is managed by a community regime. If it were possible to isolate a section of the atmosphere for pollution, the analogy might hold, but a better parallel would be trash cans and litter. Trash and atmospheric pollutants are both unfortunate by-products of human society. Trash cans are placed throughout communities as legal receptacles for waste, although sometimes people choose to litter instead of disposing of their waste properly. This is not a common property resource regime, even if the areas in which the trash cans are placed are within a commons. Similarly, the atmosphere may be used for disposal of waste under legal permits or by illegal emissions, but that fact does not necessarily make it a commons.

Trying to use analytic frameworks applicable to commons to discuss atmospheric pollution regimes requires us to stretch the definitions and concepts almost beyond recognition. Yet excluding those regimes from analysis does not cast them into analytic darkness: they are easily placed under the policy analysis umbrella already widely used for pollution problems.[86] The atmospheric pollution regime is a clear example of *protective regulatory policy*, defined as public policy that regulates the conditions under which certain activities may occur, prohibiting activities thought to be harmful (e.g., carbon emissions) and requiring activities thought to be helpful (e.g., use of chlorofluorocarbon [CFC] substitutes).[87]

International cooperation in the reduction of externalities occurs when the political pressure and economic costs of continuing to pollute no longer outweigh the costs of control. The loss of stratospheric ozone has high costs in public health, shifts in agricultural patterns due to global temperature change, and ecosystem damage. Transboundary air pollution not only kills trees; it also erodes building and automobile paint, aggravates respiratory diseases in all animals, including humans, and reduces agricultural productivity.

The costs of cooperation in reducing these activities are high, but they are also readily passed on. Nations that agree to reduce the production and use of CFCs, for example, impose regulatory controls on the producers, who in turn charge the consumers of their products for the costs of compliance. Nations that cannot afford the new technologies or the loss of income effectively use the international negotiating processes to avoid or to delay compliance; they may also rely on subsidies from other nations to help them achieve the desired goals.

If atmospheric pollution regimes are to be excluded from future discussions of the commons, should we retain the marine pollution treaties in our analysis of the ocean commons? (See the discussion of marine pollution in chapter 4.) There are two primary reasons why marine pollution treaties are properly included in the global ocean regime. First, the marine pollution treaties are a *legal*, integral part of the oceans commons regime. Second, the pollution problems these treaties address have a direct effect on the sustainability of the living resources of the sea. In other words, pollution of the resource domain has negative consequences for the extractable resources found in the domain. Neither rationale applies to the atmosphere. There is no substantial legal link between the atmospheric pollution treaties and a larger commons regime with natural resources or spatial-extension resources, and the environmental harm done by atmospheric pollution affects only common pool resources found in other resource domains.[88]

Two conclusions emerge from this discussion. First, the physical characteristics of atmospheric resources (clean air and stratospheric ozone) are not analogous to resources in commons domains, and the atmosphere regime therefore is not a commons regime. Second, public policy analysis that approaches atmospheric pollution as a negative externality controlled by protective regulatory policy provides a better approach to the problems of the regime and their analysis.

Suggested Reading

Adger, W. Neil, and Katrina Brown. *Land Use and the Causes of Global Warming*. New York: Wiley, 1994. A rigorous and technical book that challenges conventional understanding of the ways in which land should be managed to mitigate possible climate changes.

Benedick, Richard Elliot. *Ozone Diplomacy: New Directions in Safeguarding the Planet*. Cambridge, Mass.: Harvard University Press, 1991. Benedick was chief of the U.S. negotiators for the Montreal Protocol, so this book is detailed and accurate.

Newton, David. *Global Warming*. Oxford: ABC-CLIO, 1993. A great reference work with statistical information, biographical sketches, a thorough chronology, and a bibliography.

Paterson, Matthew. *Global Warming and Global Politics*. New York: Routledge, 1996. An extremely detailed description and analysis of climate change policy. Paterson has excellent insights into the North–South debates.

Soroos, Marvin. *The Endangered Atmosphere: Preserving a Global Commons*. Columbia: University of South Carolina Press, 1997. A comprehensive look at the atmosphere utilizing four case studies: atmospheric testing of nuclear weapons, acid precipitation, depletion of the ozone layer, and global climate change. Soroos is an internationally recognized scholar on atmospheric politics.

Further information can be obtained from the World Wide Web sites of the United Nations Environmental Programme (http://www.unep.org) and the United Nations Ozone Secretariat (http://www.unep.org/unep/secretar/ozone/finmech.htm).

Notes

1. The legal maxim is *Cujus est solum, ejus est usque ad coelum et ad inferos,* or "Whose is the soil, his it is up to the sky and to the depths."

2. S. Houston Lay and Howard Taubenfeld, *The Law Relating to Activities of Man in Space* (Chicago: University of Chicago Press, 1970), 37. Lay and Taubenfeld note that Grotius held this position. Note 3, citing *De jure belli ac Pacis,* trans. Ralph Van Deman Magoffin, in *Classics of International Law,* ed. James Brown Scott (New York Carnegie Endowment for International Peace, 1925).

3. Lay and Taubenfeld, *Activities of Man in Space,* 37.

4. Jeremy Rifkin, *Biosphere Politics* (New York: Crown, 1991), 59–60.

5. Andrew Haley, *Space Law and Government* (New York: Appleton-Century-Crofts, 1963), 43, citing Netherlands, Ministry of Foreign Affairs, *Recueil de diverses communications du Ministre des Affaires Etrangères aux Etats-Généraux par rapport à las neutralité des Pays-Bas et au respect du droit des gens* (1916), trans., 144–145.

6. Haley, *Space Law and Government,* 43–45, In 1939, the Dutch went even further, claiming the airspace above the Netherlands "to an unlimited altitude." The Minister of The Netherlands (Loudon) to the Under Secretary of State (Wells), 5 September 1939, MS. Dept. of State File 740.00111 European War 1939/600, cited by Haley, 52. Later events in international law made this position untenable.

7. Haley, *Space Law and Government,* 45.

8. The administrative organ for the convention, the International Commission for Air Navigation, was under the authority of the League of Nations, and the United States was not a member of the league.

9. John Cooper, *The Right to Fly* (New York: Holt, 1947), 34.

10. 20 February 1928, 47 Stat. 1901, T.S. No. 840.

11. Convention on International Civil Aviation, 7 December 1944, 61 Stat. 1180, T.I.A.S. No. 1591, 15 U.N.T.S. 295 (the Chicago Convention). An example of this notion taken to extremes existed in the United States in the 1970s, when airliners flying over states that prohibited the sale of alcoholic beverages (such as Kansas) were not allowed to sell such beverages to

passengers. Needless to say, a brisk business was conducted on either side of the Kansas state lines.

12. Lay and Taubenfeld, *Activities of Man and Space*, 37.

13. Philip C. Jessup and Howard Taubenfeld, *Controls for Outer Space and the Antarctic Analogy* (New York: Columbia University Press, 1959), 205.

14. Morris R. Cohen and Felix S. Cohen, eds., "Introduction," in *Readings in Jurisprudence and Legal Philosophy* (Boston: Little, Brown, 1951), 18.

15. See, for example, Peter H. Sand, *Lessons Learned in Global Environmental Governance* (Washington, D.C.: World Resources Institute, 1990), especially 14–18.

16. Lynton Caldwell, "International Environmental Politics: America's Response to Global Imperatives," in *Environmental Policy in the 1990s*, eds. Norman Vig and Michael Kraft (Washington, D.C.: Congressional Quarterly Books, 1990), 308.

17. In the United States, crop losses due to acid deposition are estimated at $5 billion per year. Daniel Chiras, *Environmental Science: Action for a Sustainable Future*, 4th ed. (New York: Benjamin-Cummings, 1994), 387.

18. See Bruce A. Forster, *The Acid Rain Debate: Science and Special Interests in Policy Formation* (Ames: Iowa State University Press, 1993), chapter 6.

19. Chiras, *Environmental Science*, 380.

20. Robert Angus Smith, *Air and Rain: The Beginning of a Chemical Climatology* (London: Longmans, Green, 1872), cited in "Editor's Preface," in Forster, *The Acid Rain Debate*, ix.

21. Walter Rosenbaum, *Energy, Politics, and Public Policy*, 2nd ed. (Washington, D.C.: Congressional Quarterly Books, 1987), 117.

22. Gareth Porter and Janet Welsh Brown, *Global Environmental Politics*, 2nd ed. (Boulder, Colo.: Westview Press, 1996), 69.

23. Organization for Economic Cooperation and Development, *The OECD Program on Long-Range Transport of Air Pollutants* (Paris: Organization for Economic Cooperation and Development, 1977).

24. Memorandum of Intent Between Canada and the United States Concerning Transboundary Air Pollution, 32 U.S.T. 2521, T.I.A.S. No. 9856, 20 I.L.M. 690 (1980).

25. *New York Times*, 28 June 1983, quoted in Walter Rosenbaum, *Environmental Politics and Policy* (Washington, D.C.: Congressional Quarterly Books, 1985), 135. The most comprehensive report on acid deposition is that of the National Acid Precipitation Assessment Program (NAPAP), a ten-year study sponsored jointly by the Environmental Protection Agency, the National Oceanic and Atmospheric Association, the Departments of Agriculture, Energy, and the Interior, and the Council on Environmental

Quality. Patricia Irving, ed., *Acid Deposition: State of Science and Technology, Summary Report of the United States National Acid Precipitation Assessment Program* (Washington, D.C.: Government Printing Office, September 1991). Cited in Jacqueline Vaughn Switzer, *Environmental Politics: Domestic and Global Dimensions* (New York: St. Martin's Press, 1994), 259.

26. Patricia Birnie and Alan Boyle, *International Law and the Environment* (Oxford: Clarendon Press, 1993), 398.

27. Porter and Brown, *Global Environmental Politics*, 69.

28. Birnie and Boyle, *International Law and the Environment*, 399.

29. Porter and Brown *Global Environmental Politics*, 71.

30. Birnie and Boyle, *International Law and the Environment*, 394.

31. In the United States, the Clean Air Act Amendments (1990) strengthened existing legislation and added several new areas to federal regulatory control. It also established an innovative emissions trading program that applies market-based strategies to the problems of air pollution. Each major coal-fired plant is allocated a set amount of permissible sulfur dioxide emissions, which may be traded, bought, or sold. A delightful twist occurred in March 1995, when students from seven law schools pooled their resources to buy the rights to 16.3 metric tons (18 short tons) of sulfur dioxide emissions. The students' plan is ingenious: they intend to let the permits expire unused, thus reducing pollution and simultaneously driving up the price of other permits. The students, from law schools at the University of Maryland, the City University of New York, the University of Detroit, Duke and Hamline Universities, and the University of New England spent $3,256. The project was organized by Robert Percival, a professor of environmental law at the University of Maryland. "Law Students Buy and Hold Pollution Rights," *New York Times*, 31 March 1995, B13.

32. Lynton Caldwell, *International Environmental Policy* (Durham, N.C.: Duke University Press, 1990), 191.

33. Clive Ponting, *A Green History of the World* (New York: Penguin, 1991), 387–388.

34. David Newton, *Global Warming* (Oxford: ABC-CLIO, 1993), 15–19.

35. Caldwell, *International Environmental Policy*, 263.

36. Penelope ReVelle and Charles ReVelle, *The Global Environment: Securing a Sustainable Future* (Boston: Jones and Bartlett, 1992), 374.

37. William Stevens, "Study of Ocean Currents Offers Clues to Global Climate Shifts," *New York Times*, 18 March 1997 (http://www.nytimes.com).

38. Jean-Baptiste-Joseph Fourier, "Mémoire sur les températures du globe terrestre et des espace planétaires," *Mémoires de l'Acadmie Royal de Science de*

l'Institut de France 7 (1827): 659–704. Cited in Matthew Paterson, *Global Warming and Global Politics* (New York: Routledge, 1996), 17.

39. Paterson, *Global Warming and Global Politics*, 18–19.

40. Svante Arrhenius, *Worlds in the Making* (New York: Harper, 1908). Cited in Paterson, *Global Warming and Global Politics*, 19–20.

41. Roger Revelle and Hans Suess, "Carbon Dioxide Exchange Between Atmosphere and Ocean, and the Question of an Increase in Atmospheric CO_2 During the Past Decade," *Tellus* 9 (1957): 18–27. Cited in Paterson, *Global Warming and Global Politics*, 22.

42. Paterson, *Global Warming and Global Politics*, 24–25.

43. G.A. Res. on Protection of the Global Climate for Present and Future Generations of Mankind, U.N. Doc. A/RES/44/207.

44. Ian Rowlands, *The Politics of Global Atmospheric Change* (Manchester, England: Manchester University Press, 1995), 79.

45. The first conference was held in Geneva in 1979.

46. Unless otherwise noted, this discussion is from Paterson, *Global Warming and Global Politics*, 78–110.

47. Arjun Makhijani and Kevin Gurney, *Mending the Ozone Hole: Science, Technology, and Policy* (Cambridge, Mass.: MIT Press, 1995), 29.

48. Chiras, *Environmental Science*, 380.

49. Richard Stolarski and Ralph Cicerone, "Stratospheric Chlorine: A Possible Sink for Ozone," *Canadian Journal of Chemistry* 52 (1974): 1610–1615; Mario Molina and F. Sherwood Rowland, "Stratospheric Sink for Chlorofluoromethanes: Chlorine Atom Catalysed Destruction of Ozone," *Nature* 249 (1974): 810–812. Both are cited in Richard Elliot Benedick, *Ozone Diplomacy: New Directions for Safeguarding the Planet* (Cambridge, Mass.: Harvard University Press, 1991), 10.

50. Caldwell, *International Environmental Policy*, 263.

51. Clean Air Act, 42 U.S.C. §7457(b).

52. Benedick, *Ozone Diplomacy*, 24.

53. Markus Jachtenfuchs, "The European Community and the Protection of the Ozone Layer," *Journal of Common Market Studies* 28, 3 (March 1980): 263; David Pearce, "The European Community Approach to the Control of Chlorofluorocarbons" (paper presented at UNEP Workshop on the Control of Chlorofluorocarbons, Leesburg, Va., 8–12 September 1986), 12. Both are cited in Benedick, *Ozone Diplomacy*, 24–25.

See also Thomas B. Stoel Jr., Alan S. Miller, and Breck Milroy, *Fluorocarbon Regulation* (Lexington, Mass.: Heath, 1980), 205, and J.T.B. Tripp, D.J. Dudek, and Michael Oppenheimer, "Equality and Ozone Protection," *Environment* 29, 6 (1987): 45. Both are cited in Benedick, *Ozone Diplomacy*, 28.

54. Benedick, *Ozone Diplomacy*, 42–44.

55. Convention for the Protection of the Ozone Layer (Vienna), U.N. Doc. 1G.53/5, 26 I.L.M. 1529 (1987). In force 22 September 1988.

56. Birnie and Boyle, *International Law and the Environment*, 406; Benedick, *Ozone Diplomacy*, 45.

57. J. C. Farnau, B. G. Gardiner, and J. D. Shanklin, "Large Losses of Total Ozone in Antarctica Reveal Seasonal ClO_x/NO_x Interaction," *Nature* 315 (1985): 207–210.

58. Benedick, *Ozone Diplomacy*, 18–19.

59. Joel S. Levine, "A Planet at Risk" (public lecture, 20 February 1993, Greensboro, N.C.) According to Dr. Levine, global warming will do nothing to alleviate this problem, as the impact of global warming is felt at Earth's surface and, in fact, leads to increasingly colder temperatures in the upper atmosphere.

60. Alexandre Kiss and Dinah Shelton, *International Environmental Law* (Ardsley-on-Hudson, N.Y.: Transnational, 1991), 339.

61. World Meteorological Organization et al., *Atmospheric Ozone 1985: Assessment of Our Understanding of the Processes Controlling Its Present Distribution*, 3 vols., Global Ozone Research and Monitoring Project Report No. 16 (Geneva: World Meteorological Organization, 1986). Cited in Benedick, *Ozone Diplomacy*, 13, n. 14.

62. Benedick, *Ozone Diplomacy*, 14.

63. World Meteorological Organization et al., *Atmospheric Ozone*, chapter 13, cited in Benedick, *Ozone Diplomacy*, 14.

64. World Meteorological Organization, *Atmospheric Ozone*, chapter 15, cited in Benedick, *Ozone Diplomacy*, 15, n. 18.

65. Protocol (to 1985 Vienna Convention) on Substances That Deplete the Ozone Layer (Montreal), 26 I.L.M. 1540 (1987). In force 1 January 1989.

66. Orval Nangle, "Stratospheric Ozone: United States Regulation of Chlorofluorocarbons," *Environmental Affairs* 16 (1989): 546.

67. Halons are used in fire extinguisher systems. They have bromine in place of the chlorine in CFCs and are more damaging to stratospheric ozone than are CFCs. Chiras, *Environmental Science*, 380.

68. Benedick, *Ozone Diplomacy*, 1.

69. James Koehler and Scott Hajost, "1989: Advent of a New Era for EPA's International Activities," *Colorado Journal of International Environmental Law and Policy* 1, 1 (summer 1990): 183.

70. Peter Sand, "International Cooperation: The Environmental Experience," in *Preserving the Global Environment: The Challenge of Shared Leader-*

ship, ed. Jessica Tuchman Mathews (New York: Norton, 1991), 242.

71. Richard Elliot Benedick, "Protecting the Ozone Layer: New Directions in Diplomacy," in Mathews, *Preserving the Global Environment*, 113–153, especially 143–149.

72. See Forest Reinhardt, "Du Pont Freon® Products Division," in *Managing Environmental Issues: A Casebook*, eds. Rogene Buchholz, Alfred Marcus, and James Post (Englewood Cliffs, N.J.: Prentice-Hall, 1992), 261–286, for an excellent case study on the Du Pont decision.

73. David Vogel, "Environmental Policy in Europe and Japan," in *Environmental Policy in the 1990s*, eds. Norman Vig and Michael Kraft (Washington, D.C.: Congressional Quarterly Books, 1990), 273.

74. 28 I.L.M. 1335 (1989).

75. Koehler and Hajost, "Advent of a New Era," 183.

76. United Nations, Ozone Secretariat, "The Financial Mechanism," 27 March 1997 (http://www.unep.org/unep/secretar/ozone/finmech.htm).

77. Makhijani and Gurney, *Mending the Ozone Hole*, 30–32.

78. Keith Schneider, "Ozone Depletion Harming Sea Life," *New York Times*, 16 November 1991, 6, col. 6.

79. "Fish Damage Linked to UV," *New York Times*, 18 March 1997 (http://www.nytimes.com).

80. Porter and Brown, *Global Environmental Politics*, 77.

81. Caldwell, *International Environmental Policy*, 259; Birnie and Boyle, *International Law and the Environment*, especially, 387–393.

82. A quick reading of many books that deal exclusively with problems in atmospheric policy shows little or no mention of common pool resources, although the construct is well known among scientists and policy analysts. See, for example, W. Neil Adger and Katrina Brown, *Land Use and the Causes of Global Warming* (New York: Wiley, 1994); Benedick, *Ozone Diplomacy*; Derek Elson, *Atmospheric Pollution: Causes, Effects, and Control Policies* (Oxford: Basil Blackwell, 1987); David Feldman, ed., *Global Climate Change and Public Policy* (Chicago: Nelson-Hall, 1997), although in this volume Emery Roe ("Global Warming as Analytic Tip," 19–38) raises the commons issue only to reject it, and Ronnie Lipschutz ("Bioregional Politics and Local Organization in Policy Responses to Global Climate Change," 102–122) uses some commons literature to discuss *local* responses to climate change; Bruce Forster, *Acid Rain Debate*; Karen Litfin, *Ozone Discourses: Science and Politics in Global Environmental Cooperation* (New York: Columbia University Press, 1994); Makhijani and Gurney, *Mending the Ozone Hole*; and Newton, *Global Warming*.

83. See especially Marvin Soroos, "The Atmosphere as an International

Common Property Resource" (paper presented at the annual meeting of the American Political Science Association, Washington, D.C., September 1988), and Michael McGinnis and Elinor Ostrom, "Institutional Analysis and Global Climate Change: Design Principles for Robust International Regimes," in *Global Climate Change: Social and Economic Research Issues* (Chicago: Midwest Consortium for International Security Studies and Argonne National Laboratory, 1992), 45–85. Lynton Caldwell also categorizes the atmosphere as a global commons, but his assessment is based on a frequently encountered confusion between a commons and an open-access resource domain (see chapter 1 for definitions). (See Susan J. Buck, "No Tragedy on the Commons," *Environmental Ethics* 7, 1 [spring 1985]: 49–61.) Caldwell defines an international commons as "open to use by any nation with the requisite technological capability" (*International Environmental Policy*, 257). This is *not* a commons. Later on, he recognizes the analytic problem: "[The] difficulty with management of the atmosphere as an international commons is that, for most effects, it is only a medium or a carrier" (259).

84. McGinnis and Ostrom, "Institutional Analysis," 58.

85. Larry Martinez, *Communication Satellites: Power Politics in Space* (Dedham, Mass.: Artech, 1985), 116.

86. See, for example, Gary Bryner, *Blue Skies, Green Politics*, 2nd ed. (Washington, D.C.: Congressional Quarterly Books, 1995).

87. Randall Ripley and Grace Franklin, *Congress, the Bureaucracy, and Public Policy*, 5th ed. (Belmont, Calif.: Wadsworth), 21.

88. It is true that the atmosphere covers everything on the surface of the planet and thus trees harmed by acid deposition, crops destroyed by global warming, and cancers caused by increased ultraviolet radiation all exist *in* the atmosphere. However, legally and analytically, these things are not considered a part of the atmosphere.

Chapter 6

Outer Space and Telecommunications

E pur si muove! (But it does move!)

—Galileo Galilei (1633)

Most common pool resources discussed in this volume, such as ocean fisheries and deep seabed minerals, are subject to consumption and exclusion. Scientific research stations in the Antarctic are an exception to the general rule; they are not consumed, and their primary value is access to the domain rather than to any resource flow. Most of the current space regime involves a similar type of resource. For example, geostationary orbits are limited in number and may be occupied by only one user at a time, but they are not consumed or extracted. Geostationary orbits are spatial-extension resources that lack corporeal existence.[1] The resource domain—space—and the resource itself—geostationary orbits—are the same in real terms. They differ only in the analytic framework we erect about them.

Unlike the Law of the Sea, which is rooted in customary law and until quite recently resisted efforts at codification, space law is based almost exclusively on national statutes and international treaties.[2] The international community did not have the luxury of several hundred years of exploration, with law following in its wake.[3] This is not to say that there have not been great and even violent controversies in the ocean regime (see chapter 4). However, the *law* of the sea has developed incrementally and—when compared with the law of outer space—relatively slowly. Custom has been able to discard those rules that proved unworkable or outmoded. In contrast, space law has developed in a short time, often under the pressures of dramatic technological advances.[4]

As described in this chapter, the influence of the two superpowers during the cold war skewed the development of space law and the sudden increase in the number and power of developing countries has placed an ideological shell around the process. Rapid changes in science and technology, and the pressures brought to bear by the threat of nuclear weapons in space, have had an extraordinary impact on space law, accelerating the pace of legislation and negotiation and arousing interest throughout the world community.

As exploration of the solar system and beyond becomes more commonplace, the special conditions that operate in space become unique and without legal parallel on Earth. We have seen the first glimmerings of this with rejection of national sovereignty on the Moon and international sharing of data gained from long-range telemetry. Perhaps it is time to separate planetary policy from outer space policy.

The telecommunications regime is Earth-focused. Satellites are designed primarily to relay information to Earth, and issues in the regime revolve around national sovereignty, technology transfer, economic development, and political control. In contrast, the outer space regime looks away from Earth, with considerable uncertainty about the definition and resolution of future issues. The two regimes have different physical boundaries and user pools. Telecommunications requires highly structured international, national, and regional organizations that make institutional choices at the constitutional, collective, and operational levels of choice. The space regime is much less structured, with users including multinational corporations, national governments and agencies, and even private persons. Membership in the telecommunications regime is strictly controlled, whereas anyone with the resources to do so may use the space domain, subject to rules that coordinate activities in the domain.

Only a decade ago, the term *environmental policy* meant both natural resources policy and pollution policy. The field expanded so rapidly, however, that the two areas have become semantically separate. *Environmental policy* now refers to pollution policy issues, and *natural resources policy* addresses issues such as land use, wildlife, endangered species, and parks. The range and complexity of issues that are considered part of space policy have also expanded, and for analytic purposes, it may be more useful to distinguish between outer space policies and planetary policies. Policies related to activities carried out beyond Earth's gravitational field, such as manned exploration of Mars would be outer space policies. Policies related to activities carried out within Earth's gravitational field, such as telecommunications, operations of orbiting space stations, and activities on the Moon, would be planetary policies.

This chapter is therefore divided into two main sections. The first examines the outer space regime. It begins with a discussion of how national sovereignty over superjacent airspace evolved into the existing mix of open access and nonappropriation. It continues with the political and historical development of the space regime, examining the effect of military uses of space, the role of special interest groups, and the extraordinary effect of the Committee on the Peaceful Uses of Outer Space (COPUOS). Finally, the five treaties that make up the outer space regime are discussed. This first section concludes with an analysis of the regime itself.

The second section examines the international telecommunications regime: the development and role of the International Telecommunication Union (ITU), geostationary orbits, and the major international satellite systems. This section also concludes with an analysis of the regime.

Outer Space Regime

Since World War I, the clear rule has been that nations can regulate flight over their own territories or territorial seas. Seemingly, no one was seriously concerned about satellites and space vessels when the various conventions addressing overflight were drawn. However, outer space issues soon became significant. One of the earliest issues was just how far national sovereignty extends: at what point does *airspace* stop and *outer space* begin? (See box 6.1, The Solar System.)

Sovereignty in Outer Space

The international community recognized rather quickly the potential dangers of unregulated space. The United Nations took the position in 1957 that outer space was to be used for peaceful purposes only and that no one nation could assert sovereignty over territory in outer space.[5] This latter issue was agreed on with an astonishing lack of fanfare, but for those familiar with the history of human exploration, it was little short of miraculous. Other issues were more practical: Who is responsible for debris falling on Earth? How should Earth be protected from contamination by objects brought from space? How should space itself be protected from earthly contamination? How will governments keep track of what has been launched and where it is? One question that received a great deal of attention but in the end remained unresolved was the demarcation line between the atmosphere and outer space.

Box 6.1 The Solar System

Beyond Earth's atmosphere are other forms of space: *solar space*, the area in which the remainder of the solar system is located; *galactic space*, the space occupied by our galaxy, the Milky Way, and including solar space; and *extra-galactic space*, all space beyond the Milky Way.

Earth is the fifth largest of the nine planets orbiting the sun. Not only do the planets orbit the sun, but the sun itself also revolves around a central point in the galaxy, an orbit that takes about 200 million year. Within the solar system, current technology can support human travel. A trip from Earth to the moon takes less than 5 days, whereas a trip to Venus takes 140 days, and a trip to Mercury, 210 days. Travel to Pluto, the farthest known planet, takes forty-six years. Although estimates of travel time outside the solar system vary, the numbers are so immense that the disagreements seem irrelevant: 30,000–70,000 years to reach the nearest star, and 15 billion years to reach the Andromeda Galaxy, the closest spiral galaxy.

Source: Lay and Taubenfeld, *Activities of Man in Space*

Although the physical characteristics of Earth's atmosphere and outer space certainly differ, there is no sharp physical demarcation between the two regions. The functional criteria used most often has been the altitude limit of conventional aircraft operations, usually between 10 and 20 kilometers (6.2–12 miles), but this designation becomes symbolically problematic when American pilots receive astronaut wings for flying aircraft such as the X-15 above an altitude of 80 kilometers (50 miles).[6]

The issue has not been resolved with any clarity; it was still on the agenda of the legal subcommittee of the Committee on the Peaceful Uses of Outer Space (COPUOS) in 1992.[7] Some have suggested that Earth satellites are still sufficiently terrestrial that the limits of outer space begin beyond the range of satellite orbits, at about 35,400 kilometers (22,000 miles). The United States objected to this position because if the satellites were included within airspace, they would be in violation of national sovereignty throughout most of their orbits. Following this logic, in 1976, eight equatorial nations claimed national sovereignty over the geosynchronous orbits above their countries under the Bogotá Declaration (discussed later in this chapter). However, no consensus has emerged about the line between airspace and outer space, and perhaps, given the development of the space regime, no consensus is necessary.[8] The world legal community has not been so cavalier, however, about issues of sovereignty in outer space.

In July 1969, humans first set foot on the Moon, and the event was hailed as a milestone in scientific exploration. However, especially interesting was what did *not* occur: the United States did not claim territorial sovereignty. Throughout recorded history, whenever humans have landed on an uninhabited shore (or, indeed, often when making landfall on an inhabited one), they have claimed the land for the sovereign who had sent them or to which they felt nationalistic loyalty. Here, on the Moon, was truly virgin territory, which had never before seen so much as a human footprint. Why, then, were centuries of human behavior and international law overturned by the crew of the *Apollo 11*?

The rule of national sovereignty over airspace has never been applied to outer space.[9] There were no protests, even from the non-Communist countries, over *Sputnik*'s occupation of the atmosphere above other nations' sovereign territories. In 1962, President John F. Kennedy and Premier Nikita Khrushchev began negotiations for a joint meteorological satellite for global weather forecasting. Thus, the outer space regime began to assume a definite form; in the weather satellite program, there was "again a reinforcement of and conformity to the emerging principle . . . : *outer space may be used for peaceful and scientific purposes without regard to subjacent sovereignty.*"[10]

Although the practical value of this position is obvious, it is not clear why this should be the legal case. One explanation is that protests would have little efficacy because it would be impossible to enforce regulations prohibiting such overflights; the ability to destroy an orbiting satellite came well after overflights had become customary behavior. The mind-set that saw cannon range as an acceptable definition of territorial sea might balk at an extension of national territory into outer space. It might also be simply that even though neither national laws nor international law has set a legal definition distinguishing between the atmosphere and outer space (except among parties to the Bogotá Declaration), common sense indicates that the two are not the same, so nations did not at first attempt to apply airspace law to outer space. A third reason may be that there were obvious advantages to allowing some passages, such as, telecommunications satellites, which provide useful services to many nations, and it would be difficult to establish a regime that permitted some overflights and not others.

A fourth explanation is more practical. The technical difficulty of extending national barriers into outer space is enormous. Indeed, some have argued not only that airspace law is inappropriate in outer space but also that territorial claims are both physically and technically impossible. Early arguments were made that outer space could not be constrained by national territorial claims because it has no fixed physical limits.[11] Further arguments were raised in 1956, noting not only the absurdity of territorial claims to space but also their technical impossibility: if nations were to claim the outer space above them, their physical areas of outer space would be constantly changing as Earth rotates.[12] The legal regime that finally evolved is "essentially negative. It is a regime of self-denying, self-policed rules accepted today by most if not all the states of the world."[13]

This raises the sort of question that is universally beloved by lawyers and other philosophers: can there be property rights on celestial bodies if there is no sovereignty? On Earth, governments convey property rights to a resource, usually through some form of government recognition or claim-recording process. These property rights consist of the legal right to conduct such activities as alienating the property, inheriting it, or leasing it to a second party. So, if there are no sovereign governments to register claims and to formalize property rights, can anyone *legally* exploit the resources? It is one thing to sail on the wide ocean in order to capture fugitive fish but quite another to invest resources in, for example, mines on Saturn's rings if there is no legal recourse against claim-jumpers. The outer space regime, discussed in the following section, has begun to answer these questions.

Development of the Outer Space Regime

An international law for outer space began with international acceptance of the satellite program sponsored during the International Geophysical Year (IGY) in 1957–1958.[14] (See box 6.2, Chronology for Outer Space.) During the IGY, the United States proposed that the United Nations work toward the peaceful scientific development of outer space, proposing a project sponsored jointly by the National Academy of Sciences and the National Science Foundation, with technical support from the Department of Defense. The plan called for "construction of a small, unmanned, earth-circling satellite vehicle to be used for basic scientific observation."[15] Efforts at international cooperation received a boost in 1958 when the United States House of Representatives issued *International Cooperation in the Exploration of Space*, a report of the Select Committee on Astronautics and Space Exploration.[16]

Several regional joint ventures for space exploration were established in the 1960s. These joint ventures, located in western Europe, were carried out by nations accustomed to dominating new technology. However, they soon lost their preeminent position as the United States and the USSR poured military funds into the space race.[17]

Box 6.2 Chronology for Outer Space

1957–1958 International Geophysical Year (IGY)

1957   USSR launches *Sputnik I*

1958   United Nations Resolution 1348 (XIII) establishes the Ad Hoc Committee on the Peaceful Uses of Outer Space

1959   Committee on the Peaceful Uses of Outer Space (COPUOS) becomes a permanent body of the United Nations

1967   Treaty on Principles Governing the Activities of States in the Exploration and Use of Outer Space, Including the Moon and Other Celestial Bodies (Outer Space Treaty) (in force 1967)

1968   Agreement on the Rescue of Astronauts, the Return of Astronauts, and the Return of Objects Launched into Outer Space (Rescue Agreement) (in force 1968)

1969   First moon landing

1972   Convention on International Liability for Damage Caused by Space Objects (Liability Convention) (in force 1973)

1974   Convention on Registration of Objects Launched into Outer Space (Registration Convention) (in force 1976)

1979   Agreement Governing the Activities of States on the Moon and Other Celestial Bodies (Moon Treaty) (in force 1984)

Military Effects on the Space Regime

Much of the story of space law has been defined by the pressures of the cold war. The United States and the USSR had the technology and the resources to mount a space race, although the cost to the Soviet people of sustaining that effort became painfully clear in the early 1990s. Other members of the United Nations pushed for a demilitarized regime, motivated in part by the specter of nuclear weapons raining indiscriminate destruction on their territories. The space race began in October 1957, when the USSR launched *Sputnik I*, and since then, the pace of space exploration has increased dramatically. In 1957, 2 space vessels were launched; in 1984, 129 launches were successful.[18] The pace of development has been amazing: less than four years after *Sputnik I*, the Russians had a man in orbit around Earth. Eight years later, the United States placed two men on the Moon.

Despite the nonmilitary dedication of space, American nuclear strategy during the cold war rested on the notion of mutual assured destruction (MAD): the idea that a first strike would be illogical because each side had sufficient nuclear capability to destroy the other even after the initial launch of weapons. President Ronald Reagan proposed an amendment to this policy with the Strategic Defense Initiative (SDI), or, to use the popular name, Star Wars. SDI would rely on defensive weapons in outer space that could destroy any first launch by the Soviets before their weapons struck the United States. However, questions of technical feasibility and reliability called the SDI plan into question almost immediately.[19] Just as important, however, were concerns that the Star Wars system violated the spirit, if not the letter, of the 1967 Treaty on Principles Governing the Activities of States in the Exploration and Use of Outer Space, including the Moon and other Celestial Bodies (Outer Space Treaty). Proponents countered that Star Wars was a defensive policy and did not use any "weapons of mass destruction" as prohibited by the treaty. Interest in SDI eventually faded, and President Bill Clinton terminated the program.

Still, the impact of military potential on the development of outer space cannot be underestimated. The potential of space for surveillance and attack, and the necessity to develop defensive technology, fueled space exploration throughout the cold war. The explosion in computer and communications technology led to satellite development that dwarfed the military aims of the superpowers. It is difficult to segregate peaceful scientific uses of outer space from those uses with potential military applications. For example, meteorological observations are clearly useful during times of war, but the same technology provides essential information on storms and crops. Satellites that facilitate broadcasts of benefit concerts may also be used for military communications. This is not a problem that is unique to issues of space. Many peaceful scientific endeavors have violent parallels, such as, the use of herbicides to control crop-destroying weeds and to clear jungle foliage for more efficient bombing.

The Role of Special Interest Groups

Space law is largely negotiated law, found in statutes and treaties. Although customary law has had a substantial influence, the extremely rapid pace at which the law has developed and the prominence of the United Nations have given legislation the preeminent role.[20] Equally important has been the role of science and technology. Formal treaties are negotiated in part on shared understandings of scientific and technical parameters. In national politics, expert witnesses are often in opposition to each other, providing scientific support for the policy preferences of their own side. However, in the global arena, the uses of scientific and technological information are somewhat different. Negotiators strive to understand the scientific information so they can protect their national interests from encroachment and their economic interests from preemption. There is no jury or judge to be convinced; rather, the negotiators must make informed guesses on development and political-economic returns before they complete the bargaining process. This gives an extraordinary weight to technical expertise in the development of outer space law.[21] Two groups are especially important: scientists and members of the military-industrial complexes.[22]

The scientific community interested in the exploration of space has tried hard and with some success to emulate their Antarctic colleagues by stressing the scientific value of their work over its practical applications. However, space research is much more expensive than is work in Antarctica, and national governments are often reluctant to devote substantial funding to work without immediate application. Antarctica also has mineral and energy resources that may soon be economically feasible to develop, whereas the economic potential of outer space is nebulous. There are, however, some interesting recent developments that suggest a new approach to space exploration. In February 1997, the National Aeronautics and Space Administration (NASA) held a workshop to examine the space tourism market, and a month later, aerospace trade industries held an international symposium to discuss funding options.[23] In the long run, this may work to the advantage of the outer space regime. Relieved of the political pressures of superpower conflicts, and unlikely to provoke rapacious entrepreneurial activity, the regime may have time to develop at a more considered and deliberate pace.

The military-industrial complexes see space projects as opportunities to hold their ground during an era of military retrenchment. Because scientific and technological advances in general are so closely linked with military activity, they often receive substantial portions of their funding from military sources. They are therefore almost as interested as are the armed forces in maintaining a military presence in space. Business concerns are also interested in space law, eager to be in line if profitable resources are discovered, and equally eager to use the unexplored potential of space, for example, for development of new chemicals and drugs in the weightless atmosphere of space. Thus, speculators are as interested in influencing space policy as are current entrepreneurs.

COPUOS and the Treaty Regime

The United Nations is the principal international organization for the space regime. In March 1958, following the launch of *Sputnik I*, the USSR submitted a proposal to the United Nations to organize international cooperative efforts in outer space. The United States followed in September of the same year with a similar proposal, and in December, U.S. Ambassador John Foster Dulles asked the General Assembly to establish a committee to make recommendations. The result was Resolution 1348 (XIII), which established the Ad Hoc Committee on the Peaceful Uses of Outer Space, composed of eighteen nations: Argentina, Australia, Belgium, Brazil, Canada, Czechoslovakia, France, India, Iran, Italy, Japan, Mexico, Poland, Sweden, the United Arab Republic, the United Kingdom, the United States, and the USSR.[24] This committee eventually became the Committee on the Peaceful Uses of Outer Space (COPUOS). On 12 December 1959, COPUOS became a permanent body of the General Assembly. The legal regime developed during this period comprises five major international treaties negotiated through COPUOS: the Outer Space Treaty, the Rescue Agreement, the Liability Convention, the Registration Convention, and the Moon Treaty (discussed in the following sections).

When COPUOS became a permanent body of the United Nations General Assembly in 1959, its membership expanded from the eighteen original members of the Ad Hoc Committee on the Peaceful Uses of Outer Space to twenty-four; the inclusion of Albania, Bulgaria, Hungary, and Romania satisfied Soviet concerns for representation.[25] In the early years of COPUOS, treaties were easier to negotiate because the idea of space travel—including its potential rewards—was not fully realized by the international community. As the value of participation was clarified, more nations sought membership on the committee and decision making became more difficult.

In December 1977, Benin, Colombia, Ecuador, Iraq, the Netherlands, Niger, the Philippines, Turkey, the United Republic of Cameroon, and Yugoslavia became members of COPUOS. In 1980, China followed suit. With the possible exception of China, none of these nations was likely to become spacefaring, yet all chose to invest their political resources in COPUOS. This was partly to ensure better geographical representation and partly to strengthen existing coalitions for future access to the profits—if any—to be found in outer space. In 1981, COPUOS accepted the notion of regional representation in its membership.[26] New members were allocated on the basis of regional affiliations: Upper Volta for Africa, Uruguay for Latin America, Spain for "Western Europe and Other," the Syrian Arab Republic and Vietnam for Asia. There was an increased representation for the equatorial states,[27] especially important in regard to geostationary orbits, which some equatorial nations claimed as sovereign territory.

Beginning in 1962, the primary decision rule within COPUOS has been *consensus*: a decision is accepted only when no member state objects.[28] As the developing nations became more influential within all United Nations organizations, membership in COPUOS of "space resource states" and states with advanced technology were balanced by the membership of developing nations. As membership increased, and the variety of interests to be represented increased as well, consensus became increasingly difficult to achieve.[29]

Achieving consensus is a very slow process, but it has been useful for the widespread acceptance of COPUOS's views.[30] Regardless of how severe policy disagreements may be, each member is assured of a hearing. Conflict resolution is designed to move slowly, allowing tempers to cool and crises to abate. Although majority rule could be used in the absence of consensus, COPUOS has never overridden the consensus rule. However, the unwieldy demands of the consensus rule have led to a loss in COPUOS legitimacy; in 1982, the United Nations General Assembly bypassed COPUOS and adopted a resolution regarding the use of satellites for direct television broadcasting.[31]

COPUOS is assisted by the Office for Outer Space Affairs Division of the United Nations Secretariat, which provides a liaison with other international organizations such as the International Telecommunication Union (ITU). It is also helped by several private groups: the Committee on Space Research (COSPAR), the International Council of Scientific Unions (ICSU), and the International Astronautical Federation (IAF), which is the home institution for the International Institute of Space Law (IISL).[32] Many other United Nations agencies are also involved in the space regime, primarily through their use of satellite technology: the World Meteorological Organization (WMO), the United Nations Educational, Scientific and Cultural Organization (UNESCO), the Food and Agriculture Organization (FAO) of the United Nations, the World Health Organization (WHO), the International Civil Aviation Organization (ICAO), the Intergovernmental Maritime Consultative Organization (IMCO), the International Labor Organization (ILO), the World Intellectual Property Organization (WIPO), the International Atomic Energy Agency (IAEA), and the World Bank.[33]

After the first four treaties entered into force, the regime shifted into the second phase of "international free competition."[34] The treaties provided a clear legal framework in which to regulate exploration of outer space. Issues of sovereignty and acquisition of resources were largely answered, and concerns about damages caused by launched material both in space and on Earth were quieted. The treaties reduced both uncertainty and risk. Space entrepreneurs could launch with confidence, knowing their liabilities and making intelligent guesses about profits. No one was excluded from the regime; interested parties needed only the resolve to explore and the money to finance their resolve.

Treaties

The current outer space regime is defined by five major treaties: the Outer Space Treaty, the Rescue Agreement, the Liability Convention, the Registration Convention, and the Moon Treaty.

Outer Space Treaty

Although it is tempting to draw analogies between the regimes that govern the oceans and those that govern outer space, the historical differences are substantial and cast doubt on the usefulness of the high seas model for outer space. First, until comparatively recently, many seafaring nations made extravagant claims to own (or at least to have the right to exploit) wide expanses of ocean. Faced with the impossible task of monitoring and enforcing national sovereignty, the world community accepted the concept of "freedom of the seas" for political expediency and as a maneuver for protection themselves from a loss of status. Although "freedom of the seas" was for centuries simply the right of neutral shipping, by 1958 *freedom* meant in reality the four freedoms of navigation, fishing, laying of submarine cable, and overflight.[35] This is much more restrictive than the current outer space regime. Unlike the oceans, which are clearly under pressure from resource scarcity and territorial incursion, the resources and resource domains of space seem infinite. Changes in technology are expected to increase the resource base rather than merely to improve the efficiency of exploiting it. The existing regime has successfully established open access to the resource domain; customary law as well as the treaties reinforce the doctrine.[36]

However, useful parallels have been found in the rules involving rescue of stranded astronauts, piracy, liability, and registration. These are technical problems or issues in which the analogies between marine law and space law are clear.[37] There is, for example, little difference between a shipwrecked mariner and an astronaut who lands on foreign soil.[38]

The Treaty on Principles Governing the Activities of States in the Exploration and Use of Outer Space, Including the Moon and Other Celestial Bodies (Outer Space Treaty) was negotiated and went into effect in October 1967. Article IV of the treaty follows the intent expressed in the 1958 resolution on the peaceful uses of outer space. However, in this context, "peaceful" does not exclude all military activity; it permits nonaggressive military uses. Thus the Outer Space Treaty is narrower in this regard than is the Antarctic Treaty, which absolutely prohibits military activity.[39] The language of Article IV is quite precise:

States Parties to the Treaty undertake not to place in orbit around the Earth any objects carrying nuclear weapons or any other kinds of weapons of mass destruction, install such weapons on celestial bodies or station such weapons in outer space in any other manner.

The moon and other celestial bodies shall be used by all States Parties to the Treaty exclusively for peaceful purposes. The establishment of military bases, installations and fortifications, the testing of any type of weapons and conduct of military maneuvers on celestial bodies shall be forbidden. The use of military personnel for scientific research or for any other peaceful purposes shall not be prohibited. The use of any equipment or facility necessary for peaceful exploration of the moon and other celestial bodies shall also not be prohibited.[40]

The Rescue Agreement, the Liability Convention, and the Registration Convention expand agreements reached in the Outer Space Treaty.

Rescue Agreement

In 1968, when the reality of manned flight was ensured, COPUOS drafted the 1968 Agreement on the Rescue of Astronauts, the Return of Astronauts, and the Return of Objects Launched into Outer Space (Rescue Agreement), which provides for the rescue and safe return of astronauts from both trouble in space and landing problems on Earth. This treaty is modeled on customary marine law, which led to some interesting negotiations over salvage rights to space equipment and technology.

The Rescue Agreement guarantees the return of *personnel* to the launching authority, but the return of *equipment* was problematic. The science and technology imperatives of the space race make equipment salvage very attractive; in addition, the precedent set by maritime law is to return shipwrecked or stranded mariners but to allow finders to salvage equipment. Not surprisingly, the Rescue Agreement changes that custom. Because the costs of retrieval are also likely to be high, the portions of the Rescue Agreement concerned with returning equipment are hedged with rules for reimbursement, damages, and other costs.[41]

Liability Convention

In 1972, the Convention on International Liability for Damage Caused by Space Objects (Liability Convention) was established to assess liability and

Box 6.3 Debris in Earth Orbit

At least 50,000 objects one-half inch or more in diameter are currently in orbit about Earth, ranging from spent rocket boosters and worn-out satellites to paint chips, nuts, and bolts. The Office of Technology Assessment (OTA) of the United States Congress estimates that by the year 2010, some frequently used low-Earth orbits will be too polluted to use safely. The pieces of debris can cause substantial damage even though they are quite small because their velocity, which averages 10,900 kilometers per hour (17,500 miles per hour), increases the force of impact.

The first major problem with radioactive space debris occurred in January 1978, when the Soviet satellite *Cosmos 954*, powered by a nuclear reactor, disintegrated over western Canada. The USSR finally agreed to pay Canada $3 million to defray recovery costs. Radioactive space debris poses problems on Earth as well as in space because of possible environmental damage once the debris reenters Earth's atmosphere. More than fifty satellites with radioactive components have been launched; at least six nuclear-powered satellites have had uncontrolled reentries, and at least two of these contained dangerous radioactive material. Estimates of hazardous material in orbit range as high as 1 metric ton (1.1 short tons) of highly enriched U-235, Pu-239, and other fission products.

Source: Bosco, "International Law"; Curtis, *Space Almanac*; Fawcett, *Outer Space*

Box 6.4 Project West Ford

Some debris has been placed in orbit deliberately. One example is Project West Ford (1961), a communications experiment in which small copper filaments or needles (dipoles) were launched into space to reflect radio waves at a frequency of 8,000 megacycles. The experiment primarily tested the usefulness of the dipoles as passive reflectors. The project generated substantial controversy, partly because of scientific objections to the underlying theory and partly because those conducting the experiment did not retrieve the dipoles, thus perhaps interfering with other forms of communications and space activities. The experiment was a failure, as the dipoles did not form the reflective belt anticipated; however, 350 million copper filaments continue to orbit Earth.

Source: Johnson, "Pollution and Contamination in Space"

compensation through an international legal regime for damages, death, or injury resulting from space activities. (See box 6.3, Debris in Earth Orbit and box 6.4, Project West Ford.) This treaty quieted the concerns of "non-launching" states over damages caused by the "space-resource nations" in two ways. First, it provides a readily accessible process for presenting claims against a launching state, and second, it promulgates a substantive body of law governing the rights and obligations of launching states and states asserting damage claims.[42] This was not a matter of codification but rather the creation of new law for situations with only the weakest of extant analogies—a remarkable achievement.

Although only states and some international organizations (e.g., the International Telecommunications Satellite Organization, or INTELSAT) are liable under the Liability Convention and the Registration Convention, municipal law (issues of ownership, insurance, etc.) also affects space law in much the same way as municipal law affects maritime shipping.

Registration Convention

Registration of objects launched into space is needed in part to provide evidence for liability charges. The 1974 Convention on Registration of Objects Launched into Outer Space (Registration Convention) responds to a difficulty arising under Article XI of the Outer Space Treaty, which requires parties to the treaty to report the "nature, conduct, locations, and results" of space-related activities to the United Nations, the public, and the international scientific community. Even when states followed this article, the results were not satisfactory; most problems arose from the Soviet Union's ongoing lack of candor. The Registration Convention elaborates on the regime originally set forth in the 1967 Outer Space Treaty. It has accomplished regularized markings of launched objects, centralized registration of national and other international registries, and full access to the information in the registry.

Moon Treaty

One of the more controversial space treaties is the 1979 Agreement Governing the Activities of States in the Moon and Other Celestial Bodies (Moon Treaty): it was the last of the five space treaties to enter into force, although none of the major spacefaring nations is a member. Enacted after the discussions on the Law of the Sea, the Moon Treaty includes language extolling the common heritage of mankind (CHM) principle (see chapter 2). It is partially because of this controversial provision that ratification of the treaty was delayed. Although commercial exploitation of the resources of outer space is not currently economically feasible, spacefaring nations are understandably reluctant to share their rights to resources that might become extremely valuable in the near future. A similar concern over seabed minerals led the United States to refuse to sign the Law of the Sea Treaty after the election of Ronald Reagan to the presidency (see the discussion of the deep seabed mineral regime in chapter 4).

The removal of moon rocks by American astronauts in 1969 gave rise to concerns that the resources of the Moon, mineral or otherwise, might be appropriated by other explorers or claimed by visiting nations. Developing nations were especially sensitive to this issue. Having seen their victory at the seabed-mining negotiations dissipate in the face of special interests and rapidly developing technology, they were anxious to establish the CHM principle in space before technology and potential profits overcame them again.[43] The 1979 Moon Treaty struck a precarious balance, prohibiting appropriation of "natural resources *in place*" (emphasis added) while retaining the possibility of appropriation of resources that had been moved, such as, mined ore. However, as discussed in chapter 4, the seabed regime has been substantially modified from the common heritage of mankind principle, and it is probable that the Moon Treaty will also be revised if the possibility of profitable resource extraction develops.

Discussion

The space law regime has evolved in a remarkably short time, achieving "enormous maturity in an exceedingly brief moment."[44] This has been possible for several reasons. First, the international institutions for devising law are in place and are perceived as legitimate sources of law by those affected by the law. Second, it was advantageous for every state and interest group to establish a stable regime as soon as possible. The nonnuclear states had a vital interest in the demilitarization of space, and the nuclear powers were willing to forgo a potential area of conflict without appearing to bow to the opposition. Third, there were precedents in the Law of the Sea, existing and customary air law, and, to a lesser extent, the Antarctic Treaty System; it was not necessary to start from scratch.

Constitutional choice decisions were made through the United Nations, and in the early days, COPUOS was the primary vehicle for this level of institutional choice. Just as the Antarctic regime is protected by physical conditions on the Antarctic continent, both collective choice and operational choice decisions in space policy were largely dictated by advances in space technology. These advances were relatively predictable, so collective choice and operational choice rules for future circumstances could be made with some confidence.

Monitoring is difficult in the space regime, although since the collapse of the Soviet Union, voluntary compliance from the former Communist bloc nations has apparently improved. Sanctioning is even more difficult; for example, Canada was unable to collect all of the $3 million dollars in damages it was awarded after the Soviet satellite *Cosmos 954* crashed there.[45] National operations are nested within the international regime, although it is not as essential that national space activities are coordinated to the extent the telecommunications activities are (see the following discussion of the telecommunications regime).

The Moon Treaty is the most vulnerable part of the space regime. The major spacefaring nations are not parties to the Treaty, and recent modifications to the deep seabed mineral regime signal a reluctance to accept the economic implications of the common heritage of mankind principle articulated in this treaty. The moon has the potential to be governed under a commons regime: it has clear boundaries, limiting local conditions, and a preexisting regime that defines institutional choice mechanisms. However, the major spacefaring nations must be parties to whatever decisions are made, or a sustainable regime cannot be created.

International Telecommunications Regime

From the beginning, it was clear that use of the radio spectrum must be regulated for both efficient use and effective political control of information technology. The first international agreements regulated the wire services; the most recent ones control the use of geostationary orbits.

International Telecommunication Union (ITU)

The radio spectrum may be considered a form of natural resource. (See box 6.5, The Electromagnetic Spectrum.) It is never consumed (although portions in use are temporarily unavailable to other users), so it is not a renewable resource, but it is limited because overcrowding can reduce or eliminate its usefulness. The radio spectrum is also affected by external forces. It may be "polluted" by artificial or natural disturbances, by interference, or by wasteful use. The radio spectrum is *res communes*[46] rather than *res nullius*

Box 6.5 The Electromagnetic Spectrum

Radio frequencies range from very low frequencies (VLF) of 3 to 30 kilohertz (kHz) to very high frequencies (VHF) of 30 to 300 gigahertz (GHz). The frequency spectrum is divided into various bands, each with characteristics that make it especially suitable for various telecommunications services, such as AM and FM radio, television, radar, and electronic mail. Higher-frequency waves, which carry the most information, must be bounced back to Earth by either satellites or relay stations or they will continue traveling through the atmosphere and into space. Lower-frequency waves are reflected back by the ionosphere and therefore are cheaper to use, but the possibilities of spillover and interference are greatly increased.

---

because allocation of the spectrum to various users is not permanent. Users receive usufructuary rights rather than a full bundle of proprietary rights. In 1965, the ITU (Montreux) Convention described the International Frequency Registration Board (IFRB), which registers frequency assignments, "as custodians of an international public trust."[47]

The International Telecommunication Union (ITU) is one of the oldest international organizations, founded in 1865 as the International Telegraph Union to regulate the wire services. (See box 6.6, Chronology for Telecommunications.) International cooperation in radio telecommunications began

---

Box 6.6 Chronology for Telecommunications

1865	International Telegraph Union (ITU) founded
1901	Marconi receives the first transatlantic wireless signal
1906	First Radiotelegraph Convention (Berlin)
1927	First Table of Allocations issued
1932	Madrid Plenipotentiary Conference forms International Telecommunication Union from old International Telegraph Union, effective 1934
1947	ITU becomes a specialized agency of the United Nations
1957	USSR launches *Sputnik I*, first artificial satellite
1963	First World Space Radiocommunication Conference (Geneva)
1992	Geneva Plenipotentiary Conference reorganizes the ITU into three new sectors

shortly after 1901, when Italian physicist Guglielmo Marconi hoisted a kite into the air at St. John's, Newfoundland, to receive the first transatlantic wireless signal. The need for communications among vessels at sea and their land bases led to several international conferences at which agreements were reached on distress and weather signals and on coastal stations. The first International Radiotelegraph Conference on the radio spectrum, held in Berlin in 1906, issued telecommunications guidelines. The first Table of Allocations was issued at the 1927 Radiotelegraph Conference in Washington. It defined the radio frequencies for each radio service and specified procedures each service should use to regularize its legal rights to the specific channels.[48]

The present-day ITU was formed in 1932 at the Madrid Plenipotentiary Conference and assumed its new name in 1934. It became a specialized agency of the United Nations in 1947. Unlike most international governmental organizations (IGOs), the ITU is not defined by a permanent charter. It is instead governed by a series of conventions that are reviewed at periodic Plenipotentiary Conferences (held no more often than every five years). The ITU has permanent organs in the General Secretariat and the Administrative Council of the United Nations. These administer the daily operations of the ITU.

Until 1992, regulations were set and amended by four subunits: the International Radio Consultative Committee (CCIR), the International Telephone and Telegraph Consultative Committee (CCITT), the Administrative Conferences (the World Administrative Radio Conferences [WARCs] and the World Administrative Telephone and Telegraph Conferences), and the International Frequency Regulation Board (IFRB). However, in recent years, the ITU has struggled with increasing political pressures. The ITU has been a relatively unpoliticized organization, primarily because most appointments to it are based on technical and scientific expertise. The IFRB was the dispute resolution organ for the ITU, and even it was composed mostly of engineers chosen for their technical abilities rather than for their negotiating skills.[49] The scientific focus of the ITU caused political problems during the 1970s and 1980s when the developing countries sought strategic advantages in a number of different arenas, including telecommunications. They had come to realize that previous ITU decisions made on technical grounds were not necessarily in their own best interests.

Rights to the radio spectrum were originally allocated on a basis familiar to water users in the American Southwest: first in time, first in right. The developing nations were concerned that the more advanced countries would establish a permanent monopoly over the resources. They argued that this rule led to unfair allocation of access to the regime because in the past they had lacked financial and technical resources to achieve entry and to establish their rights. The developing countries advocated a change in the procedures for assigning access rights, suggesting instead that each member of the ITU receive an allotment of orbits and frequencies. Predictably, the developed countries objected, noting that no satellite system had been refused access, that changing technology continues to expand the possible uses, and that the proposed change would result in an inefficient use of the resource. Of course, such arguments also support the *status quo*, which gives an advantage to the developed countries. Arguments that rest on the infinite capacity of technology to resolve problems of access and resource scarcity are seen by the developing countries as of dubious value, in part because the technology may be too expensive to adopt.

New trends in international communications, such as globalization and deregulation, as well as the enhanced role of telecommunications in such activities as banking, tourism, and information systems, seemed to require reorganization of the ITU. New members, particularly those representing developing countries, wanted an increased role for the ITU in development assistance. In response to these demands, at the 1989 Nice Plenipotentiary Conference, a review committee was created to recommend reforms enabling the organization to respond to its new international telecommunications environment. As a result, the ITU structure was revised by the Geneva Plenipotentiary Conference in Geneva in December 1992.

Three sectors were created. The Telecommunications Development Sector is charged with improving telecommunications by offering and coordinating technical assistance activities among international, regional, and national development and investment agencies. The Standardization Sector took all of the CCITT's responsibilities and the standardization portions the CCIR's responsibilities. The Radiocommunication Sector took over the CCIR's radio frequency spectrum management. It also took responsibility for the regulatory activities formerly conducted by the IFRB.

One unique aspect of the telecommunications regime is the role of sector members that are not countries. These are international organizations, operating agencies, and scientific or industrial organizations that wish to participate in sector activities, Plenipotentiary Conferences, World Conferences on International Telecommunications (which are not part of any sector), and WARCs. Access to ITU activities is contingent on payment of a fee, which varies with the extent of participation.[50] This gives the sector members access to policy decisions and provides the ITU with both technical information and money.

Although the structure of the ITU has changed, its responsibilities remain the same. The ITU adopts international regulations and treaties governing global telecommunications, including radio, telephone, telegraph, facsimile, and television relay services through satellites, as well as the use of geostationary satellite orbits, within which countries adopt their own national radio spectrum regulations. Because the ITU coordinates worldwide communications, it seeks to ensure that interference is minimized. This is important to all participants, and therefore most nations accede to the ITU regulations. Additional incentives to comply with ITU regulations are extensive. States that violate ITU protocols may be excluded from access to technological innovations, and interference with their illegitimate broadcasts is likely. International sanctions against "pirate" broadcasters are stringent; the Law of the Sea even permits nations to take punitive measures on the high seas against broadcasters targeting their territories.[51]

How did the ITU, which was originally designed for telegraph, radio, and telephone communications, become involved in the issues of outer space? The ITU's involvement is a logical extension of its telecommunications mission; early satellite launches used a number of communications functions, such as guidance systems and voice and television links, each of which has a different spectrum requirement.[52]

Geostationary Orbits

Technology has played a prominent role in the use of geostationary orbits. (See box 6.7, Geostationary Orbits.) Until the late 1980s, access to the orbits was limited in practice to the advanced spacefaring powers, primarily the United States and the Soviet Union. These were the countries with political and commercial incentives to develop military-based technology as part of the cold war arms race. However, the political and economic value of access to telecommunications satellites was absolutely clear to the developing countries, which were determined to obtain guaranteed access to satellite orbits and the radio spectrum so that when their technologies improved, they would be able to use them.

In 1971, the World Administrative Radio Conference on Space Telecommunications (WARC-ST) formally brought geostationary orbits under ITU control. The Radio Regulations were revised; in a dramatic departure from the old "first in time" protocol, all countries were given equal access to the use of space radio communication service frequencies and to the related geostationary orbits. In 1979, developing countries were allocated frequencies for broadcast satellites (despite the fact that they had no satellites) as well as

Box 6.7 Geostationary Orbits

Geosynchronous orbits are located approximately 35,786 kilometers (22,366 miles) above Earth's surface; a satellite in these orbits moving in the same direction as Earth's rotation takes twenty-four hours to complete one pass and remains above the same point on Earth. The orbits may be equatorial, polar, or inclined. Although the terms *geosynchronous* and *geostationary* are often used interchangeably, they are not synonymous in law. Under regulations of the International Telecommunication Union (ITU), a geostationary orbit is a geosynchronous orbit over the equator.

To work effectively, satellites must be at least 18 kilometers (11.2 miles) apart and operate on different radio frequencies, although to some extent this depends on the technology used for intersatellite communication. In theory, 2,000 satellites could operate in geostationary orbit, but this is more than necessary: as few as three satellites placed in orbit could serve the entire globe. The first satellite to be placed in a very high geostationary orbit was the American communications satellite *Syncom 2* in 1963.

Sources: Bosco, "International Law"; Finch, "Limited Space"; Gehrig, "Geostationary Orbit"; Herter, "Electromagnetic Spectrum"; Martinez, *Communication Satellites*; Soroos, "International Commons"; Vogler, *Global Commons*

guaranteed "parking places" if they ever did acquire satellites. (See box 6.8, the Bogotá Declaration.) This action was prompted by perceived inequities in the allocation of resources and by the addition of sixty-five new member nations to the 1979 General WARC, most of which were developing countries.[53] By 1989, an "arc allotment plan" had been devised that ensured that each nation would receive at least one orbital slot.

Communications satellites have been the most lucrative space activity to date.[54] There are three global satellite networks: INTELSAT (International Telecommunications Satellite Organization), INTERSPUTNIK (International Organization of Space Communications), and INMARSAT (International Mobile Satellite Organization). Multipurpose regional systems have been established for Europe (the European Telecommunications Satellite, EUTELSAT) and the Middle East (the Arab Satellite Communications Organization, ARABSAT).[55]

Box 6.8 The Bogotá Declaration

In the 1976 Bogotá Declaration, Brazil, Colombia, Congo, Ecuador, Indonesia, Kenya, Uganda, and Zaire tried to stake claims to the geostationary orbits above their countries, claiming that geostationary orbits are natural resources linked to the gravitational field generated in their countries at the equator. Nonequatorial nations countered that other factors affect geostationary orbits: the attraction of the moon and sun, solar radiation pressure, and launch and propulsion character- istics of each satellite. Even if gravity were solely responsible for the orbits, the in- dividual contribution of each country would be small. The parties to the Bogotá Declaration also claimed permanent sovereignty over geostationary orbits because the orbits are within their territorial boundaries, although they recognized the right of innocent passage through their space. Although in the end, the declaration is only an interesting footnote to history, it did put the world community on no- tice that the developing countries recognized access to and use of the telecom- munications regime as very serious issues.

Sources: Christol, *Modern International Law;* Finch, *"Limited Space"*

Global Satellite Networks

The International Telecommunications Satellite Organization (INTELSAT) began operations in 1965 with the *Early Bird* (INTELSAT I) satellite. INTELSAT supplies international and domestic telecommunications, and the only requirement for membership is membership in the ITU. A number of factors led to the creation of INTELSAT: increasing international concern over the development of space telecommunications; the preeminence of American technology and experience, which virtually compelled the western European allies to cooperate with American interests; and a desire on the part of some of these allies, especially France, to establish a framework within which they could successfully compete with the United States.[56]

INTELSAT is unique organization because it is an IGO for *commercial* use of satellite communications. Revenue shares are based on investment shares and the amount of traffic on the INTELSAT system. Although it is nominally a nonprofit cooperative of more than 170 countries and territo- ries, it is actually a profit-seeking enterprise. INTELSAT itself owns the satellites, tracking and telemetry control facilities, and administrative machinery that constitutes the space segment. Member countries are in effect stockholders, "owning" a share of the space segment in proportion to their investment and traffic volume. They pay INTELSAT for the volume of traffic they generate, and they receive dividends in proportion to their shares. The Earth segments are owned by the member countries or by the organizations designated by the member countries. The members in turn bill their customers for use of the system; each country sets its own tariffs. This may generate high profits; for example, in 1980 the West German Bundespost profit was more than $40 million.[57] The United States is represented by the COMSAT Corporation, a parastatal (i.e., a mix of public and private) corporation created by Congress in 1962.[58]

Developing countries may become members of INTELSAT by leasing space on INTELSAT satellites. This is a strong investment strategy for countries that do not have substantial telecommunications infrastructures. These countries charge very high tariffs to their own consumers, which keeps demand for services inside their countries low. This practice balances demand with the infrastructure capacity while generating revenue. In addition, the global increase in INTELSAT traffic continues to pay substantial dividends to the developing countries that are members, providing a second source of income from the investment.[59]

INTERSPUTNIK, although carrying only a fraction of the volume carried by INTELSAT, uses Russian *Stationar* satellites that utilize smaller and cheaper Earth stations than are used by INTELSAT. INTERSPUTNIK was established by the USSR in 1971 as an alternative to INTELSAT membership (although the USSR did join INTELSAT in 1991). The Soviets had objected to INTELSAT because it was managed by a private corporation and undergirded by commercial ideology.[60] This does not, however, mean that INTERSPUTNIK is averse to making money; in 1992, its revenues were $10 million.[61] The INTERSPUTNIK organization follows more democratic lines than does INTELSAT; each country has one vote regardless of the volume of traffic it generates on the system, whereas on INTELSAT, the size of the vote is commensurate with the amount of volume used by the country.[62] Only nine countries have joined INTERSPUTNIK: Bulgaria, Cuba, Czechoslovakia, the German Democratic Republic, Hungary, Mongolia, Poland, Romania, and the Soviet Union.[63] However, INTERSPUTNIK now has Western corporate members such as AT&T and CNN.[64]

The International Mobile Satellite Organization (INMARSAT) was established in July 1979 and began operations in February 1982. It provides communications between ships and from ship to shore, relying on leased access to INTELSAT and U.S. Navy *Marisat* satellites.[65] The Soviet Union was a member of INMARSAT, partly because its substantial fishing fleet and corresponding level of use would give it the second largest vote in the governing council. This also gave the Soviets access to Western satellite technology through their offer to sell launch services for INMARSAT satellites on the Soviet *Proton* rocket.[66]

Multipurpose Systems: ARABSAT, the ESA, and EUTELSAT

In 1976, the twenty-two members of the Arab League established the Arab Satellite Communications Organization (ARABSAT) to provide telephone, data, television, and radio services in the Middle East and North Africa. ARABSAT has cultural as well as instrumental goals of telecommunications, information exchange among members, and rural education.[67] This is clearly a politically motivated organization; it not only provides reliable telecommunications and direct broadcast television to the Arab states but also offers access to advanced technology while demonstrating Arab independence from Western institutions.[68]

The European Space Agency (ESA) was created in October 1980. It replaced the European Space Research Organization (ERSO, 1962) and the European Launcher Development Organization (ELDO, 1964). Its mandate under the European Space Agency Convention is to regulate inter-European competition in space activities. EUTELSAT is the weather satellite system established in 1982 and managed by the ESA.

A third system was established by the Soviets. Intercosmos is now dissolved and has been replaced by the Commonwealth of Independent States (CIS) Interstate Space Council. It is dominated by Russia, Kazakhstan, and Ukraine.[69]

Discussion

The military implications of communications satellites are obvious, but the tremendous strides in environmental analysis they make possible are just as important. For example, remote sensing data have become extremely important in agricultural management. Crops reflect different amounts of solar radiation, and details such as the health of a crop and its water content may be measured by the color it radiates; remote sensing detects crop patterns for drug interdiction, geological exploration, and assessment of moisture levels in plants for irrigation monitoring. Weather patterns are detected from space, aiding in the provision of advance warnings for severe weather conditions, and stratospheric ozone levels are monitored.

Data transmission via satellite has brought the dubious benefits of radio, television, and telephone to virtually the entire planet, and the economic impact of independent information control is substantial. Improved access to information increases the amount and accuracy of information for both domestic and international markets and strengthens the role of developing countries. In 1982, a study conducted by the ITU and the OECD reported a 200:1 return as economic growth for investment in telecommunications in Kenya and an 85:1 return in rural Egypt.[70] Satellite-based systems are practical for several reasons: one satellite transponder can broadcast to a large geographical region; maintenance costs are independent of the size of the region covered; and the system is much more flexible than are terrestrial or cable systems.[71]

The North–South separation in telecommunications is striking. Countries that lack the infrastructure or the technical demand for communications satellites will fight bitterly to gain access to such resources. The satellites' symbolic value and political weight are virtually independent of their use as communications technology. Developing countries see the Western technology lock on telecommunications as one more case of developed nations trying to maintain a pool of cheap labor and resources. They also perceive restrictions on technology transfer as an attempt to keep them dependent on suppliers from developed countries. Although international cooperation is necessary for efficient use of telecommunications, nations are instinctively reluctant to relinquish regulatory control of their own communications systems to external actors.[72]

Problems occur along the East–West continuum as well. Within the former Communist bloc countries and the republics within the former Soviet Union, computers and other forms of communications technology have not been widely available, even to most government organizations. This lack of access was, of course, intended partly to restrict the flow of information to non-Communist groups: it is difficult to have a repressive, information-hoarding government if teenagers have modems on their computers. Western countries were equally interested in protecting Western technology, in part to maintain their perceived technological superiority in the cold war. Restrictions on telecommunications technology were imposed on both exports (from the Western side) and imports (from the Communist side). These fears were probably exaggerated. Even in the larger Soviet cities, the quality of the telephone lines and the vagaries of the power system would have made serious hacking extremely difficult; the scarcity of supplies such as paper and printer ribbons also limited the utility of computer access. What communications systems did exist were used primarily by the military and to support communications between the periphery and the central government core of the Soviet system.[73]

A slightly different issue is posed by the developing nations' fight to gain reserved access to geostationary orbits. Countries that barely have telephones are claiming and even leasing out their access rights to geostationary orbits. For example, in 1990, Tonga claimed the last sixteen slots for orbits linking Asia, the Pacific, and the North American continent; observers concluded that the claim was an exercise in financial speculation prompted by an American entrepreneur.[74] One explanation for this sort of behavior is that the developing countries are not actually pursuing *access* but instead are using these claims as bargaining chips in their negotiations with the developed countries in other policy areas.[75]

It is equally plausible that the developing countries have recognized the peculiar relationship between spatial-extension resources and issues of access. Exploitation of most resources requires access as the first of many stages before benefits are realized, but to exploit spatial-extension resources may require *only* access, without any subsequent activities. In the past, the more powerful nations and interest groups have gained preferential access to the resources because they had the technology to exploit them. The development of access rights independent of the ability to utilize the spatial-extension resources has given the developing nations a powerful argument in their efforts to gain parity with the developed world. They now participate in making decisions at all three levels of institutional choice.

The telecommunications regime presents the clearest case of nested enterprises of any of the regimes examined in this volume.

The ITU allocates services to nations and to satellite organizations, which in turn make allocations to their citizens and members under their own specialized rules. The telecommunications regime meets many of the design principles that characterize sustainable regimes. The tidy mechanisms that allow local conditions for resource use while preserving international collective and constitutional choices are a model for good institutional design.

Suggested Reading

Cooper, John. *The Right to Fly.* New York: Henry Holt, 1947. Cooper writes in the grand tradition of public servants who have been in the policy trenches and come back to tell us what they have learned. He wouldn't approve of the current regime, and it is well worth your while to find out why.

Reynolds, Glenn, and Robert Merges. *Outer Space: Problems of Law and Policy*, 2nd ed. Boulder, Colo.: Westview Press, 1997. This new edition addresses commercial trade in space-launch services and space-related goods and services as well as current developments in international space law. The World Wide Web site of the International Telecommunication Union (http://www.itu.int) provides access to ITU publication as well as information about meetings, conferences, and current issues.

Notes

1. Myres McDougal, "The Prospects for a Regime in Outer Space," in *Law and Politics in Space*, ed. Maxwell Cohen (Montreal: McGill-Queen's University Press, 1964), 121.

2. Morris R. Cohen and Felix S. Cohen, "Introduction," in *Readings in Jurisprudence and Legal Philosophy* (Boston: Little, Brown, 1954), 12.

3. Ibid., 13.

4. The first article calling attention to the coming need for an outer space regime appeared in 1910, written by Emile Laude, a Belgian jurist. Joseph Bosco, "International Law Regarding Outer Space: An Overview," *Journal of Air Law and Commerce* 55 (1990): 612, n. 17, citing E. R. C. Van Bogaert, *Aspects of Space Law* (Boston: Kluwer, 1986), 3. The first book devoted to space law was Vladimir Mandl, *Das Weltraumrecht, ein Problem der Raumfahrt* (1932). Nathan A. Goldman, *American Space Law: International and Domestic* (Ames: Iowa State University Press, 1988), 66, n. 2.

5. *Sputnik I* was launched on 4 October 1957, and on 14 November, the United Nations General Assembly approved a resolution that "the sending of objects through outer space should be exclusively for peaceful and scientific purposes" (G.A. Res. 1148 [XII] of 14 November 1957, para. I[f]). A year later, the General Assembly affirmed "the common interest of mankind in outer space and . . . the common aim that outer space should be used for peaceful purposes only" (G.A. Res. 1348, 13 U.N. GABR Supp. (no. 18) at 5 U.N. Doc. A/4090 (1958).

6. S. Houston Lay and Howard Taubenfeld, *The Law Relating to Activities of Man in Space* (Chicago: University of Chicago Press, 1970), 44.

7. John Vogler, *The Global Commons: A Regime Analysis* (New York: Wiley, 1995), 102.

8. J. E. S. Fawcett, *Outer Space: New Challenges to Law and Policy* (Oxford: Clarendon Press, 1984), 17.

9. Bosco, "International Law," 621. Bosco notes that "The only opposition to this principle has been enunciated in the Bogotá Declaration of December 3, 1976, whereby eight developing countries attempted to claim

sovereign rights over corresponding segments of the geostationary orbit" (621, n. 63, citing Van Bogaert, *Aspects of Space Law*, 58). However, the Bogotá Declaration has not been accepted by the major spacefaring nations. See also Andrew Haley, *Space Law and Government* (New York: Appleton-Century-Crofts, 1963), 67. It is difficult to tell whether Haley's assertion was uniformly accepted. Scrupulously fair, he notes several objections, such as Becker, "The Control of Space," *Department of State Bulletin* 39 (1958): 416, and Gorove, "On the Threshold of Space: Toward Cosmic Law," 4 N.Y.L.F. 305 (1958). However, developments since the publication of Haley's book in 1963 would seem to support his position.

10. Haley, *Space Law and Government*, 73.

11. Alex Mayer, address to the International Astronautical Federation, 1952, cited in C. Wilfred Jenks, *Space Law* (New York: Praeger, 1965), 97–98.

12. Jenks, *Space Law*, 98–99.

13. Lay and Taubenfeld, *Activities of Man in Space*, 51.

14. Haley, *Space Law and Government*, 62.

15. National Academy of Sciences, press release, 29 July 1955, cited in Haley, *Space Law and Government*, 65–66.

16. House Select Committee on Astronautics and Space Exploration, *International Cooperation in the Exploration of Space*, 85th Cong., 2nd Sess., Title 1, 1958 (Committee Print), cited in Haley, *Space Law and Government*, 71, n. 114.

17. Jenks, *Space Law*, 74.

18. Bosco, "International Law," 610.

19. Goldman, *American Space Law* (1988), 14–15.

20. Carl Q. Christol, *The Modern International Law of Outer Space* (Elmsford, N.Y.: Pergamon Press, 1982), 13.

21. Christol, *Modern International Law*, 13.

22. The telecommunications regimes, which are also part of the outer space regime, generate their own set of interests. These are discussed later in the chapter.

23. "Symposium Launches Space Tourism Industry," *Greensboro News and Record*, 22 March 1997, B6, B9. This is not as futuristic or silly as it might seem at first glance. The Japanese Rocket Society estimates it will cost $10 billion to develop passenger vehicles for outer space, or about half the cost of developing the mobile phone market over Japan in a two-year period.

24. G.A. Res. 1348, 13 U.N. GAOR Supp. (No. 18) at 5, U.N. Doc. A/4090 (1958). Cited in Bosco, "International Law," 613.

25. Lay and Taubenfeld, *Activities of Man in Space*, 219.

26. U.N. Doc. A/35/791 (12 January 1981), cited in Christol, *Modern International Law*, 16.

27. As of 1992, the following fifty-three nations were members of COP-UOS: Albania, Argentina, Australia, Austria, Belgium, Benin, Brazil, Bulgaria, Burkina Faso, Cameroon, Canada, Chad, Chile, China, Colombia, Czechoslovakia, Ecuador, Egypt, France, Germany, Hungary, India, Indonesia, Iran, Iraq, Italy, Japan, Kenya, Lebanon, Mexico, Mongolia, Morocco, the Netherlands, Niger, Nigeria, Pakistan, the Philippines, Poland, Portugal, Romania, the Russian Federation, Sierra Leone, Sudan, Sweden, the Syrian Arab Republic, Turkey, Ukraine, the United Kingdom, the United States, Uruguay, Venezuela, Vietnam, and Yugoslavia. United Nations, Department of Public Information (New York), *Yearbook of the United Nations 1992*, vol. 46 (Boston: Martinus Nijhoff, 1992), 1203.

28. Christol, *Modern International Law*, 18. This rule was chosen in 1962.

29. Goldman, *American Space Law* (1988), 30.

30. Christol, *Modern International Law*, 18.

31. Goldman, *American Space Law: International and Domestic* (San Diego: Univelt, 1996), 26.

32. Christol, *Modern International Law*, 19.

33. Goldman, *American Space Law* (1996), 28.

34. Lay and Taubenfeld, *Activities of Man in Space*, 74.

35. These four "freedoms" were set out at the 1958 Convention on the Law of the Sea (Geneva). Philip C. Jessup and Howard Taubenfeld, *Controls for Outer Space and the Antarctic Analogy* (New York: Columbia University Press, 1959), 211 (notes omitted).

36. Christol, *Modern International Law*, 846.

37. Jessup and Taubenfeld, *Controls for Outer Space*, 213.

38. One area in which the analogy has, unfortunately, failed is advertising. I know of no seagoing vessel that carries commercial advertising (except racing vessels, which may carry product endorsements from sponsors), but Columbia Pictures paid $500,000 to advertise Arnold Schwarzenegger's 1993 movie *The Last Action Hero* on an American Conestoga rocket scheduled for launch in June 1993. Peter Carlson, "Has NASA Lost Its Way?," *The Washington Post Magazine*, 30 May 1993, 12.

39. Antarctic Treaty (Washington), 402 U.N.T.S. 71, Gr. Brit. T.S. No. 97 1961 (Cmd. 1535), 12 U.S.T. 794, T.I.A.S. No. 4780. In force 23 June 1961.

Article I(1): Antarctica shall be used for peaceful purposes only. There shall be prohibited, *inter alia*, any measures of a military nature, such as the establishment of military bases and fortifications, the carrying out of military manoeuvres, as well as the testing of any type of weapons.

Article V(1): Any nuclear explosions in Antarctica and the disposal there of radioactive waste material shall be prohibited.

40. Ibid., Article IV.
41. Christol, *Modern International Law*, 203.
42. Ibid., 119.
43. Ibid., 247.
44. Ibid., 843.
45. *Cosmos 954 Claim*, 18 I.L.M. 899 (1979), cited in Patricia Birnie and Alan Boyle, *International Law and the Environment* (Oxford: Clarendon Press, 1993), 416–417, n. 166.
46. Fawcett, *Outer Space*, 52.
47. Article 13, cited in Fawcett, *Outer Space*, 52.
48. The Table of Allocations was the forerunner of the Master Frequency Register, which is administered by the International Frequency Registration Board (IFRB).
49. Marvin Soroos, *Beyond Sovereignty* (Columbia: University of South Carolina Press, 1986), 341.
50. See the ITU's World Wide Web site (http://www.itu.int).
51. Horace B. Robertson, "The Suppression of Pirate Radio Broadcasting," *Law and Contemporary Problems* 45, 1 (winter 1982): 71–101.
52. Larry Martinez, *Communication Satellites: Power Politics in Space* (Dedham, Mass.: Artech, 1985), 115.
53. Marvin Soroos, "The Commons in the Sky: The Radio Spectrum and Geosynchronous Orbit as Issues in Global Policy," *International Organization* 36, 3 (summer 1982): 673.
54. Bosco, "International Law," 621.
55. Goldman, *American Space Law* (1988), 8–9.
56. Fawcett, *Outer Space*, 54–55.
57. Martinez, *Communication Satellites*, 5, citing "INTELSAT macht Telefonieren billiger," *Astronautik*, 2 (1981): 33.
58. Goldman, *American Space Law* (1996), 50.
59. Martinez, *Communication Satellites*, 5.
60. Fawcett, *Outer Space*, 44.
61. Goldman, *American Space Law* (1996), 49.
62. Martinez, *Communications Satellites*, 3.

63. Fawcett, *Outer Space*, 45.

64. Goldman, *American Space Law* (1996), 48.

65. Martinez, *Communication Satellites*, 2.

66. Ibid., 2.

67. Fawcett, *Outer Space*, 46. See also Martinez, *Communication Satellites*, 9.

68. Ali Al-Mashat, "The Arab Satellite Communications System," *AIAA 9th Satellite Communications Conference Proceedings* (San Diego, March 1982), 191, cited in Martinez, *Communication Satellites*, 10.

69. Goldman, *American Space Law* (1996), 46–47.

70. W. Pierce and N. Jequier, *Telecommunications and Development: General Synthesis Report on the Contribution of Telecommunications to Economic and Social Development* (Geneva and Paris: International Telecommunication Union and Organization for Economic Cooperation and Development, 1982), cited in Martinez, *Communications Satellites*, 35.

71. Martinez, *Communication Satellites*, 38.

72. Edward Miles, "Transnationalism in Space: Inner and Outer," *International Organization* 25 (summer 1971): 602.

73. Martinez, *Communication Satellites*, 15.

74. Edmund Andrews, "Tiny Tonga Seeks Satellite Empire in Space," *New York Times*, 28 August 1990, 1, C17.

75. Martinez, *Communication Satellites*, 12–13.

Chapter 7

Conclusion

Of making many books there is no end; and much study is a
weariness of the flesh. Let us hear the conclusion of the whole
matter.

—Ecclesiastes 12:12–13

The material in this volume has ranged across a wide variety of historical
eras, resources, and regimes. This conclusion addresses two sets of questions.
First, is the modified analytic framework used here a useful approach for
analyzing the global commons? What is the next step? And second, after
reviewing the history and structure of these global commons, do current
trends point to the Grotian moment suggested in chapter 1, "a time in which
a fundamental change of circumstances [creates] the need for a different
world structure and a different international law"?[1]

The Analytic Framework

Sustainable management of global commons requires an analytic framework
that recognizes fundamental institutional characteristics defining all common pool resource regimes. The analytic framework developed in chapter 2
provides an excellent starting point, although the multitude of regime
designs discussed in this book presents a formidable problem for the analyst.
   The first component of the analytic framework addresses three levels of
institutional choice: constitutional, collective, and operational. (See box 7.1,
Analytical Framework for the Global Commons.) Constitutional choices
(e.g., who will be a member of the regime) are free choices made by nation-
states. Any country may enter into treaty arrangements, subject to interna-

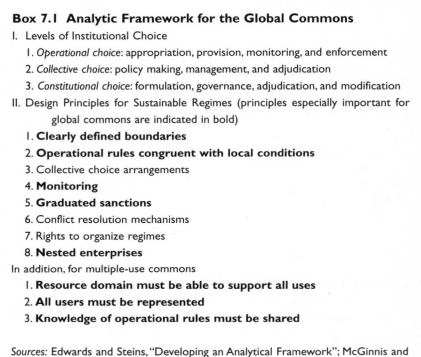

Box 7.1 Analytic Framework for the Global Commons

I. Levels of Institutional Choice

   1. *Operational choice*: appropriation, provision, monitoring, and enforcement

   2. *Collective choice*: policy making, management, and adjudication

   3. *Constitutional choice*: formulation, governance, adjudication, and modification

II. Design Principles for Sustainable Regimes (principles especially important for global commons are indicated in bold)

   1. **Clearly defined boundaries**

   2. **Operational rules congruent with local conditions**

   3. Collective choice arrangements

   4. **Monitoring**

   5. **Graduated sanctions**

   6. Conflict resolution mechanisms

   7. Rights to organize regimes

   8. **Nested enterprises**

In addition, for multiple-use commons

   1. **Resource domain must be able to support all uses**

   2. **All users must be represented**

   3. **Knowledge of operational rules must be shared**

Sources: Edwards and Steins, "Developing an Analytical Framework"; McGinnis and Ostrom, "Institutional Analysis"; Ostrom, *Governing the Commons*

tional recognition of that country as a sovereign nation. However, participation in a treaty regime is also limited by factors peculiar to each nation-state. Regardless of the regime or any of its characteristics, goals, and outcomes, a nation is a party to the regime only if its internal national ratification processes are also satisfied. Thus, for international agreements, constitutional choice is complicated by external acceptance of eligibility for regime membership and internal willingness to agree to the central government's decision to participate in the regime.

Collective choices for a regime may be made at the international level (e.g., the International Telecommunications Union) or the national level (e.g., the U.S. Federal Communications Commission). More rarely, collective choice decisions are made at the subnational level; for example, in the United States, some state governments exercise considerable control over anadromous fish.

Operational choices, which carry the heaviest burden for monitoring and sanctioning, may also be made at several levels, and the problem of implementation of international treaties by national and subnational units permeates any discussion of institutional choice. For example, national governments may monitor compliance with ocean dumping regulations under the International Convention for the Prevention of Pollution from Ships (MARPOL) or they may delegate the responsibility to various port authorities. In the United States, state governments have substantial authority for wildlife management, an area that is subject to numerous international agreements.

Thus, the levels of institutional choice are enormously complex regarding global commons. This is not the same dynamic that exists in *nested enterprises*, which rest on the idea that institutions develop in hierarchial levels that are sustained to some extent by successful management of their constituent parts. If the resource domains are composed of nested domains, each with its own regime, but constitutional and collective institutional choices are made in institutional arenas that do not match the domains, analytical chaos erupts. This is why *clearly defined boundaries* are so important. The telecommunications regime is effective because its institutional choice levels and resource domains are well matched. Constitutional choices are made at the international level. Broad collective choice decisions are also made at the international level, with input and agreement from national actors who then turn to their own governments for more focused collective choice decisions on allocation of telecommunications resources. Limits agreed to at the international level minimize the chances of international conflicts arising from national allocations, so the national telecommunications decisions are more easily made at the collective and operational levels.

Fisheries regimes are harder to establish because fish are a fugitive resource, sharing and moving among political jurisdictions. It is difficult to nest management enterprises because nesting is generally hierarchical and fish domains are a mixture of nested and overlapping domains. This leads to the second design principle, *operational rules congruent with local conditions*. In other words, regulations that control everyday regime activities must fit the physical conditions where the activities take place. For example, allowable fish catches for a section of ocean must be adjusted for wind, tides, currents, water temperatures, fish food stocks, previous catches, and a number of similar conditions. This is awkward enough in small resource domains, but in complex, multijurisdictional domains, it is extremely troublesome, especially for global regimes in which determination of "local conditions" is often subject to limited data and scientific uncertainty (see chapter 1). This helps explain why the living resources of the ocean have proven so intractable to sustainable management.

Another complication for analysis of global commons regimes is the definition of the user pool. For example, fishermen are the obvious users of fisheries; the consumers of fish products (e.g., human diners, pet cats, or fertilizer companies) are not usually incorporated as "users" of the resource. However, what about fish processors on land or on mother ships at sea? Where is the boundary drawn between users/appropriators and consumers? Are the paying sector members of the telecommunications regime also resource appropriators? They are certainly participants at the levels of collective and operational choice. Definition of how the boundaries of the user pool (design principle 1) must be thought through very carefully for large-scale common pool resource regimes.

The design principles established for multiple-use commons discussed in chapter 2 require that all users are represented in the regime. For global commons, this must also include all formal participants, not just actual appropriators. Thus, noncountry sector members who have access to collective and operational institutional choices in the telecommunications regimes and multinational corporations that participate in the space regime are all considered "users" in an analysis of their global commons regimes. This is not to say that they necessarily have equal voices with other participants, but they should be allowed some voice in institutional decisions.

It is, of course, no surprise that analysis of global commons is more complex than analysis of small-scale common pool resource regimes, which are already remarkably complicated. Before the full utility of the analytic framework can be assessed, it needs to be measured against the historical and descriptive details of a single global commons regime. This is a daunting challenge, especially since such an undertaking will require examination of all the nested and overlapping institutions within the larger regime. Sustainable global commons regimes probably do not rest on commons regimes at all levels; an important analytic task will be to discover the characteristics of the levels at which commons regimes and other types of regimes intersect and the ways in which this affects sustainability.

The cost of including so many common pool resource regimes in one volume is the sacrifice of detail. To be applied constructively, the analytic framework developed in chapter 2 must include a depth of detail that is simply unattainable in this book. However, the modified framework used here demonstrates how such an analysis may increase understanding of global commons regimes; for example, application of the framework in chapter 5 clarified the difficulties in classifying the atmospheric pollution regime as a global commons.

The analytic framework certainly shows great promise for application to large-scale multiple-use commons, providing a unique perspective from which to examine global and international regimes.

Grotian Moment or Incremental Change?

Every generation sees itself as the last bastion of some valued way of life, viewing the preceding generation with nostalgia and the succeeding generation with dismay. Sometimes generational changes are significant, as when the Industrial Revolution transformed European agrarian society, but even such significant changes do not indicate a Grotian moment. They do not reorient the international order or require fundamental change in international law. The first Grotian moment was defined by the passing of feudal society, the rise of the nation-state, and the development of a law among nations. How can a Grotian moment be recognized, especially if the only one in history occurred four centuries ago? Possible indicators include today's globalized view of the environment, technological revolution in communications, and ascendancy of economic considerations in all political spheres, particularly in the heightened value of the world's natural resources.

Government policy makers are increasingly forced toward a globalized view of the world environment, triggered by recognition of impending disasters: the depletion of atmospheric ozone, global warming, acid deposition, and destruction of the rain forests. This recognition has increased the influence of the developing countries in designing and implementing international and global property regimes for several reasons. First, as the economies of developing countries improve, they will generate more of the same environmental problems now plaguing the globe unless the developed nations provide financial and technical assistance. Second, developing countries are reservoirs of valued natural resources that the developed world lacks or has exhausted. Powerful developed nations can no longer make environmental policy decisions without considering the developing nations' interests.

The technological revolution in communications may be a second indicator. Instant telecommunications, independent of cables and other physical connections, allows organizations and nations to make global assessments of environmental conditions. Electronic information exchange is rapid and difficult to control politically. This provides equal access to information and a common vocabulary of events and interpretation that may overwhelm regional and national differences. The developing nations have been able to capitalize on their growing influence in the global arena by insisting on their rights to the telecommunications regime even without the technology to take advantage of those rights. In 1992, the International Telecommunication Union was reorganized to provide more assistance to developing countries and to protect their access to the telecommunications regime.

A final sign that a Grotian moment might be in the wings is the dominance of economic considerations and economic analysis in public policy debates and outcomes.[2] Multinational corporations overshadow national governments in many international spheres; never before in world history have corporate interests unconnected with the interests of a nation-state regularly determined international structures and policies.[3]

Certainly, the developing countries have forged stronger positions in environmental regime negotiations, partly because they have been able to capitalize on both their resource reserves and the danger that they will become producers of significant industrial pollution. In other words, they have learned to work within the current system. Their more radical proposals, however, have not been so successful; for example, international law has not bent to accommodate the common heritage of mankind (CHM) principle in any meaningful way. In addition, the growing power of several Asian nations, especially China, is based not on environmental issues but on economic ones. Thus, it is not yet clear whether the new leverage of the developing nations reflects a profound shift in power and attitudes in the international community or simply indicates a variation of the usual waxing and waning of international coalitions and their influence.

The first Grotian moment occurred at the end of the feudal period as nation-states became the dominant international actors. Examination of the historical development of the global commons, from wide-ranging exploration of ocean law to the recent rapid development of space law, does not seem to indicate such a striking revolution. The law is evolving incrementally; dramatic changes such as the CHM principle have been modified when confronted with practical considerations or have yet to face serious challenges from economic forces. Multinational corporations have not broken out of the old legal mode and continue to operate within the context of international law among nations.

It is probably as difficult to recognize a Grotian moment as it is to recognize a paradigm shift. The entire point of being in a paradigm is that we are not conscious of it, and a Grotian moment may only be recognizable only when it is long past. If the current era is indeed such a moment, we will be forced to come to a new understanding of the international order and to make new institutional arrangements to work within it. International cooperation in environmental issues has become a practical matter of survival rather than a mere philosophical position. Even if the changes described here are not of Grotian magnitude, they do presage a shift in international structures and law that will affect the management of the international and global commons. Reputedly, an ancient Chinese curse is "May you live in interesting times." To live through a Grotian moment would certainly be interesting, but if this is *not* a Grotian moment, we should perhaps be thankful.

Suggested Reading

Stone, Deborah. *Policy Paradox: The Art of Political Decision Making*. New York: Norton, 1997. This is the second edition of *Policy Paradox and Political Reason* (1988), which was so good that readers were buttonholing virtual strangers at conferences in an almost evangelical fervor: "You simply *must* read this!" It explores the role of values and politics in policy making with a fresh and lively style. Although the focus is on American politics, the application is global.

Susskind, Lawrence. *Environmental Diplomacy: Negotiating More Effective Global Agreements*. New York: Oxford University Press, 1994. Susskind draws on analyses of past efforts in negotiating environmental treaties to offer guidelines for improving negotiation efforts. It is an excellent reference, and the techniques work.

Wapner, Paul. *Environmental Activism and World Civic Politics*. Albany: State University of New York Press, 1996. An important and informative book on the roles of transnational environmental activist groups. This one is worth buying.

Notes

1. B. V. A. Röling, "Are Grotius' Ideas Obsolete in an Expanded World?," in *Hugo Grotius and International Relations*, eds. Hedley Bull, Benedict Kingsbury, and Adam Roberts (Oxford: Oxford University Press, 1990), 297–298. Röling credits Richard Falk for the term *Grotian moment*. Richard Falk, "On the Recent Further Decline of International Law," in *Legal Change: Essays in Honour of Julius Stone*, ed. A. R. Blackshield (Sidney, Australia: N.P., 1983), 272.

2. Steven Lee Myers, "Trade Overshadows Human Rights, Survey Says," *New York Times*, 5 December 1996 (http://www.nytimes.com). Myers reports a study by Human Rights Watch that rebuked the United States, members of the North Atlantic Treaty Organization (NATO), and Middle Eastern Nations for ignoring human rights to protect markets. See also Michael McGinnis and Elinor Ostrom, "Institutional Analysis and Global Climate Change: Design Principles for Robust International Regimes," in *Global Climate Change: Social and Economic Research Issues* (Chicago: Midwest Consortium for International Security Studies and Argonne National Laboratory, 1992), 67.

3. The modern corporation itself is a relatively recent legal invention. To give a profit-oriented enterprise the legal rights of a human being is a development that does not astonish us only because we have grown accustomed to its face.

Acronyms

AAOE	Airborne Antarctic Ozone Experiment (1987)
ACMRR	Advisory Committee on Marine Resources Research
AEC	Atomic Energy Commission (United States)
AOSIS	Alliance of Small Island States
ARABSAT	Arab Satellite Communication Organization
ASOC	Antarctic and Southern Ocean Coalition (1978)
ATCM	Antarctic Treaty Consultative Meeting
ATS	Antarctic Treaty System
BIOMASS	Biological Investigation of Marine Antarctic Systems and Stocks
CCAMLR	Convention on the Conservation of Antarctic Marine Living Resources
CCIR	International Radio Consultative Committee (Comité Consultatif International des Radio Communications)

CCITT	International Consultative Committee for Telephony and Telegraphy (Comité Consultatif International Telegraphique et Telephonique)
CCOL	Coordinating Committee on the Ozone Layer
CEP	Chile, Ecuador, and Peru
CFC	Chlorofluorocarbon
CHM	Common heritage of mankind
CIS	Commonwealth of Independent States
CITEJA	International Technical Committee for Aerial Legal Experts (1925)
CITES	Convention on International Trade in Endangered Species of Wild Fauna and Flora
CLS	Critical legal studies
COP1	First Conference of the Parties to the United Nations Framework Convention on Climate Change (1995)
COPUOS	Committee on the Peaceful Uses of Outer Space (also UNCOPUOS)
COSPAR	Committee on Space Research
COSTED	Committee on Science and Technology in Developing Countries
CRAMRA	Convention on the Regulation of Antarctic Mineral Resource Activities
CSAGI	Special Committee on the Geographical Year (Comité Spécial de l'Année Géophysique)
DBS	Direct broadcast satellites

DSDP	Deep Sea Drilling Program
DSIR	Department of Scientific and Industrial Research (New Zealand)
DVDP	Dry Valley Drilling Project
EAMREA	Environmental Impact Assessment of Mineral Resource Exploration and Exploitation in the Antarctic (Group of Specialists, SCAR)
EC	European Community (*see also* EEC and EU)
EEC	European Economic Community (*see also* EC and EU)
EEZ	Exclusive Economic Zone
ELDO	European Launcher Development Organization
EOSAT	Earth Observation Satellite Company
EPA	Environmental Protection Agency (United States)
ERSO	European Space Research Organization
ESA	European Space Agency
EU	European Union (*see also* EC and EEC)
EURATOM	European Community of Atomic Energy
EUTELSAT	European Telecommunications Satellite
FAO	Food and Agriculture Organization of the United Nations
FCCC	Framework Convention on Climate Change
FDA	Food and Drug Administration (United States)

FIBEX   First International BIOMASS Experiment (1981)

GARP   Global Atmospheric Research Programme (*see* WRCP)

GEF   Global Environmental Facility

GEMS   Global Environment Monitoring System

IAA   International Academy of Astronautics

IAATO   International Association of Antarctic Tour Operators

IAD   Institutional analysis and development

IAEA   International Atomic Energy Agency (United Nations)

IAF   International Astronautical Federation

IATA   International Air Traffic Association (1919)

IBEA   International Biomedical Expedition to the Antarctic (1980 and 1981)

IBISO   International Biological Investigation of the Southern Ocean (renamed BIOMASS, 1976)

IBRD   International Bank for Reconstruction and Development (World Bank) (United Nations)

IBTA   International Bureau of Telegraph Administrations

ICAO   International Civil Aviation Organization (1947) (United Nations)

ICJ   International Court of Justice

ICSU   International Council of Scientific Unions

IDNDR	International Decade for Natural Disaster Reduction
IFRB	International Frequency Registration Board
IGBP	International Geosphere-Biosphere Programme
IGC	International Geophysical Cooperation (1959)
IGO	International governmental organization
IGY	International Geophysical Year (1957–1958)
IISL	International Institute of Space Law
ILO	International Labour Organization (United Nations)
IMCO	Intergovernmental Maritime Consultative Organization (United Nations) (*see* IMO)
IMF	International Monetary Fund (United Nations)
IMO	International Maritime Organization (United Nations) (formerly IMCO)
IMOF	Interim Multilateral Ozone Fund
INMARSAT	International Mobile Satellite Organization
INTELSAT	International Telecommunications Satellite Organization
INTERSPUTNIK	International Organization of Space Communications
IOC	Intergovernmental Oceanographic Commission
IPCC	Intergovernmental Panel on Climate Change (United Nations)
IPY	International Polar Year (First, 1882–1883; Second, 1932–1933)

IRPTC	International Register of Potentially Toxic Chemicals
IRU	International Radiotelegraph Union (1906 predecessor to the ITU)
ISA	International Seabed Authority (UNCLOS III)
ISAS	International Survey of Antarctic Seabirds
ISC	Interdisciplinary Scientific Commission (of the Committee on Space Research)
ITU	International Telecommunication Union (formerly International Telegraph Union, 1865 predecessor to the IRU)
IUBS	International Union of Biological Sciences
IUCN	World Conservation Union (formerly International Union for the Conservation of Nature and Natural Resources; name changed 1988)
IUG	International Union of Geography
IUGG	International Union of Geodesy and Geophysics
IWC	International Whaling Commission
LANDSAT	Land satellites (United States)
LOS	Law of the Sea
MAD	Mutual assured destruction
MARPOL	International Convention for the Prevention of Pollution from Ships
MSY	Maximum sustainable yield
NAPAP	National Acid Precipitation Assessment Program (United States)

NAS	National Academy of Sciences (United States)
NASA	National Aeronautics and Space Administration (United States)
NASC	National Advisory Space Council (United States)
NCP	Nonconsultative party
NGO	Nongovernmental organization
NIC	Newly industrialized country
NIEO	New International Economic Order
NOAA	National Oceanic and Atmospheric Administration (United States)
OAS	Organization of American States
OECD	Organization for Economic Cooperation and Development
OPEC	Organization of Petroleum Exporting Countries
OTA	Office of Technology Assessment (United States)
PICAO	Provisional International Civil Aviation Organization (1944–1947)
RARC	Regional Administrative Radio Conference
RISP	Ross Ice Shelf Project
RPOA	Recognized Private Operating Agency (of the International Telecommunication Union)
SARA	Superfund Amendment and Reauthorization Act (1986, United States)
SCAR	Scientific Committee on Antarctic Research (of the

International Council of Scientific Unions) (formerly Special Committee on Antarctic Research; name changed 1961)

SCOR   Special Committee on Oceanic Research (see SCAR)

SDI   Strategic Defense Initiative

SIBEX   Second International BIOMASS Experiment

SPA   Specially Protected Area (Antarctica)

SSSI   Site of Special Scientific Interest (Antarctica)

SST   Supersonic Transport

STEP   Solar-Terrestrial Energy Programme

UNCED   United Nations Conference on the Environment and Development (Rio Conference, Earth Summit)

UNCHE   United Nations Conference on the Human Environment

UNCLOS   United Nations Conferences on the Law of the Sea (UNCLOS I, UNCLOS II, UNCLOS III)

UNCOPUOS   *See* COPUOS

UNDP   United Nations Development Programme

UNECE   United Nations Economic Commission for Europe

UNEP   United Nations Environment Programme

UNESCO   United Nations Educational, Scientific and Cultural Organization

UNFPA   United Nations Population Fund (formerly Fund for Population Activities)

UNIDO   United Nations Industrial Development Organization

UNISPACE '82	Second United Nations Conference on the Exploration and Peaceful Uses of Outer Space
URSI	International Scientific Radio Union (Union Radio Scientifique International)
USGS	United States Geological Survey
VHF	Very high frequency
VLF	Very low frequency
WARC	World Administrative Radio Conference
WARC-ORB	World Administrative Radio Conference on the Use of the Geostationary Satellite Orbits and the Planning of the Space Services Utilizing It (1985)
WARC-ST	World Administrative Radio Conference on Space Telecommunications
WCC	World Climate Conference
WCP	World Climate Programme
WCRP	World Climate Research Programme (formerly GARP)
WHO	World Health Organization
WIPO	World Intellectual Property Organization (United Nations)
WMO	World Meteorological Organization (United Nations)
WWF	Worldwide Fund for Nature
WWW	World Weather Watch

Treaties

Note: The treaties in this list are the major treaties referred to in the text. Readers may wish to consult the World Wide Web site maintained by the Consortium Information Network (CIESIN) for International Earth Science for more detailed information about treaty status (sedac.ciesin.org/pidb/pidb-home.html).

1954   International Convention for the Prevention of Pollution of the Sea by Oil (London). In force 26 July 1958. Amended 1962, 1969.

1958   Convention on the High Seas (Geneva). In force 30 September 1962.

1958   Convention on the Continental Shelf (Geneva). In force 10 June 1964.

1958   Convention on the Territorial Sea and the Contiguous Zone (Territorial Seas Convention) (Geneva). In force 10 September 1964.

1958   Convention on Fishing and Conservation of the Living Resources of the High Seas (Conservation Convention) (Geneva). In force 20 March 1966.

1959   Antarctic Treaty (Washington). In force 23 June 1961.

1964   Agreed Measures for the Conservation of Antarctic Fauna and Flora (Agreed Measures) (Brussels). In force 1 November 1982.

1967   Treaty on Principles Governing the Activities of States in the Exploration and Use of Outer Space, Including the Moon and Other Celestial Bodies (Outer Space Treaty). In force 10 October 1967.

1968   Agreement on the Rescue of Astronauts, the Return of Astronauts, and the Return of Objects Launched into Outer Space (Rescue Agreement). In force 3 December 1968.

1969   International Convention on Civil Liability for Oil Pollution Damage (Brussels). In force 19 June 1975. 1976 Protocol in force 8 April 1981.

1969   International Convention Relating to Intervention on the High Seas in Cases of Oil Pollution Casualties (Brussels). In force 6 May 1975. 1973 Protocol, in force 30 March 1983.

1971   Convention on the Establishment of an International Fund for Compensation for Oil Pollution Damage (Brussels). Amended 1976, not in force. In force 16 October 1978. 1984 Protocol not in force.

1972   Convention for the Conservation of Antarctic Seals (Seal Convention) (London). In force 11 March 1978.

1972   Convention for the Prevention of Marine Pollution by Dumping from Ships and Aircraft (Oslo Convention) (Oslo). In force 7 April 1974. Amended 2 March 1983, in force 1 September 1989. 1989 Protocol not in force.

1972   Convention on International Liability for Damage Caused by Space Objects (Liability Convention). In force 9 October 1973.

1972   Convention on the Prevention of Marine Pollution by Dumping of Wastes and Other Matter (London Convention) (London). In force 30 August 1975. Amended 1978, in force 11 March 1979. Amended 1980, in force 11 March 1989. Amended 1989, not in force.

1973   International Convention for the Prevention of Pollution from Ships (MARPOL). Amended by Protocol of 1978 before entry into force. In force 2 October 1983.

1973   Convention on International Trade in Endangered Species of Wild Fauna and Flora (CITES) (Washington). In force 1 July 1975.

1974   Convention on the Protection of the Marine Environment of the Baltic Sea Area (Helsinki). In force 3 May 1980.

1974   Convention on Registration of Objects Launched into Outer Space (Registration Convention). In force 15 September 1976.

1978   Protocol Relating to the Convention for the Prevention of Pollution from Ships (MARPOL). In force 2 October 1983.

1979   Agreement Governing the Activities of States on the Moon and Other Celestial Bodies (Moon Treaty). In force 11 July 1984.

1979   Convention on the Conservation of European Wildlife and Natural Habitats (Bern). In force 1 June 1982.

1979   Convention on Long-Range Transboundary Air Pollution (Geneva Convention) (Geneva). In force 16 March 1983.

1979   Convention on the Conservation of Migratory Species of Wild Animals (Bonn). In force 1 November 1983.

1980   Convention on the Conservation of Antarctic Marine Living Resources (CCAMLR, Southern Ocean Convention) (Canberra). In force 7 April 1982.

1980   Memorandum of Intent Between Canada and the United States Concerning Transboundary Air Pollution.

1980   Protocol for the Protection of the Mediterranean Sea against Pollution from Land-Based Sources (Athens). In force 17 June 1983.

1982   Memorandum of Understanding on Port State Control (Paris).

1982   United Nations Convention on the Law of the Sea (Law of the Sea Treaty). In force 16 November 1994.

1985   Protocol (to 1979 Geneva Convention) on the Reduction of Sulphur Emissions or Their Transboundary Fluxes by at Least 30 Percent (Helsinki Protocol). In force 2 September 1987.

1985   Convention for the Protection of the Ozone Layer (Vienna Convention) (Vienna). In force 22 September 1988.

1987   Protocol (to 1985 Vienna Convention) on Substances That Deplete the Ozone Layer (Montreal Protocol) (Montreal). In force 1 January 1989. Amended 1990 (London), in force 10 August 1992. Amended 1992 (Copenhagen), in force 14 June 1994.

1988   Protocol (to 1979 Geneva Convention) Concerning the Control of Emissions of Nitrogen Oxides or Their Transboundary Fluxes (Sofia Protocol). In force 2 February 1991.

1988   Convention on the Regulation of Antarctic Mineral Resource Activities (CRAMRA) (Wellington). Not in force.

1991   Protocol (to the Antarctic Treaty) on Environmental Protection (Environmental Protocol) (Madrid). Not in force.

1992   Convention on Biological Diversity (Biodiversity Convention). In force 29 December 1993.

1992   Framework Convention on Climate Change. In force 21 March 1994.

1994   Agreement Relating to the Implementation of Part XI of the United Nations Convention on the Law of the Sea of 10 December 1982. In force 16 November 1994.

Glossary

biological diversity   The extent of variety in plants, animals, and microorganisms and the ecosystems of which they are a part.

black letter law   An informal, nonlegal term indicating the general principles of law accepted by courts or found in statutory law.

Common heritage of mankind (CHM) principle   Identification of some resources, such as deep seabed minerals, as the property of the global human population. CHM proponents then argue that since a community already holds most of the bundle of property rights to the resources, the resources cannot legally be appropriated by any one individual or state.

common pool resources   Subtractable resources managed under a property regime in which a legally defined user pool cannot be efficiently excluded from the resource domain.

commons   Resource domains in which common pool resources are found (for example, Antarctica or outer space).

competitive regulatory policy   A type of public policy that limits the provision of specific goods and services to a few companies or agencies chosen from a group of competitors; the selected companies or agencies are then regulated (for example, the allocation of broadcast frequencies).

convention   A binding written agreement between two or more nations. Conventions may also be called **treaties** or **protocols**, although protocols are usually additions to existing treaties.

distributive policy   A type of public policy that supports private activities that are beneficial to society as a whole but that would not usually be undertaken by the private sector (for example, grazing subsidies).

epistemic community   A policy network formed by scientists, technical experts, and international organizations specializing in a particular policy area.

externality   An effect or consequence, either negative or positive, that is transferred from one party to another without the consent of the recipient. An example of a negative externality is transboundary pollution.

framework convention   A treaty that lays down very general requirements for state actions.

free riders   People or groups who benefit from the efforts of others without bearing any of the costs.

frontier ethic   The perceptions that (1) nature is a cornucopia, (2) science and technology will always find a way to reverse or bypass any environmental problem, and (3) the human species is independent of the world ecosystem.

global commons   Resource domains to which all nations have legal access, such as outer space.

international commons   Resource domains shared by several nations, such as the Mediterranean Sea and Antarctica.

jurisprudence   The science of law. Its function is to clarify the principles on which the law is based.

multilateral treaty   A binding agreement among three or more nations.

natural resource   Material that has economic or social value when extracted from its natural state (for example, fish).

parastatal organization   A quasi-government, quasi-private organization.

party (to a treaty)   A nation-state that has agreed to a treaty and for which the treaty is in force.

precautionary principle   The normative position that when faced with scientific uncertainty about the outcome of a proposed environmental policy, the alternative that poses the least risk should be chosen. In lay terms, "Better safe than sorry."

property   (1) A collection or bundle of rights to a resource that are guaranteed and protected by the government, such as rights of access, exclusion, extraction, or sale of the captured resources; (2) any tangible item to which the owner has an enforceable right of use or any intangible right to which the owner has legal title.

protective regulatory policy   A type of public policy that regulates the conditions under which private activities may take place, such as the setting of emission standards for coal-fired plants.

protocol   A binding written agreement between two or more nations, usually an addition to an existing treaty and often specifying technical standards for the treaty. Protocols must be ratified separately. They may also be called **treaties** or **conventions**.

redistributive policy   A type of public policy that changes the allocation of valued goods and services such as money, property, or rights among different groups (for example, the distribution of welfare benefits).

resource   Anything that is used to meet the needs of an organism.

resource domain   The fixed spatial dimension in which resources are found. For example, research stations (resources) are found in Antarctica (resource domain).

shirking   Uncooperative behavior in which a group member fails to perform as promised on the assumption that he will not be caught.

soft-law approaches   Customary procedures that are not formalized through treaties.

spatial-extension resources   Resources that have value because of their location (for example, geostationary orbits or Antarctic research stations).

transaction costs   Costs of negotiation, execution, and enforcement incurred in creating and sustaining institutions (for example, time and opportunity costs).

treaty   A binding written agreement between two or more nations. Treaties may also be called **conventions** or **protocols**, although protocols are usually additions to existing treaties.

umbrella treaty   A framework convention linked to one or more protocols that address specific issues.

Bibliography

Adger, W. Neil, and Katrina Brown. *Land Use and the Causes of Global Warming*. New York: Wiley, 1994.

Akehurst, Michael. *A Modern Introduction to International Law*. 6th ed. London: Unwin Hyman, 1987.

Allen, Scott. "National Interest and Collective Security in the Ocean Regime." In *Ocean Governance: Strategies and Approaches for the 21st Century*, ed. Thomas Mensah, 20–34. Honolulu: Law of the Sea Institute, 1996.

Al-Mashat, Ali. "The Arab Satellite Communications System." *AIAA 9th Satellite Communications Conference Proceedings* (San Diego, March 1982), 191. Cited in Larry Martinez, *Communication Satellites: Power Politics in Space*. (Dedham, Mass.: Artech, 1985) 10.

Amado, F. V. Garcia. *The Exploitation and Conservation of the Resources of the Sea: A Study of Contemporary International Law*. Leiden: A. W. Sijthoff, 1963.

Anand, R. P. *Origin and Development of the Law of the Sea*. The Hague: Martinus Nijhoff, 1983.

Andrews, Edmund. "Tiny Tonga Seeks Satellite Empire in Space." *New York Times*, 28 August 1990, 1, C17.

Arrhenius, Svante. *Worlds in the Making*. New York: Harper, 1908. Cited in Matthew Paterson, *Global Warming and Global Politics* (New York: Routledge, 1996), 19–20.

Ashford, Douglas E. "Historical Context and Policy Studies." In *History and Context in Comparative Public Policy*, ed. Douglas E. Ashford. Pittsburgh: University of Pittsburgh Press, 1992.

Auburn, F. M. *Antarctic Law and Politics*. Bloomington: Indiana University Press, 1982.

Austin, John. *Lectures on Jurisprudence on the Philosophy of Positive Law*, 5th ed., ed. R. Campbell. London: John Murray, 1885.

———. "The Province of Jurisprudence Determined" (1832). In *The Province of Jurisprudence Determined and the Uses of the Study of Jurisprudence* (London: Wiedenfeld and Nicholson, 1955), 1–361.

———. "The Uses of the Study of Jurisprudence" (1863). In *The Province of Jurisprudence Determined and the Uses of the Study of Jurisprudence* (London: Wiedenfeld and Nicholson, 1955), 363–393.

Baird, Douglas, Robert Gertner, and Randal Picker. *Game Theory and the Law*. Cambridge, Mass.: Harvard University Press, 1994.

Bardach, John. "Sustainable Development of Fisheries." In *Ocean Yearbook 9*, eds. Elisabeth Mann Borgese, Norton Ginsburg, and Joseph Morgan, 57–72. Chicago: University of Chicago Press, 1991.

Barkenbus, Jack N. *Deep Seabed Resources*. New York: Free Press, 1979.

Baty, Thomas. "The Three-Mile Limit." *American Journal of International Law* 22 (July 1928): 503–537.

Bean, Michael J. *The Evolution of National Wildlife Law*. New York: Praeger, 1983.

Benedick, Richard Elliot. *Ozone Diplomacy: New Directions in Safeguarding the Planet*. Cambridge, Mass.: Harvard University Press, 1991.

———. "Protecting the Ozone Layer: New Directions in Diplomacy." In *Preserving the Global Environment: The Challenge of Shared Leadership*, ed. Jessica Tuchman Mathews, 112–153. New York: Norton, 1991.

Berkes, Fikret, ed. *Common Property Resources: Ecology and Community-Based Sustainable Development*. London: Belhaven Press, 1989.

Berlins, Marcel. "A Sea of Troubles for International Law Makers." *The Times*, (London), 12 June 1974, 16(a).

Berman, Harold. *Law and Revolution: The Formation of the Western Legal Tradition*. Cambridge, Mass.: Harvard University Press, 1983.

Bewes, Wyndham. *The Romance of the Law Merchant*. London: n.p., 1923.

Birnie, Patricia, and Alan Boyle. *International Law and the Environment*. Oxford: Clarendon Press, 1993.

Blomkvist, Hans. "The Soft State: Making Policy in a Different Context." In *History and Context in Comparative Public Policy*, ed. Douglas E. Ashford, 117–150. Pittsburgh: University of Pittsburgh Press, 1992.

Bodenheimer, Edgar. *Jurisprudence: The Philosophy and Method of the Law*. Cambridge, Mass.: Harvard University Press, 1962.

Bodin, Jean. *Les six livres de république de J. Bodin Anquein (De république)*. Paris: Chez I. du Puis, 1583.

Borgese, Elisabeth Mann. *The Mines of Neptune*. New York: Abrams, 1985.

Bosco, Joseph. "International Law Regarding Outer Space: An Overview." *Journal of Air Law and Commerce* 55 (1990): 609–651.

Bozeman, Adda. *Politics and Culture in International History.* Princeton, N.J.: Princeton University Press, 1960.

Bryner, Gary. *Blue Skies, Green Politics.* 2nd ed. Washington, D.C.: Congressional Quarterly Books, 1995.

Buchholz, Rogene, Alfred Marcus, and James Post, eds. *Managing Environmental Issues: A Casebook.* Englewood Cliffs, N.J.: Prentice-Hall, 1992.

Buck, Susan J. "Multijurisdictional Resources: Testing a Typology for Program Structuring." In *Common Property Resources: Ecology and Community-Based Sustainable Development,* ed. Fikret Berkes, 127–147. London: Belhaven Press, 1989.

———. "No Tragedy on the Commons." *Environmental Ethics* 7, 1 (spring 1985): 49–61.

Buck, Susan J., and Edward Hathaway. "Designating State Natural Resource Trustees Under the Superfund Amendments." In *Regulatory Federalism, Natural Resources, and Environmental Management,* ed. Michael Hamilton, 83–94. Washington, D.C.: American Society for Public Administration, 1990.

Bull, Hedley. "The Importance of Grotius in the Study of International Relations." In *Hugo Grotius and International Relations,* eds. Hedley Bull, Benedict Kingsbury, and Adam Roberts, 65–93. Oxford: Oxford University Press, 1990.

Cairns, Huntington. *Legal Philosophy from Plato to Hegel.* Baltimore: Johns Hopkins University Press, 1949.

Caldwell, Lynton. "Beyond Environmental Diplomacy: The Changing Institutional Structure of International Cooperation." In *International Environmental Diplomacy,* ed. John Carroll, 13–27. Cambridge: Cambridge University Press, 1988.

———. *International Environmental Policy.* Durham, N.C.: Duke University Press, 1984.

———. *International Environmental Policy.* 2nd ed. Durham, N.C.: Duke University Press, 1990.

———. "International Environmental Politics: America's Response to Global Imperatives." In *Environmental Policy in the 1990s,* eds. Norman Vig and Michael Kraft, 301–321. Washington, D.C.: Congressional Quarterly Books, 1990.

Carlson, Peter. "Has NASA Lost Its Way?" *The Washington Post Magazine,* 30 May 1993, 10–15, 22–28.

Chandler, Melinda. "The Biodiversity Convention: Selected Issues of Interest to the International Lawyer." *Colorado Journal of International Environmental Law and Policy* 4 (1993): 141–175

Chapman, Wilbert McLeod. "Food from the Sea and Public Policy." In *Ocean Resources and Public Policy,* ed. T. Saunders English, 64–75. Seattle: University of Washington Press, 1973.

"'Chilean Antarctica' Stamp." *New York Times*, 5 December 1946, 43.

Chiras, Daniel. *Environmental Science: Action for a Sustainable Future*. 4th ed. New York: Benjamin-Cummings, 1994.

Christol, Carl Q. *The Modern International Law of Outer Space*. Elmsford, N.Y.: Pergamon Press, 1982.

"Chronological Summary: Events of 1992." *Colorado Journal of International Environmental Law and Policy* 4 (1993): 229–239.

Churchill, Winston. *The Birth of Britain*. New York: Dodd, Mead, 1958.

Coase, Ronald. "The Lighthouse in Economics." *Journal of Law and Economics* 17 (1974): 357–376.

———. "The Nature of the Firm." *Economica* 4 (1937): 386–405.

Cohen, Morris R., and Felix S. Cohen, eds. *Readings in Jurisprudence and Legal Philosophy*. Boston: Little, Brown, 1951.

"Collective Action Needed to Protect Fish Stocks." *Greensboro News and Record*, 7 August 1993, A20.

Commons, J. R. *Legal Foundations of Capitalism*. New York: Macmillan, 1924; Madison: University of Wisconsin Press, 1968.

Congressional Research Service. *Ocean Manganese Nodules*. Washington, D.C.: Government Printing Office, February 1976.

Cooper, John. *The Right to Fly*. New York: Holt, 1947.

Couratier, Josyane. "The Regime for the Conservation of Antarctica's Living Resources." In *Antarctic Resources Policy: Scientific, Legal, and Political Issues*, ed. Francisco Orrego Vicuña, 139–148. Cambridge: Cambridge University Press, 1983.

Crutchfield, James. "Resources from the Sea." In *Ocean Resources and Public Policy*, ed. T. Saunders English, 105–133. Seattle: University of Washington Press, 1973.

Curtis, Anthony, ed. *Space Almanac*. Woodsboro, Md: ARCsoft, 1989.

D'Amato, Anthony. *The Concept of Custom in International Law*. Ithaca, N.Y.: Cornell University Press, 1971.

———. "What 'Counts' as Law?" In *Law-Making in the Global Community*, ed. Nicholas Onuf, 83–107. Durham, N.C.: Carolina Academic Press, 1982.

Darman, Richard. "The Law of the Sea: Rethinking U.S. Interests." *Foreign Affairs* 56 (1978): 373–395.

De Soares Guimaraes, L. F. Macedo. "The Antarctic Treaty System from the Perspective of a New Consultative Party." In Polar Research Board, *Antarctic Treaty System: An Assessment*, 337–344. Washington, D.C.: National Academy Press, 1986.

Diamond, Martin. "Ethics and Politics: The American Way." In *Moral Foundations of the American Republic*, 3rd ed., ed. Robert Horwitz, 75–108. Charlottesville: University of Virginia Press, 1986.

Douglas, Mary, and Aaron Wildavsky. *Risk and Culture*. Berkeley: University of California Press, 1982.

Downes, David. "Global Trade, Local Economies, and the Biodiversity Convention." In *Biodiversity and the Law*, ed. William Snape III, 202–216. Washington, D.C.: Island Press, 1996.

Drewry, David. "Conflict of Interest in the Use of Antarctica." In *Antarctic Science: Global Concerns*, eds. Gotthilf Hempel, 12–30. New York: Springer-Verlag, 1994.

Dubs, Marne. "Minerals of the Deep Sea: Politics and Economics." In *Ocean Yearbook*, eds. Elisabeth Mann Borgese and Norton Ginsburg, 55–84. Chicago: University of Chicago Press, 1986.

Eastman, Joseph T., and Arthur Devries. "Antarctic Fishes." *Scientific American* 255, 5 (November 1986): 106–114.

Eckert, Ross. *The Enclosure of Ocean Resources: Economics and the Law of the Sea*. Stanford, Calif.: Hoover Institution Press, 1979.

Edwards, Victoria, and Nathalie Steins. "Developing an Analytical Framework for Multiple-Use Commons." Paper presented at conference of the International Association for the Study of Common Property, Berkeley, Calif., 5–8 June 1996 (Department of Land and Construction Management, University of Portsmouth, Portsmouth, Hampshire PO1 2LF, United Kingdom).

Elson, Derek. *Atmospheric Pollution: Causes, Effects, and Control Policies*. Oxford: Basil Blackwell, 1987.

Falk, Richard. "On the Recent Further Decline of International Law." In *Legal Change: Essays in Honour of Julius Stone*, ed. A. R. Blackshield, 272. Sidney, Australia: n.p., 1983. Cited in B. V. A. Röling, "Are Grotius' Ideas Obsolete in an Expanded World?," in *Hugo Grotius and International Relations*, eds. Hedley Bull, Benedict Kingsbury, and Adam Roberts (Oxford: Oxford University Press, 1990), 297–298.

Farnau, J. C., B. G. Gardiner, and J. D. Shanklin. "Large Losses of Total Ozone in Antarctica Reveal Seasonal ClO_x/NO_x Interaction." *Nature* 315 (1985): 207–210.

Fawcett, J. E. S. *Outer Space: New Challenges to Law and Policy*. Oxford: Clarendon Press, 1984.

Feldman, David, ed. *Global Climate Change and Public Policy*. Chicago: Nelson-Hall, 1997.

Finch, Michael. "Limited Space: Allocating the Geostationary Orbit." *Northwestern Journal of International Law and Business* 7 (1986): 788–802.

"Fish Damage Linked to UV." *New York Times*, 18 March 1997 (http://www.nytimes.com).

Forster, Bruce. *The Acid Rain Debate: Science and Special Interests in Policy Formation*. Ames: Iowa State University Press, 1993.

Fourier, Jean-Baptiste-Joseph. "Mémoire sur les températures du globe terrestre et des espace planétaires." *Mémoires de l'Académie Royal de Science de l'Institut de France* 7 (1827): 659–704. Cited in Matthew Paterson, *Global Warming and Global Politics* (New York: Routledge, 1996), 17.

Fuchs, V. E. "Antarctica: Its History and Development." In *Antarctic Resources Policy: Scientific, Legal, and Political Issues*, ed. Francisco Orrego Vicuña, 13–19. Cambridge: Cambridge University Press, 1983.

Fulton, Thomas Wemyss. *The Sovereignty of the Sea.* Edinburgh and London: William Blackwood, 1911; Millwood, N.Y.: Kraus Reprint, 1976.

Gehrig, James J. "The Geostationary Orbit—Technology and Law." *19th Proceedings of the Colloquium on the Law of Outer Space* 19 (1976): 267–277.

Goldman, Nathan. *American Space Law: International and Domestic.* Ames: Iowa State University Press, 1988.

———. *American Space Law: International and Domestic.* San Diego, CA: Univelt, 1996.

Goldwin, Robert A. "Common Sense vs. 'The Common Heritage.'" In *Law of the Sea: U.S. Policy Dilemma*, eds. Bernard Oxman, David Caron, and Charles Buderi, 59–75. San Francisco: ICS Press, 1983.

Goodsell, Charles. "Administration as Ritual." *Public Administration Review* 49 (1989): 161–166.

Gow, Anthony. "The Ice Sheet." In *Antarctica*, ed. Trevor Hatherton, 221–258. New York: Praeger, 1965.

Griffiths, Robert J. "From the Ocean Floor to Outer Space: The Third World and Global Commons Negotiations." *Journal of Third World Studies* 9, 2 (1992): 375–389.

———. *Freedom of the Seas or The Right Which Belongs to the Dutch to Take Part in the East Indian Trade (Mare liberum)*, (1608), trans. Ralph Van Deman Magoffin. New York: Oxford University Press, 1916; New York: Arno Press, 1972.

Grotius, Hugo. *The Freedom of the Seas, or The Right Which Belongs to the Dutch to Take Part in the East Indian Trade (Mare liberum)*, (1608), trans. Ralph Van Deman Magoffin. In *Classics of International Law*, ed. James Brown Scott. New York: Carnegie Endowment for International Peace, 1925.

Haas, Peter. *Saving the Mediterranean: The Politics of International Environmental Cooperation.* New York: Columbia University Press, 1990.

Haley, Andrew. *Space Law and Government.* New York: Appleton-Century-Crofts, 1963.

Hamilton, Alexander, James Madison, and John Jay. *The Federalist Papers* (1788). New York: New American Free Library, 1961.

Hatherton, Trevor. "Antarctica Prior to the Antarctic Treaty—A Historical Perspective." In Polar Research Board, *Antarctic Treaty System: An Assessment*, 15–32. Washington, D.C.: National Academy Press, 1986.

Hawkes, Nigel. "Science Briefing: Long Lost Lake." *The Times* (London), 20 May 1996, 14.

Heap, John A., and Martin Holdgate. "The Antarctic Treaty System as an Environmental Mechanism—An Approach to Environmental Issues." In Polar Research Board, *Antarctic Treaty System: An Assessment*, 195–210. Washington, D.C.: National Academy Press, 1986.

Henderson-Sellars, B. *Pollution of Our Atmosphere*. Bristol, England: Adam Higler, 1984.

Henkin, Louis. *International Law: Politics and Values*. Boston: Martinus Nijhoff, 1995.

Herter, Christian A. "The Electromagnetic Spectrum: A Critical Natural Resource." In *Transboundary Resources Law*, eds. Albert Utton and Ludwik Teclaff, 89–101. Boulder, Colo.: Westview Press, 1987.

Hewison, Grant. "The Role of Environmental Non-Governmental Organizations." In *Ocean Governance: Strategies and Approaches for the 21st Century*, ed. Thomas Mensah, 115–137. Honolulu: Law of the Sea Institute, 1996.

Hey, E. "The Precautionary Concept in Environmental Policy and Law: Institutionalizing Caution." *Georgetown International Environmental Law Review* 4 (1992): 303–318.

Holling, C. S. "Myths of Ecological Stability: Resilience and the Problem of Failure." In *Studies in Crisis Management*, eds. C. F. Smart and W. T. Stanbury, 97–109. Montreal: Butterworth and Institute for Research on Public Policy, 1978.

Horwitz, Morton. "The Transformation in the Conception of Property in American Law, 1780–1860." *University of Chicago Law Review* 40 (1973): 248–290.

Hosking, Eric. *Antarctic Wildlife*. New York: Facts on File, 1982.

Hoskins, W. G., and L. Dudley Stamp. *The Common Land of England and Wales*. London: Collins, 1965.

"How Do You Mean, 'Fair'?" *The Economist*, 29 May 1993, 71.

Hughes, Charles Evans. Letter to A. W. Prescott. In G. H. Hackworth, *Digest of International Law*, vol. 1, 1245. Washington, D.C.: Government Printing Office, 1963. Cited in Jeffrey D. Myhre, *The Antarctic Treaty System: Politics, Law, and Diplomacy* (Boulder, Colo.: Westview Press, 1986), 24.

Hutchinson, Alan C. "Introduction." In *Critical Legal Studies*, ed. Alan C. Hutchinson, 1–14. Totowa, N.J.: Rowman and Littlefield, 1989.

Irving, Patricia, ed. *Acid Deposition: State of Science and Technology, Summary Report of the United States National Acid Precipitation Assessment Program*. Washington, D.C.: Government Printing Office, September 1991. Cited in Jacqueline Vaughn Switzer, *Environmental Politics: Domestic and Global Dimensions* (New York: St. Martin's Press, 1994), 260, n. 10.

Jachtenfuchs, Markus. "The European Community and the Protection of the

Ozone Layer." *Journal of Common Market Studies* 28, 3 (March 1980): 263. Cited in Richard Elliot Benedick, *Ozone Diplomacy: New Directions in Safeguarding the Planet*, (Cambridge, Mass.: Harvard University Press, 1991), 24.

Jenks, C. Wilfred. *Space Law*. New York: Praeger, 1965.

Jennings, R. Y. *The Acquisition of Territory in International Law*. Manchester, England: University of Manchester Press, 1963. Cited in Jeffrey D. Myhre, *The Antarctic Treaty System: Politics, Law, and Diplomacy* (Boulder, Colo.: Westview Press, 1986), 8.

Jessup, Philip C., and Howard J. Taubenfeld. *Controls for Outer Space and the Antarctic Analogy*. New York: Columbia University Press, 1959.

Johnson, John. "Pollution and Contamination in Space." In *Law and Politics in Space*, ed. Maxwell Cohen, 37–53. Montreal: McGill-Queens University Press, 1964.

Jones, Thomas. "Manganese." In U.S. Department of the Interior, Bureau of Mines, *Minerals Yearbook*, Vol. 1, *Metals and Minerals*, 691–704. Washington, D.C.: Government Printing Office, 1991.

Kelly, John M. *A Short History of Western Legal Theory*. Oxford: Clarendon Press, 1992.

Kent, George. "Global Fisheries Management." In *The Global Predicament: Ecological Perspectives on World Order*, eds. David Orr and Marvin Soroos, 232–248. Chapel Hill: University of North Carolina Press, 1979.

Keohane, Robert, Peter Haas, and Marc Levy. "The Effectiveness of International Environmental Institutions." In *Institutions for the Earth: Sources of Effective International Environmental Protection*, eds. Peter Haas, Robert O. Keohane, and Marc A. Levy, 3–24. Cambridge, Mass.: MIT Press, 1993.

King, H. G. R. *The Antarctic*. New York: Arco, 1970.

Kingsbury, Benedict, and Adam Roberts. "Introduction: Grotian Thought in International Relations." In *Hugo Grotius and International Relations*, eds. Hedley Bull, Benedict Kingsbury, and Adam Roberts, 1–64. Oxford: Oxford University Press, 1990.

Kiss, Alexandre, and Dinah Shelton. *International Environmental Law*. Ardsley-on-Hudson, N.Y.: Transnational, 1991.

Koehler, James, and Scott Hajost. "1989: Advent of a New Era for EPA's International Activities." *Colorado Journal of International Environmental Law and Policy* 1, 1 (summer 1990): 181–187.

Krasner, Stephen. "Sovereignty: An Institutional Perspective." *Comparative Political Studies* 21, 1 (1988): 55–94.

———. "Structural Causes and Regime Consequences: Regimes as Intervening Variables." *International Organization* 36 (1982): 185–205.

Lansdown, Lord. Speech to the House of Lords, 18 February 1960. *Parliamentary Debates*, Lords, vol. 221 cols. 188–191. Cited in M. J. Peterson, *Man-*

aging the Frozen South: The Creation and Evolution of the Antarctic Treaty System (Berkeley: University of California Press, 1988), 75.

"Latins Ask Widening of Offshore Limits." *New York Times*, 20 July 1965, n.p.

"Law Students Buy and Hold Pollution Rights." *New York Times*, 31 March 1995, B13.

Lay, S. Houston, and Howard Taubenfeld. *The Law Relating to Activities of Man in Space*. Chicago: University of Chicago Press, 1970.

"Leaving the Feeding Grounds." *The Economist*, 7 August 1993, 40.

Lehman, John. "The Navy and the Law of the Sea." Letter to the editor, *Washington Post*, 30 July 1982.

Leopold, Aldo. *Sand County Almanac*. Oxford: Oxford University Press, 1949, 1977.

Lerman, Matthew. *Marine Biology*. Menlo Park, Calif.: Benjamin-Cummings, 1986.

Levine, Joel S. "A Planet at Risk." Public lecture, 20 February 1993, Greensboro, N.C.

Li, Yuwen. *Transfer of Technology for Deep Sea-Bed Mining: The 1982 Law of the Sea Convention and Beyond*. Boston: Martinus Nijhoff, 1994.

Lipschutz, Ronnie. "Bioregional Politics and Local Organization in Policy Responses to Global Climate Change." In *Global Climate Change and Public Policy*, ed. David Feldman, 102–122. Chicago: Nelson-Hall, 1997.

Litfin, Karen. *Ozone Discourses: Science and Politics in Global Environmental Cooperation*. New York: Columbia University Press, 1994.

McCay, Bonnie, and James Acheson, eds. *The Question of the Commons: The Culture and Ecology of Communal Resources*. Tucson: University of Arizona Press, 1987.

McDougal, Myres S. "International Law and the Law of the Sea." In *The Law of the Sea: Offshore Boundaries and Zones*, ed. Lewis Alexander, 1–23. Columbus: Ohio State University Press, 1967.

———. "The Prospects for a Regime in Outer Space." In *Law and Politics in Space*, ed. Maxwell Cohen, 105–123. Montreal: McGill-Queens University Press, 1964.

McGinnis, Michael. "Collective Action, Governance, and International Relations: The MAORCA Framework." Unpublished paper, November 1996 (Michael McGinnis, Department of Political Science, Indiana University, Bloomington, Ind. 47405).

McGinnis, Michael, and Elinor Ostrom. "Institutional Analysis and Global Climate Change: Design Principles for Robust International Regimes." In *Global Climate Change: Social and Economic Research Issues*, 45–85. Chicago: Midwest Consortium for International Security Studies and Argonne National Laboratory, 1992.

Maine, Sir Henry Sumner. *Ancient Law* (1861) N.p.: Dorset Press, 1986.

———. *Lectures on the Early History of Institutions*. London: John Murray, 1889.

Makhijani, Arjun, and Kevin Gurney. *Mending the Ozone Hole: Science, Technology, and Policy*. Cambridge, Mass.: MIT Press, 1995.

Maley, P. D. "Communications Satellites in Geostationary Orbit." In *Cambridge Encyclopedia of Space*, ed. Michael Rycroft, 244. Cambridge: Cambridge University Press, 1990.

Martinez, Larry. *Communication Satellites: Power Politics in Space*. Dedham, Mass.: Artech, 1985.

Marx, Wesley. *The Oceans: Our Last Resource*. San Francisco: Sierra Club Books, 1981.

Meinzen-Dick, Ruth, and Lee Ann Jackson. "Multiple Uses, Multiple Users of Water Resources." Paper presented at conference of the International Association for the Study of Common Property, Berkeley, Calif., 5–8 June 1996 (International Food Policy Research Institute, 1200 17th St. NW, Washington, D.C. 20036)

Mensah, Thomas, ed. *Ocean Governance: Strategies and Approaches for the 21st Century*. Honolulu: Law of the Sea Institute, 1996.

Miles, Edward. "Transnationalism in Space: Inner and Outer." *International Organization* 25 (summer 1971): 602–625.

"Milestone for Law of Sea Treaty." *The InterDependent* 19, 4 (winter 1993–1994): 4.

Miller, G. Tyler Jr. *Living in the Environment*. 5th ed. Belmont, Calif.: Wadsworth, 1988.

Molina, Mario, and F. Sherwood Rowland. "Stratospheric Sink for Chlorofluoromethanes: Chlorine Atom Catalysed Destruction of Ozone." *Nature* 249 (1974): 810–812. Cited in Richard Elliot Benedick, *Ozone Diplomacy: New Directions in Safeguarding the Planet* (Cambridge, Mass.: Harvard University Press, 1991), 10.

"Multinationals: Back in Fashion." *The Economist*, 27 March 1993, 5–8.

Myers, Steven Lee. "Trade Overshadows Human Rights, Survey Says." *New York Times*, 5 December 1996 (http://www.nytimes.com).

Myhre, Jeffrey D. *The Antarctic Treaty System: Politics, Law, and Diplomacy*. Boulder, Colo.: Westview Press, 1986.

Nangle, Orval. "Stratospheric Ozone: United States Regulation of Chlorofluorocarbons." *Environmental Affairs* 16 (1989): 531–580.

Nash, Roderick. *Wilderness and the American Mind*. 3rd ed. New Haven, Conn.: Yale University Press, 1982.

———. ed. *American Environmentalism: Readings in Conservation History*. 3rd ed. New York: McGraw-Hill, 1990.

Nelson, L. D. M. "Some Observations on the Agreement Implementing Part XI of the 1982 Convention on the Law of the Sea." In *Ocean Governance: Strate-*

gies and Approaches for the 21st Century, ed. Thomas Mensah, 233–218. Honolulu: Law of the Sea Institute, 1996.

Netting, Robert. *Balancing on an Alp.* Cambridge: Cambridge University Press, 1981.

Neustadt, Richard, and Ernest R. May. *Thinking in Time: The Uses of History for Decision Makers.* New York: Free Press, 1988.

Newton, David. *Global Warming.* Oxford: ABC-CLIO, 1993.

Oakerson, Ronald. "Analyzing the Commons: A Framework." In *Making the Commons Work: Theory, Practice, and Policy,* ed. Daniel Bromley, 41–59. San Francisco: ICS Press, 1992.

———. "A Model for the Analysis of Common Property Problems." In National Research Council, *Proceedings of the Conference on Common Property Resource Management.* Washington, D.C.: National Academy Press, 1986.

Oliver, John E., and John J. Hidore. *Climatology: An Introduction.* Columbus, Ohio: Merrill, 1984.

O'Riordan, Timothy, and J. Cameron, eds. *Interpreting the Precautionary Principle.* London: Earthscan, 1994.

———. "The Rudiments of a Theory of the Origins, Survival, and Performance of Common-Property Institutions." In *Making the Commons Work: Theory, Practice, and Policy,* ed. Daniel Bromley. San Francisco: ICS Press, 1992, 293–318.

Ostrom, Elinor, Roy Gardner, and James Walker. *Rules, Games and Common Pool Resources.* Ann Arbor: University of Michigan Press, 1994.

Ostrom, Elinor. *Governing the Commons: The Evolution of Institutions for Collective Action.* Cambridge: Cambridge University Press, 1990.

Oxman, Bernard H. "Summary of the Law of the Sea Convention." In *The Law of the Sea: U.S. Policy Dilemma,* eds. Bernard Oxman, David Caron, and Charles Buderi, 147–161. San Francisco: ICS Press, 1983.

Paterson, Matthew. *Global Warming and Global Politics.* New York: Routledge, 1996.

Pearce, David. "The European Community Approach to the Control of Chlorofluorocarbons." Paper presented UNEP Workshop on the Control of Chlorofluorocarbons, Leesburg, Va., 8–12 September 1986). Cited in Richard Elliot Benedick, *Ozone Diplomacy: New Directions in Safeguarding the Planet* (Cambridge, Mass.: Harvard Univerity Press, 1991), 25.

Peterson, M. J. *Managing the Frozen South: The Creation and Evolution of the Antarctic Treaty System.* Berkeley: University of California Press, 1988.

Philbrick, Francis S. "Changing Conceptions of Property in Law." *University of Pennsylvania Law Review* 86 (1938): 691ff. In *Readings in Jurisprudence and Legal Philosophy,* eds. Morris R. Cohen and Felix S. Cohen, 38–48. Boston: Little, Brown, 1951.

Pierce, W., and N. Jequier. "Telecommunications and Development: General

Synthesis Report on the Contribution of Telecommunications to Economic and Social Development." Geneva and Paris: International Telecommunication Union and Organization for Economic Cooperation and Development, 1982. Cited in Larry Martinez, *Communication Satellites: Power Politics in Space* (Dedham, Mass.: Artech, 1985), 35.

Pitt, David. "Talks at U.N. Combat Threat to Oceans' Species from Overfishing." *New York Times*, 25 July 1993, 7.

Ponting, Clive. *A Green History of the World: The Environment and the Collapse of Great Civilization.* New York: Penguin, 1991.

Porter, Gareth, and Janet Welsh Brown. *Global Environmental Politics.* 2nd ed. Boulder, Colo.: Westview Press, 1996.

Qasim, S. Z., and H. P. Rajan. "The Antarctic Treaty System from the Perspective of a New Member." In Polar Research Board, *Antarctic Treaty System: An Assessment*, 345–374. Washington, D.C.: National Academy Press, 1986.

Quigg, Philip. *A Pole Apart: The Emerging Issue of Antarctica.* New York: McGraw-Hill, 1983.

Reiff, Henry. *The United States and the Treaty Law of the Sea.* Minneapolis: University of Minnesota Press, 1959.

Reinhardt, Forest. "Du Pont Freon® Products Division." In *Managing Environmental Issues: A Casebook*, eds. Rogene Buchholz, Alfred Marcus, and James Post, 261–286. Englewood Cliffs, N.J.: Prentice-Hall, 1992.

ReVelle, Penelope, and Charles ReVelle. *The Environment: Issues and Choices for Society.* Boston: Jones and Bartlett, 1988.

———. *The Global Environment: Securing a Sustainable Future.* Boston: Jones and Bartlett, 1992.

Revelle, Roger, and Hans Suess, "Carbon Dioxide Exchange Between Atmosphere and Ocean, and the Question of an Increase in Atmospheric CO_2 During the Past Decade." *Tellus* 9 (1957): 18–27. Cited in Matthew Paterson, *Global Warming and Global Politics* (New York: Routledge, 1996), 22.

Rifkin, Jeremy. *Biosphere Politics.* New York: Crown, 1991.

Ripley, Randall, and Grace Franklin. *Congress, the Bureaucracy, and Public Policy*, 5th ed. Belmont, Calif.: Wadsworth, 1991.

Robertson, Horace B. "The Suppression of Pirate Radio Broadcasting," *Law and Contemporary Problems* 45, 1 (winter 1982): 71–101.

Robinson, David. "Common Pool Resources, Heritage, and the Global Commons: Observations and Management Suggestions." Master's thesis, Sydney University Law School, Sydney, Australia, 1991.

Roe, Emery. "Global Warming as Analytic Tip." In *Global Climate Change and Public Policy*, ed. David Feldman 19–38. Chicago: Nelson-Hall, 1997.

Röling, B. V. A. "Are Grotius' Ideas Obsolete in an Expanded World?" In *Hugo Grotius and International Relations*, eds. Hedley Bull, Benedict Kingsbury, and Adam Roberts, 281–299. Oxford: Oxford University Press, 1990.

Roots, E. Fred. "The Role of Science in the Antarctic Treaty System." In Polar

Research Board, *Antarctic Treaty System: An Assessment*, 169–184. Washington, D.C.: National Academy Press, 1986.

Rose, Carol M. *Property and Persuasion: Essays on the History, Theory, and Rhetoric of Ownership.* Boulder, Colo.: Westview Press, 1994.

——. "Property as Storytelling: Perspectives from Game Theory, Narrative Theory, Feminist Theory." *Yale Journal of Law and the Humanities* 2 (1990): 27–57.

Rosenbaum, Walter A. *Energy, Politics, and Public Policy.* 2nd ed. Washington, D.C.: Congressional Quarterly Books, 1987.

——. *Environmental Politics and Policy.* Washington, D.C.: Congressional Quarterly Press, 1985.

Rosenblum, Mort. "Plan to Develop Antarctica Leaves Environmentalists Cold." *Greensboro News and Record*, 8 October 1989, 1, A16.

Rowlands, Ian. *The Politics of Global Atmospheric Change.* Manchester, England: Manchester University Press, 1995.

Rutford, Robert H. "Summary of Science in Antarctic Prior to and Including the International Geophysical Year." In Polar Research Board, *Antarctic Treaty System: An Assessment*, 87–101. Washington, D.C.: National Academy Press, 1986.

Sahlins, Marshall. *Stone Age Economics.* Chicago: Aldine-Atherton, 1972.

Sand, Peter. "International Cooperation: The Environmental Experience." In *Preserving the Global Environment: The Challenge of Shared Leadership*, ed. Jessica Tuchman Mathews, 236–279. New York: Norton, 1991.

——. *Lessons Learned in Global Environmental Governance.* Washington, D.C.: World Resources Institute, June 1990.

Sanger, Clyde. *Ordering the Oceans: The Making of the Law of the Sea.* Toronto: University of Toronto Press, 1987.

Satchell, Michael. "The Rape of the Oceans." *U.S. News and World Report* 112, 24 (22 June 1992): 64–75.

Schneider, Keith. "Ozone Depletion Harming Sea Life." *New York Times*, 16 November 1991, 6, col. 6.

Sebenius, James. *Negotiating the Law of the Sea.* Cambridge, Mass.: Harvard University Press, 1984.

Seitz, John. *Global Issues: An Introduction.* Cambridge, Mass.: Blackwell Publishing, 1995.

Selden, John. *Mare clausum (The right and dominion of the sea).* London: Richard Meighen, 1635.

Shapley, Deborah. *The Seventh Continent: Antarctica in a Resource Age.* Washington, D.C.: Resources for the Future, 1985.

Smith, Herbert A., ed. *Great Britain and the Law of Nations: A Selection of Documents Illustrating the Views of the Government in the United Kingdom upon Matters of International Law.* 2 vols. London: P. S. King, 1932–1935.

Smith, Robert Angus. *Air and Rain: The Beginnings of a Chemical Climatology*. London: Longmans, Green, 1872.

Soroos, Marvin. Beyond Sovereignty. Columbia: University of South Carolina Press, 1986.

———. "The Commons in the Sky: The Radio Spectrum and Geosynchronous Orbit as Issues in Global Policy." *International Organization* 36, 3 (summer 1982): 665–677.

———. "The International Commons: A Historical Perspective." *Environmental Review* 12, 1 (spring 1988): 1–21.

———. "Conflict in the Use and Management of International Commons." In *Perspectives on Environmental Conflict and International Relations*, ed. Jyrki Käkönen, 31–43. London: Pinter, 1992.

Steiner, Henry J., and Detlev F. Vagts. *Transnational Legal Problems: Materials and Texts*. Mineola, N.Y.: Foundation Press, 1986.

Stevens, William. "Study of Ocean Currents Offers Clues to Global Climate Shifts." *New York Times*, 18 March 1997 (http://www.nytimes.com).

Stoel, Thomas B. Jr., Alan S. Miller, and Breck Milroy. *Fluorocarbon Regulation*. Lexington, Mass.: Heath, 1980. Cited in Richard Elliot Benedick, *Ozone Diplomacy: New Directions in Safeguarding the Planet* (Cambridge, Mass.: Harvard University Press, 1991), 28.

Stolarski, Richard, and Ralph Cicerone. "Stratospheric Chlorine: A Possible Sink for Ozone." *Canadian Journal of Chemistry* 52 (1974): 1610-1615. Cited in Richard Elliot Benedick, *Ozone Diplomacy: New Directions in Safeguarding the Planet* (Cambridge, Mass.: Harvard University Press, 1991), 10.

Stonehouse, B. "Birds and Mammals." In *Antarctica*, ed. Trevor Hatherton, 153–186. New York: Praeger, 1965.

Sugden, David. *Arctic and Antarctica*. Totowa, N.J.: Barnes and Noble, 1982.

Sullivan, Walter. "Antarctica in a Two-Power World." *Foreign Affairs* 36, 1 (1957): 154–166.

Sunquist, Fiona. "Two Species, One Design." *International Wildlife* 26, 5 (September–October 1996): 28–33.

Swarztrauber, Sayre A. *The Three-Mile Limit of Territorial Seas*. Anapolis, Md.: Naval Institute Press, 1972.

Switzer, Jacqueline Vaughn. *Environmental Politics: Domestic and Global Dimensions*. New York: St. Martin's Press, 1994.

"Symposium Launches Space Tourism Industry." *Greensboro News and Record*, 22 March 1997, B6, B9.

Taylor, Lawrence. "'The River Would Run Red with Blood': Community and Common Property in an Irish Fishing Settlement." In *The Question of the Commons: The Culture and Ecology of Communal Resources*, eds. Bonnie McCay and James Acheson, 290–307. Tucson: University of Arizona Press, 1987.

Thompson, Michael. "The Cultural Construction of Nature and the Natural Destruction of Culture." Working paper prepared for the International Institute for Applied Systems Analysis, Laxenberg, Austria, 1984.

Thompson, Michael, Richard Ellis, and Aaron Wildavsky. *Cultural Theory*. Boulder, Colo.: Westview Press, 1990.

Tonnessen, J. N., and O. A. Johnsen. *A History of Modern Whaling*. Abridged English ed. Berkeley: University of California Press, 1982.

Tripp, J. T. B., D. J. Dudek, and Michael Oppenheimer. "Equality and Ozone Protection." *Environment* 29, 6 (1987): 45. Cited in Richard Elliot Benedick, *Ozone Diplomacy: New Directions in Safeguarding the Planet* (Cambridge, Mass.: Harvard University Press, 1991), 28.

United Nations Ozone Secretariat. "The Financial Mechanism," 27 March 1997 (http://www.unep.org/unep/secretar/ozone/finmech.htm).

U.S. Department of State. *Foreign Relations of the United States, 1948*. Vol. 1, part 2. National Security Council paper of 18 July 1948, H.920.5 Bethesda, Md.: Congressional Information Service, 1980. Cited in Jeffrey D. Myhre, *The Antarctic Treaty System: Politics, Law, and Diplomacy* (Boulder, Colo.: Westview Press, 1986), 27.

Van Zandt, David. "The Lessons of the Lighthouse: 'Government' or 'Private' Provision of Goods." *Journal of Legal Studies* 22 (January 1993): 47–72.

Villarroel, Enrique Gajardo. "Apuntes para un libro sobre la historia diplomática del tratado antártico y de la participación chilena en su elaboración." *Revista de difusión INACH* 10 (1977): 40ff. Cited in F. M. Auburn, *Antarctic Law and Politics* (Bloomington: Indiana University Press, 1982), p. 86.

Vogel, David. "Environmental Policy in Europe and Japan." In *Environmental Policy in the 1990s*, eds. Norman Vig and Michael Kraft, 257–278. Washington, D.C.: Congressional Quarterly Books, 1990.

Vogler, John. *The Global Commons: A Regime Analysis*. New York: Wiley, 1995.

Von Glahn, Gerhard. *Law Among Nations*. 6th ed. New York: Macmillan, 1992.

Wacke, Andreas. "Freedom of Contract and Restraint of Trade Clauses in Roman and Modern Law." *Law and History Review* 11, 1 (spring 1993): 1–19.

Walker, P. M. B., ed. *Cambridge Air and Space Dictionary*. Cambridge: Cambridge University Press, 1990.

Walton, D. W. H. *Antarctica Science*. Cambridge: Cambridge University Press, 1987.

Wamsley, Gary, et al. "The Public Administration and the Governance Process: Refocusing the American Dialogue." In A *Centennial History of the American Administrative State*, ed. Ralph Clark Chandler, 291–317. New York: Free Press, 1987.

Wapner, Paul. *Environmental Activism and World Civic Politics*. Albany: State University of New York Press, 1996.

Wilder, Robert Jay. "The Three-Mile Territorial Sea: Its Origins and Implications for Contemporary Offshore Federalism." *Virginia Journal of International Law* 32, 3 (spring 1992): 681–746.

Woolcott, Richard A. "The Interaction Between the Antarctic Treaty System and the United Nations System." In Polar Research Board, *Antarctic Treaty System: An Assessment,* 375–390. Washington, D.C.: National Academy Press, 1986.

World Commission on Environment and Development. *Our Common Future.* New York: Oxford University Press, 1987.

World Meteorological Organization et al. *Atmospheric Ozone 1985: Assessment of Our Understanding of the Processes Controlling Its Present Distribution.* 3 vol. Global Ozone Research and Monitoring Project Report No. 16. Geneva: World Meteorological Organization, 1986. Cited in Richard Elliot Benedick, *Ozone Diplomacy: New Directions in Safeguarding the Planet* (Cambridge, Mass.: Harvard University Press, 1991), 13.

Wright, N. A. and P. L. Williams. *Mineral Resources of Antarctica.* Geological Survey Circular 705. Reston, Va.: U.S. Geological Survey, 1974.

Young, Oran. *International Cooperation: Building Regimes for Natural Resources and the Environment.* Ithaca, N.Y.: Cornell University Press, 1989.

Zacher, Mark W. "Toward a Theory of International Regimes." In *The Evolution of Theory in International Relations: Essays in Honor of William T. R. Fox,* ed. Robert L. Rothstein, 119–137. Columbia: University of South Carolina Press, 1991.

Zumberge, James. "The Antarctic Treaty as a Scientific Mechanism—The Scientific Committee on Antarctic Research and the Antarctic Treaty System." In Polar Research Board, *Antarctic Treaty System: An Assessment,* 153–184. Washington, D.C.: National Academy Press, 1986.

Index